A Critical History

of

English Literature

VOLUME I

DAVID DAICHES

A Critical History
of
English Literature

SECOND EDITION

IN FOUR VOLUMES

VOLUME I

LONDON · SECKER & WARBURG

First published in England 1960 by
Martin Secker & Warburg Limited
54 Poland Street, London W1V 3DF

Copyright © 1960 The Ronald Press Company

Reprinted 1960, 1961, 1963, 1968, 1983, 1985

436 12104 2

Made and printed in Great Britain by
Richard Clay (The Chaucer Press) Ltd, Bungay, Suffolk

To my former students
on both sides of the Atlantic

però pur va ed in andando ascolta

Preface

THIS IS AN AGE of specialist scholars, and for one man to attempt a complete history of English literature is now both rash and unusual. I cannot claim to be a specialist in all the periods on which I have written, nor, in spite of my best attempts, have I been able to keep abreast of all new developments in English studies. But I have been reading English literature continuously and closely ever since I began my studies at Edinburgh University in 1930, and I have long felt the urge to describe the whole scene as I see it. This, therefore, is one man's history of English literature; it is intended less as a work of reference than as a work of description, explanation, and critical interpretation. It is not meant to be looked up, but to be read. I have given myself generous space in dealing with major figures such as Shakespeare and Milton, without bothering whether, in strict terms of relative greatness, they deserve so much more than I have given to some other writers. Indeed, the chapters on Shakespeare and Milton can perhaps stand as independent critical studies, capable of being extracted from the rest of the *History* and read as short books on their own. Nevertheless, though the word "critical" in my title is important, I have tried never to lose sight of the fact that this is a history, not a series of separate critical studies, and the appropriate kinds of historical generalizations and the proper continuity of narrative have, I hope, been maintained throughout. I may sometimes have treated a minor writer who interests me particularly at greater length than he deserves, or rather briefly summarized something important and well known. But I have tried to see my subject steadily and see it whole; and I have tried to write interestingly, less as the impersonal scholar recording facts than as the interested reader sharing his knowledge and opinions.

On matters of pure scholarship I have, of course, often had to depend on the researches of others. On questions of emphasis and assessment I have done so as little as possible, although occasionally even the most conscientious critical historian must be content to take the word of a sympathetic expert about the value of an odd minor work to which he himself has never devoted a great deal of careful attention. Art is long and life is short, and one cannot always be wholly original in everything. I hope, however, that the pattern which a single mind imposes on this vast material will make my account more lively and suggestive than the conscientious composite works of reference by teams of experts, from which I have myself profited but which are not literary history in the sense that this book is intended to be.

I have been more liberal in quotation from the works under discussion than is usual for a literary historian; I have found that the critical side of the work demands this. I have been deliberately inconsistent in the texts of my quotations. As a rule I have modernized spelling and punctuation, though not in Middle English texts, which lose too much by such modernization. In sixteenth-, seventeenth-, and eighteenth-century texts I have retained the original spelling where it is important as giving a period flavor or indicating some historical aspects of the language or of literary convention; otherwise I have modernized it. My principle in this and other matters has been maximum ease of reading compatible with sound scholarship and intellectual responsibility.

DAVID DAICHES

Jesus College, Cambridge
February, 1960

Contents

VOLUME I

CHAPTER   PAGE

1   ANGLO-SAXON LITERATURE 3

2   THE DEVELOPMENT OF MIDDLE ENGLISH PROSE AND VERSE 31

3   MIDDLE ENGLISH LITERATURE: FABLIAU, LYRIC, DREAM ALLEGORY, BALLAD 68

4   CHAUCER, GOWER, PIERS PLOWMAN 89

5   THE END OF THE MIDDLE AGES 128

6   THE EARLY TUDOR SCENE 146

7   SPENSER AND HIS TIME 165

8   DRAMA FROM THE MIRACLE PLAYS TO MARLOWE . . 208

VOLUME II

9   SHAKESPEARE 246

10   DRAMA FROM JONSON TO THE CLOSING OF THE THEATERS 309

11   POETRY AFTER SPENSER: THE JONSONIAN AND THE META-PHYSICAL TRADITIONS 346

13   PROSE IN THE SIXTEENTH AND SEVENTEENTH CENTURIES 458

12   MILTON 390

14   SCOTTISH LITERATURE TO 1700 504

VOLUME III

CHAPTER   PAGE

15 THE RESTORATION   537

16 THE AUGUSTAN AGE: DEFOE, SWIFT, POPE   .   .   .   590

17 POETRY FROM THOMSON TO CRABBE   652

18 THE NOVEL FROM RICHARDSON TO JANE AUSTEN   .   .   700

19 EIGHTEENTH-CENTURY PHILOSOPHICAL, HISTORICAL AND
      CRITICAL PROSE, AND MISCELLANEOUS WRITING   .   766

20 SCOTTISH LITERATURE FROM ALLAN RAMSAY TO WALTER
      SCOTT   809

VOLUME IV

21 THE ROMANTIC POETS I: BLAKE, WORDSWORTH, AND
      COLERIDGE   856

22 THE ROMANTIC POETS II: SHELLEY, KEATS, AND BYRON   905

23 FAMILIAR, CRITICAL, AND MISCELLANEOUS PROSE OF THE
      EARLY AND MIDDLE NINETEENTH CENTURY   .   .   935

24 VICTORIAN PROSE: JOHN HENRY NEWMAN TO WILLIAM
      MORRIS   961

25 THE VICTORIAN POETS   993

26 THE VICTORIAN NOVEL   1049

27 DRAMA FROM THE BEGINNING OF THE EIGHTEENTH
      CENTURY   1094

28 TWENTIETH-CENTURY POETRY   1122

29 THE TWENTIETH-CENTURY NOVEL   1152

    INDEX   1179

A Critical History

of

English Literature

VOLUME I

dred years and more after their arrival, they came "from three very powerful nations of the Germans: that is, from the *Saxones, Angli,* and the *Iutae.*" We know something about the Saxons, who appear to have come from the low country south of Denmark and east of Holland, the modern Holstein. The Angles appear to have lived in modern Jutland and the neighboring islands before they appeared in Britain, while the Jutes, whose origin is the most obscure of the three, perhaps came from the country east of the lower Rhine and perhaps, though less probably (the apparent similarity of names not being the cogent argument it might appear to the modern ear), from Jutland. In Anglo-Saxon England there were Saxon kingdoms (in the south and southwest), Anglian kingdoms (in the east, north, and midlands), and the Jutish kingdom of Kent in the southeast. The cultural differences between the three groups are of comparatively little moment: their language was essentially the same, though with important dialectical differences; and they all considered themselves part of "Germania," that loosely associated group of peoples who included Goths, Burgundians, Lombards, and others, and who had a common set of heroes who might belong to any one of these.

Of the Romanized Britons whom the invading Anglo-Saxons pushed into western corners of England the historian of English literature has little to say. A Celtic people who had been taken into the Roman Empire, they were left to fend for themselves when the Romans, desperately trying to hold their empire together against barbarian invaders, withdrew from England in A.D. 410. A prey to the ruder Picts and Scots in the north, they soon found themselves more seriously threatened by the invaders from across the North Sea, to whom they were an alien people known as "Welsh," which was simply the Germanic peoples' name for foreigners who were not part of Germania. Only in Wales have these Cambro-Britons continuously preserved their language and their traditions; their contribution to specifically English literature is sporadic and oblique, and does not appear until long after the Anglo-Saxon period. If Arthur, who plays such an important part in Middle English romance, was really a historical Cambro-British character from this period—and we have no mention of him before the ninth century except for a passing remark by an early seventh-century Welsh poet that a certain warrior, while brave, "was not Arthur"—there is still no reason for considering his metamorphosis into a hero of medieval romance and a focus for a host of "Arthurian" stories as any part of a direct and continuous heritage from Celtic Britain into later times. It was not until the twelfth century, when English literature sought its inspiration from the French, that the Arthurian romances began to appear, and while it is true that it was an Englishman, Geoffrey of Monmouth, who first elaborated the Arthurian story (in his *Historia Regum Britanniae*) to provide rich material for these romances, the Anglo-French development of the material is very far removed from any Celtic origins. Whatever the origins of the Arthurian story, therefore, we are justified in beginning the history of English literature with the Anglo-Saxons.

Of surviving Anglo-Saxon literature, that which brings us most closely into contact with the Germanic origins of the invaders is the heroic poetry, which still bears traces not only of the pre-Christian heroic society of the continental Saxons and others, but also of that community of subject which linked these early English with the wider civilization of Germania. This is written in the language we know as Old English or Anglo-Saxon, which is essentially the English language in an earlier stage of its development, with inflections which have since disappeared, a relatively small vocabulary from which many words have since been lost (though some which are lost to standard English remain in altered form in Scots and in regional English dialects), and significant differences between, for example, the West Saxon dialect of the south and the Anglian dialect of Northumbria. The verse is alliterative and stressed, without rhyme, each line containing four stressed syllables and a varying number unstressed. There is a definite pause (caesura) between the two halves of each line, with two stresses in each half.

> We geascodon   Eormenrices
> wylfenne geþoht;   ahte wide folc
> Gotena rices;   þæt wæs grim cyning.
> Sæt secg monig   sorgum gebunden,
> wean on wenan,   wyscte geneahhe
> þæt þæs cynerices   ofercumen wære.

To the superficial eye this looks very far removed from modern English; and in a sense it is. (The letter þ—"thorn"—has the sound of "th.") But a literal translation helps to bring out its relation to modern English:

> We have learned of Eormanric's
> wolfish disposition; he held wide dominion
> in the realm of the Goths. That was a cruel king.
> Many a man sat bound in sorrows,
> anticipating woe, often wishing
> that his kingdom were overcome.

Some thirty thousand lines of Anglo-Saxon poetry have survived, nearly all of it contained in four manuscripts,[1] and we have no reason to believe that the older, nonreligious poetry that survives is more than a casually preserved fragment of what was written. Specifically religious poetry might be expected to have earned ecclesiastical care and preservation, but the heroic poetry which connects more directly with the Germanic origins of the Anglo-Saxons could not be expected to arouse any special ecclesiastical interest even when it had been superficially purged of its pagan feeling and in some degree Christianized in thought. The conversion of the English peoples began with the arrival of Augustine in Kent in 597; he had been sent by Gregory the Great with a band of monks in order to achieve this missionary task. But, though Æthelberht, king of Kent, was duly converted to Christianity and Augustine was soon able to establish the seat of his bishopric at Canterbury, the permanent establishment of Christianity throughout England proved a much lengthier task and one which required the active intervention of Celtic missionaries from Ireland and Scotland. Differences between the customs and practices of the Irish Church—which had remained somewhat isolated from Rome—and the Roman Church, which had sponsored Augustine's mission, made for certain difficulties between those English ecclesiastics who looked to Rome and those who looked to Iona and to Ireland, and these were not resolved until the Synod of Whitby in 663;[2] but it is sufficient for the historian of literature to note that the development of English Christianity was not continuous but sporadic for the first century and more, with certain notable setbacks such as the defeat and death of the Christian Edwin, king of Northumbria, at the hands of the pagan Penda, king of Mercia, in 632, which meant the disappearance of the Christian Church in Northumbria until its re-establishment by Aidan and his followers from Iona. If even the external ecclesiastical organization was thus unstable in the early centuries, it is not difficult to see how traces of pagan thought in varying kinds of relation to Christianity persisted for some time after the nominal conversion of the English.

---

[1] These are: (1) MS Cotton Vitellius A XV in the British Museum, which contains *Beowulf, Judith,* and three prose works. (2) The Junius Manuscript in the Bodleian Library, Oxford (MS Bodleian Junius 11), which contains *Genesis, Exodus, Daniel,* and *Christ and Satan.* (3) The Exeter Book, given by Bishop Leofric to Exeter Cathedral, containing *Christ, Juliana, The Wanderer, The Seafarer, Widsith, Deor,* and many other short pieces. (4) The Vercelli Book, preserved in the cathedral library at Vercelli, in northern Italy, which contains *Andreas, The Fates of the Apostles, Address of the Soul to the Body, The Dream of the Rood,* and *Elene.*

[2] Not 664, as is traditionally held. Bede dates it 664, but he begins his year in September, and as the Synod can be shown to have been held in late September or early October, this would mean 663 in our dating.

Unfortunately, though much is known in general about the my-thology of the Germanic and the Norse peoples, we have very little definite information about the heathen background of Old English culture. Though we can draw analogies between what we know of Scandinavian heathendom and what we surmise of its Old English equivalent, the fact remains that the common origin of the two was already far in the past by the time we find the Anglo-Saxons in Eng-land. Old English place names give some indication of pre-Christian activity associated with certain localities in Anglo-Saxon England, but tell us nothing of the larger patterns of attitude and belief which are of the most relevance for a study of the literature. That Anglo-Saxon heroic poetry, even as we have it, is the product of a pagan heroic society and in social tone and general mood bears evidence of its origins, can hardly be disputed. But debate on the degree to which *Beowulf*, for example, has been modified by a relatively so-phisticated Latin culture—not only by Christian sentiment but, as has been claimed, by a Virgilian tradition—cannot be resolved without knowledge of more details than it seems likely we shall ever possess about primitive Anglo-Saxon beliefs. On the whole, it would seem likely that *Beowulf* and such other remains of early English heroic poetry as survive are closer to their pagan origins in mood and pur-pose than is sometimes believed.

Though there are difficulties in placing the earliest extant Anglo-Saxon poetry in its cultural context, we can take some comfort from the knowledge that what has survived of Anglo-Saxon poetry, frag-mentary though it is and an arbitrary sample though it may be, is of earlier date than any extant poetry of the other Germanic literatures —of Old High German or Old Norse, for example. Anglo-Saxon he-roic poetry is the nearest we can get to the oral pagan literature of the Heroic Age of Germania. The stressed alliterative verse of Anglo-Saxon poetry is clearly the product of an oral court minstrelsy; it was intended to be recited by the *scop*, the itinerant minstrel who fre-quented the halls of kings and chiefs and sometimes found continu-ous service with one master. One of the earliest surviving Anglo-Saxon poems, *Widsith*, is the autobiographical record of such a scop. The poem as we have it is probably not homogeneous—some of the lines seem to be later interpolations—but the core of the work finely reflects the heroic attitude to the bard's function and gives us a fas-cinating glimpse of the Germanic world as it appeared to the imagi-nation of the Anglo-Saxons. The text we have of the poem is in the Exeter Book, and is thus tenth-century and in the West Saxon dia-lect; the poem—which must have been originally composed in Northumbria—dates from the late seventh or early eighth century, though parts of it must be older even than that. Widsith, the "far wanderer," tells of his travels throughout the Germanic world and mentions the many rulers he has visited. Many of the characters he mentions figure in other poems—in *Beowulf*, for example, and in the fragmentary stories of Finn and Waldhere. The princes he claims to have visited cover virtually the whole Germanic world and their lifetimes extend over two hundred years. He was, he tells us, with Eormanric (the Gothic king who died about 370); "likewise I was in Italy with Ælfwine," he tells us elsewhere in the poem, and Ælfwine is Alboin, king of the Lombards, who died about 572 (and who is, incidentally, the latest character to be mentioned in any Germanic heroic poem). The poem thus cannot be true autobiography. It is, however, something much more interesting than that: it is a view of Germanic history and geography as it appeared to a Northumbrian bard of the seventh century drawing on the traditions of his people. What strikes us most forcibly is its catholicity: praise is meted out impartially to Huns, Goths, Burgundians, Franks, Danes, Swedes, Angles, Wends, Saxons, Langobards, and many others. "Ætla [Attila] ruled the Huns, Eormanric the Goths, Becca the Bannings, Gifica the Burgundians, . . . Theodric ruled the Franks, Thyle the Rondings, Breoca the Brondings, Billing the Wærnas. Oswine ruled the Eowan, and Gefwulf the Jutes, Fin Folcwalding the race of the Frisians. . . . Offa ruled Angel, Alewih the Danes; he was the most coura- geous of all these men, but he did not excel Offa in his mighty deeds." We are given here a bird's eye view of the subject matter of Germanic heroic poetry; and we are reminded that the heroes of that poetry were not regional or national but common to all Germania.

Widsith may be primitive stuff as poetry—indeed, the first cata- logue of rulers in the poem is cast in the form of a very early type of genealogical verse and may well date from the beginning of the sixth century or even from before the coming of the Anglo-Saxons to Brit- ain—but it is this very primitive quality which is of most interest. In its combination of historical memories and heroic traditions it shows us something of the historical foundations of heroic poetry and reminds us of the nature and extent of that wide world of Ger- mania which the author of *Beowulf* was equally to take for granted as familiar to his audience and thus as suitable material for allusion and analogy. The whole world of barbarian wanderings and con- quests—the world which collided with, in a sense destroyed, and in a sense was absorbed by, the Roman Empire—is here sketched out. And that world provides the orchestration, as it were, for *Beowulf*.

Beowulf holds a special position in Anglo-Saxon literature—indeed, in older Germanic literature as a whole—because it is the only com-

plete extant epic of its kind in an ancient Germanic language. Nowhere else is a traditional theme handled in a long narrative poem
against a background which reveals to us the culture and society of
the Heroic Age of the Germanic peoples. Whether there were in fact
other Anglo-Saxon epics, which have not survived, is a question
which may well be debated forever; but the fact remains that
Beowulf survives in a single manuscript, which was damaged by fire
before it was ever studied or transcribed. If it is impossible to determine conclusively whether it was *the* Anglo-Saxon epic or simply
an Anglo-Saxon epic (though it should be mentioned that modern
opinion inclines to the belief that it was the only poem of its kind
composed in Anglo-Saxon times), it can at least be said that it is a
poem technically impressive in its handling of narrative verse, remarkably successful in rendering that combination of heroic idealism
and somber fatalism which seems to have been part of the Germanic
temper, yet structurally weak and providing insufficient unity of tone
or organization to hold together effectively the two central episodes
and the many digressions which make up the whole. Though the
ultimate origin of the story is folklore (working, as folklore does, on
history), and behind the poem probably lies a variety of popular lays,
the poem as we have it is generally agreed to be the work of a single
author writing in the first half of the eighth century, though a powerful case has been made out for its having been composed orally by a
heathen considerably earlier, with the Christian references (of which
there are about seventy) representing later revision or interpolations.
Future scholars may well return to this latter view.

    Beowulf falls into two main parts. The first deals with the visit of
Beowulf, nephew of King Hygelac of the Geats (the Geats probably
occupied what is now southern Sweden), to the court of King
Hrothgar of Denmark. The aging Hrothgar had long been plagued
by a man-eating monster, Grendel, who came regularly to the king's
great hall of Heorot to prey on his warriors, and it was to slay the
monster that Beowulf came to Denmark. He fights with and mortally
wounds Grendel in Heorot, and when Grendel's mother comes to
take revenge for the death of her son he follows her to her under-
water home and after a desperate struggle slays her too. Beowulf
and his companions then leave for home, laden with honors and presents from the Danish king. The second part takes place fifty years
later, when Beowulf has long been king of the Geats. A dragon,
guarding a hoard of treasure, has been disturbed, and has been going
out to wreak slaughter throughout the land. Beowulf, to save his
country from the dragon's ravages, undertakes to fight it, and though
he succeeds in slaying it he is himself mortally wounded in the

struggle. The poem ends with an account of Beowulf's funeral: his body is burned on an elaborate funeral pyre, amid the lamentations of his warriors.

There are historical elements in *Beowulf*, though they are seen through the folk memory and the folk imagination, in combination with a variety of marvelous legends. There are also numerous digressions and allusions which make it clear that the author is taking for granted among his readers (or auditors) knowledge of a whole body of stories concerning Germanic heroes. In the feast at Heorot celebrating Beowulf's victory over Grendel we are told how the minstrel recited the story of Hnæf's death at the hands of the sons of Finn and the subsequent vengeance taken on Finn by the Danes, whose leader Hnæf had been. Part of the minstrel's recital is given at considerable length in *Beowulf*, but it can have had little meaning to anyone without a knowledge of the whole story. We can in some degree reconstruct the sequence of events with the help of a fragmentary Anglo-Saxon lay, *The Fight at Finnsburh*, which appears to deal with other events in the same story, told on a different scale. Other stories are referred to in *Beowulf* more casually, and part of its interest lies in the thread of Germanic story that runs, through allusions, analogies, and references, through the poem. Though it is an Anglo-Saxon poem, composed in England, it harks back to the period of Germanic history before the Anglo-Saxon invasion and shows no bias toward English heroes. Geats, Danes, and Swedes occupy the foreground of the narrative, and emerging briefly from the background are a number of figures whom we also meet in Scandinavian tradition and in the poetry and legends of a variety of Teutonic peoples.

On the surface, *Beowulf* is a heroic poem, celebrating the exploits of a great warrior whose character and actions are held up as a model of aristocratic virtue. It reflects the ideals of that state of society we call the Heroic Age, and its resemblance to the *Odyssey* in this respect has often been noted. The grave courtesy with which men of rank are received and dismissed, the generosity of rulers and the loyalty of retainers, the thirst for fame through the achievement of deeds of courage and endurance, the solemn boasting of warriors before and after performance, the interest in genealogies and pride in a noble heredity—all these things are to be found in both poems. But *Beowulf* is also a record of marvels rather different in kind from those encountered by Ulysses in his adventures, and, further, its Anglo-Saxon gravity is reinforced by the introduction of Christian elements which do not, however, seriously weaken the pagan atmosphere of the poem, for they are concerned with large elemental facts such as God's creation and governance of the world and such Old Testament stories as that of Cain's murder of Abel. If the general atmosphere of *Beowulf* can be called seriously pagan, with the seriousness deepened and the pagan heroic ideal enlarged by Christian elements, it is certainly not uncivilized, though the civilization it reflects is primitive enough. There is a genuine ideal of nobility underlying its adventure stories.

It is the splendid gravity of the poem that falls most impressively on modern ears. Sometimes in a single line the poem conveys atmosphere and mood to perfection. We are given an account of Beowulf's reception at Heorot, and his confident words before his warriors lay themselves down to sleep. Then:

> Com on wanre niht
> scriðᶾan sceadu-ȝenȝa.   Sceotend swæfon,
> þa þæt horn-reced   healdan scoldon,
> ealle buton anum. . . .
>   Ða com of more   under mist-hleoþum
> Ȝrendel ȝonȝan,   Ȝodes yrre bær. . . .

> Came on the dark night
> gliding, the shadowy prowler. The warriors slept
> who were to hold the antlered hall,
> all but one. . . .
>   Then from the moor under the misty cliffs
> came Grendel marching; he bore God's anger. . . .

The tone is not uniform, but the poem is at its most effective in its moments of slow terror or suspense, and in its more elegiac moods. It has neither the larger epic conception of the *Odyssey* nor the fine polish of a "secondary" epic such as the *Aeneid*. But it is an impressive, if uneven, performance, carrying us successfully into the Anglo-Saxon heroic imagination, with its emphasis on solemn courtesy, generosity, fidelity, and sheer endurance. And underlying all is the sense of the shortness of life and the passing away of all things except the fame a man leaves behind.

There is little else surviving of Anglo-Saxon literature which makes direct contact with the older heroic view of life. *Deor*, an interesting poem of forty-two lines, is the complaint of a minstrel who, after years of service to his lord, has been supplanted by a rival, Heorrenda. He comforts himself by recounting the trials of Germanic

---

³ ð, like þ, has the sound of "th." Ð is the capital form of ð.

heroes, all of which were eventually overcome. After each reference to the troubles of some famous character there occurs the refrain

Þæs ofereode,   þisses swa mæg.
That was surmounted; so may this be.

We get fascinating glimpses of figures famous in Germanic legend— Weland the smith, Theodoric the Ostrogoth, Eormanric the Goth, and others—and of the troubles they suffered or caused; but the main interest of the poem lies in its combination of this kind of subject matter with a personal, elegiac note, not common in Anglo-Saxon poetry, though found even more intensely in *The Wanderer* and *The Seafarer*, to be discussed later.

Two fragments make up the remainder of what we have of older Anglo-Saxon heroic poetry, and the fact that both were discovered by accident illustrates the arbitrariness as well as the incompleteness of the extant body of Anglo-Saxon verse. The first is a fragment of fifty lines, incomplete both at the beginning and the end, dealing with the same Finn story which we hear of in *Beowulf*. It is part of a lay, and describes the attack on Hnæf's hall by the followers of Finn (the *Beowulf* passage being a paraphrase of a handling at much greater length of the same general subject, though there are difficulties in reconciling it with the fragment). The second fragment is part of an Anglo-Saxon treatment of the Waltharius story, a story well-known on the continent and preserved in its most complete form in the Latin epic of Waltharius by Ekkehard of St. Gall, who lived in the latter part of the tenth century. The Anglo-Saxon fragment— which, though earlier than Ekkehard's *Waltharius*, shows evidence of a Christian editing of which the Latin poem gives little sign—is generally known as *Waldhere*: it consists of two separate parts of about thirty lines each, and its chief interest is in offering further evidence of the popularity of stories of continental Germanic heroes among the Anglo-Saxons. The two leaves of manuscript which contain the fragmentary *Waldhere* were not discovered until 1860.

The Christianizing of the Anglo-Saxons had more far-reaching effects on their literature than the addition of Christian elements to heroic poems. By the eighth century the techniques of Anglo-Saxon heroic poetry were being applied to purely Christian themes, with the result that we have a substantial body of Anglo-Saxon religious poetry, representing a quite new development in English literature. Here we see the Anglo-Saxons breaking loose from their pagan origins and, instead of seeking subjects for their poetry in the heroic themes common to old Germania, turning to face the new world of Latin Christianity. It is Christianity that brought the Anglo-Saxons into touch with Christian Europe, and Christian Europe in turn had its contacts with the classical civilization of Greece and Rome. We must thus distinguish between that part of Anglo-Saxon literature which sought nourishment from "barbarian" Germanic traditions that had nothing to do with classical civilization and that part whose inspiration is Latin and which represents an English treatment of themes and attitudes common throughout Christendom and thus found all over Europe. The Christian literature of the early English shows them in touch with the new European civilization as well as with the ancient classical world. It also enabled Anglo-Saxon poets to work on biblical story and so connected them with the Hebrew imagination.

Religious poetry seems to have flourished in northern England—Northumbria—throughout the eighth century, though most of it has survived only in West Saxon transcriptions of the late tenth century. Bede, the great English ecclesiastical historian and scholar who lived from 673 to 735, tells in his *Ecclesiastical History of the English People* how in the monastery of the abbess Hilda at Whitby a lowly lay brother named Cædmon suddenly and miraculously received the gift of song and "at once began to sing in praise of God the Creator verses which he had never heard before." As the abbess Hilda died in 680, this puts the beginnings of Anglo-Saxon religious poetry before that date.

The only poem we have which is certainly by Cædmon is the nine-line poem quoted by Bede in his account of the poet's first inspiration. Bede wrote his *Ecclesiastical History* in Latin (though it was translated into Anglo-Saxon under King Alfred), but fortunately in one of the manuscripts of the work the original Northumbrian text of the poem has been preserved:

> Nu scylun hergan   hefænricæs Uard,
> Metudæs mæcti   end his modgidanc,
> uerc uuldurfadur,   sue he uundra gihuæs,
> eci Dryctin,   or astelidæ. . . .

> Now let us praise the guardian of Heaven's kingdom,
> The Creator's might and His purpose,
> The work of the Father of glory, as He of all wonders,
> Eternal Lord, established the beginning. . . .

(The difference between Northumbrian and West Saxon can be seen at a glance if we put beside the Northumbrian version, quoted above, the following later West Saxon version:

> Nu sculon herigean   heofonrices Weard,
> Meotodes meahte   ond his modgeþanc,

people to freedom and victory. The description of the drowning of
the Egyptian host in the Red Sea is done with great verve:

> . . . Streamas stodon,   storm up gewat
> heah to heofonum,   herewopa mæst;
> laðe cyrmdon,   lyft up geswearc,
> fægum stefnum;   flod blod gewod.
> Randbyrig wæron rofene,   rodor swipode
> meredeaða mæst.   Modige swulton,
> cyningas on corðre,   cyre swiðrode
> sæs æt ende. . . .

> . . . The seas reared up, the storm uprose
> High to the heavens, the great clamor of an army;
> The foe cried out (the air above grew dark)
> With doomed voices; blood spread through the waters.
> The wall of shields was pulled down; scourged the sky
> The greatest of water-deaths; brave men perished,
> Kings in their pride, their chance of return vanished
> At the sea's end. . . .

Linguistic evidence suggests that *Exodus* is the oldest of the
Anglo-Saxon biblical poems, and it perhaps dates from the beginning
of the eighth century.

Daniel is less interesting, with much less dramatic quality and a
more prosaic tone throughout. It is a paraphrase of the first five chapters of the biblical book of Daniel as it appears in the Vulgate, with
the apocryphal prayer of Azariah interpolated in the middle. The
interpolation seems to derive from a separate poem dating from the
middle or late ninth century; the main part of *Daniel* was probably
composed in Northumbria early in the eighth century.

In the same manuscript that contains the two *Genesis* poems,
Exodus and *Daniel*, there is found also an untitled religious poem
which is now generally called *Christ and Satan.* This shows an
Anglo-Saxon poet working not directly from biblical sources but
from a variety of Christian traditions. Here we get a picture of Satan
in Hell which represents him not as the defiant spirit of *Genesis B*
but as a lost soul lamenting bitterly his exclusion from the joys of
Heaven. He is given several speeches, each with considerable elegiac
eloquence; the author is clearly concerned to emphasize the difference between Heaven and Hell and the different results of following
Christ and following Satan. The latter part of the poem concentrates
on Christ, though at the very end, after an account of Satan's temptation of Christ in the wilderness, we return to Satan in his frustration.

Christ and Satan seems to have been influenced by the school of
Cynewulf, a poet who may have flourished early in the ninth century
and who is the first Anglo-Saxon poet to sign his work (by means of

runic letters woven into the poem). Four of Cynewulf's poems are extant, all showing a more self-conscious craftsmanship than is found in the Cædmonian poems and suggesting in style and structure the influence of classical models. The heroic strain, so successfully transplanted from the older poetry in such a poem as *Exodus,* is lacking in Cynewulf, and in its place we find a more meditative and contemplative tone. The four Anglo-Saxon Christian poems which have the name of Cynewulf worked into them in acrostic form are *Christ, Juliana, Elene,* and *The Fates of the Apostles.* All these poems possess both a high degree of literary craftsmanship and a note of mystical contemplation which sometimes rises to a high level of religious passion. The story of Christ as told in the poem of that title draws on a variety of ecclesiastical and patristic sources, but it handles its subject—the Advent, the Ascension, and the Last Judgment[5]—with an intensity all its own. The dialogue between Mary and Joseph in the first part, brief though it is, shows a real feeling for the dramatic situation, and is, besides, the earliest extant dramatic passage in English literature. *Juliana* is a more conventional work, a typical saint's life, following its Latin prose source without any significant deviation, while *Elene* is the story of the discovery of the true cross by St. Helena, mother of Constantine, told with a keen sense of the wonder of it all and a relish for the romantic suggestions of distant scenes and places. *The Fates of the Apostles* is a short poem of one hundred and twenty-two lines (and may be the concluding part of *Andreas,* which it follows in the manuscript: if so, then *Andreas,* too, is by Cynewulf, for *The Fates of the Apostles* contains the runic signature). The author is here meditating on the adventures of the various apostles after they dispersed to spread the Gospel, but its interest for the modern reader lies largely in the personal passages. Its opening shows an interesting mutation of the heroic into the personal elegiac strain: "Lo, weary of wandering, sad in spirit, I made this song, gathered it from far and wide, of how the bright and glorious heroes showed forth their courage."

With Cynewulf, Anglo-Saxon religious poetry moves beyond biblical paraphrase into the didactic, the devotional, and the mystical. These qualities are also exhibited by many of the religious poems which seem to have been written under his influence. The most remarkable of these is *The Dream of the Rood,* fragments of which are to be found inscribed in runic letters on the Ruthwell Cross in Dum-

[5] Some scholars maintain that only the second part, to which they give the title of *The Ascension* (or *Christ B*), is by Cynewulf, for only this part contains Cynewulf's name in runic characters. The other two parts they consider to be separate poems, giving one the title of *The Advent* (or *Nativity,* or *Christ A*) and the other the title of *Doomsday C* (or *Christ C*), grouping it together with two other poems on the Last Judgment which they call *Doomsday A* and *Doomsday B* respectively.

friesshire, Scotland (probably an early eighth century version, pre-Cynewulf), while the complete poem exists in the Vercelli Book, in a much later version (probaby late ninth century). The tone of the complete version as we have it suggests that the earlier version had been afterward adapted by a poet of the school of Cynewulf, perhaps even by Cynewulf himself. It is the oldest surviving English poem in the form of a dream or vision—a form which was later to be used for such a variety of purposes. The dreamer tells how he saw a vision of the bright cross, brilliantly adorned with gems, and goes on to tell the speech that he heard it utter. The speech of the cross, in which it tells of its origin in the forest, its removal to be made into a cross for "the Master of mankind," its horror at the role it had to play but its determination to stand fast because that was God's command, the suffering of "the young Hero" who ascends the cross resolutely in order to redeem mankind—all this is done in verse charged with a simple eloquence and sustaining a high note of religious passion and wonder. The speech ends with an exhortation to each soul to "seek through the cross the kingdom which is far from earth," and the poem then concludes with the dreamer's account of his own religious hopes. Other poems associated with the school of Cynewulf are *Andreas,* which tells of the adventures, sufferings, and evangelical successes of St. Andrew, with deliberate emphasis on the wonderful and the picturesque, and a perhaps excessive exploitation of the rhetorical devices of Anglo-Saxon poetry (the source of the poem is a Latin rendering of the apocryphal Greek *Acts of Andrew and Matthew*); two poems on the life of the English hermit St. Guthlac; *The Phoenix,* of which the first part, deriving from the Latin poem *De Ave Phoenice,* attributed to Lactantius, describes an earthly paradise in the East, the beauty of the phoenix, its flight to Syria after it has lived for a thousand years to build its nest, die, and be reborn, while the second half takes the phoenix as an allegory both of the life of the virtuous in this world and the next and as a symbol of Christ; and—following *The Phoenix* in the Exeter Book—a poem entitled *Physiologus* or *Bestiary* which belongs to the popular medieval literary form of beast allegories, where real or (more often) imaginary qualities of animals are given a moral application. *Physiologus,* which derives ultimately from a Greek original, is incomplete, and deals with the panther, the whale and, incompletely, the partridge. It has the same lushness of descriptive style that is found in *The Phoenix,* and its natural history is equally fabulous. The whale is given the charming name of Fastitocalon—a corruption of Aspidochelone, originally applied to the turtle.

Finally, there falls to be mentioned among significant Anglo-Saxon religious poems the fragmentary *Judith,* of which only the concluding sections survive, in the same manuscript that contains *Beowulf.* The poem is a version of the Vulgate text of the apocryphal book of Judith, and the extant portion tells in vigorous and rapidly moving verse of Judith's beheading of the drunken Holofernes after his confident feasting, her rallying of the Hebrews to attack the Assyrians, the consternation of the Assyrians on discovering Holofernes' headless body, the rout of the Assyrians by the Hebrews, and Judith's triumph and praise to God. *Judith* possesses a fierce energy in describing the death of Holofernes and the defeat of the Assyrians, a note of positive jubilation, which is quite different from anything in the older heroic poetry. In fluidity of movement the verse form shows itself to be fairly late, and the poem may date from the end of the ninth century or possibly even later.

Though some of the Anglo-Saxon religious poems, especially some of those by Cynewulf and his school, express a personal devotional feeling, none of them can be said to be really lyrical in character or to have been written primarily for the purpose of exploring personal emotion. Neither the heroic nor the religious poetry of the Anglo-Saxon tends toward the lyric, and though a note of somber elegy is sometimes struck, it is rarely developed for its own sake. There is, however, a group of Anglo-Saxon poems in which a mood of lyrical elegy predominates, and these stand somewhat apart from the poetry we have already discussed. Of these *The Wanderer* and *The Seafarer* are the most similar to each other. *The Wanderer* is the lament of a solitary man who had once been happy in the service of a loved lord but who now, long after his lord's death and the passing away of that earlier time of happiness and friendship, has become a wanderer journeying the paths of exile across the icy sea. The poem ends with some conventional moralizing, but the main part of the elegy is an impressive lament for departed joys, done with a plangent tone of reminiscence and an effective use of the *ubi sunt?* theme—"where are the snows of yesteryear?"—that was to become such a favorite in medieval literature. *The Seafarer,* which has the same melancholy tone, the same mingling of regret and self-pity, is the monologue of an old sailor who recalls the loneliness and hardships of a life at sea while at the same time aware of its fascination. Some critics take it to be a dialogue, in which the old sailor urges the hardships of the seafaring life against the arguments of an eager young man anxious to take to the sea and attracted by the difficulties, and the poem can indeed be read in this way; but the fluctuating moods of the poem seem more impressive if taken as the alternation of weariness and fascination in the same person. Whichever way we read it, however, it is the elegiac element that stands out from among the sometimes obscure sequence of moods, which ends, like *The Wanderer*, with a conventional religious sentiment. The date of both these poems is uncertain: they may be almost as old as *Beowulf*. Both are found in the Exeter Book.

Another poem in the Exeter Book, which is generally given the title of *The Wife's Lament*, can also be considered as belonging to this group of elegiac monologues. It is difficult to follow the precise situation the speaker is describing, but apparently the wife has been separated from her husband and forced to dwell in a cave in the forest by the plottings of his kinsmen. In spite of the comparative obscurity of the situation, the central emotion comes through strongly, and the note of personal passion—the love and longing for the absent husband, the curse on the enemy responsible for her present plight—rings out with remarkable clarity. Similar in many ways to this poem is *The Husband's Message*. Here the speaker is the piece of wood on which the letter is carved: it first tells the wife its own life story and then goes on to speak the message now carved on it. The husband reminds the wife of her earlier vows, tells her that he has been driven from her by a feud, and bids her join him across the sea. *Wulf and Eadwacer* is another dramatic monologue, existing only in a fragment of nineteen lines in the Exeter Book, which, for all the obscurity of the situation described, expresses an intense romantic passion in a way quite uncharacteristic of Anglo-Saxon poetry as it has come down to us. Wulf is the woman's outlawed lover and Eadwacer her hated husband, or at least the man with whom, against her will, she is forced to live. The passionate cry of

> Wulf, min Wulf,   wena me þine
> seoce gedydon,   þine seldcymas
> murnende mod,   nales meteliste—

> Wulf, my Wulf, my longings for thee
> Have made me sick, thy rare visits,
> It was my sorrowful heart, not want of food—

might be Iseult calling for Tristan as conceived by some nineteenth-century romantic poet. *The Wife's Lament, The Husband's Message,* and *Wulf and Eadwacer* represent all we have of Anglo-Saxon love poetry. They have not been tampered with by clerics anxious to give a moral and religious twist to the end, but have survived in all the intensity of their original utterance. How many poems in a similar style may have been lost it is impossible to tell, nor is it easy to see for what kind of an audience this kind of poetry was written. We know to what taste the Anglo-Saxon heroic poet catered, and we can understand the appeal of the religious poetry of the age; but these passionate renderings of personal emotion, devoid of either heroic atmosphere or religious teaching, must have appealed to a taste one is not accustomed to thinking of as at all prevalent in the Anglo-Saxon period of English culture.

There is one other interesting Anglo-Saxon poem with an elegiac tone; it is a description of a ruined city (perhaps Bath) in about fifty lines, found in the Exeter Book. It is a sad picture of desolation and decay set against an account of the earlier prosperity of the place, and, though the text is imperfect, the sense of passionate regret at the passing away of what was once lively and beautiful is conveyed with impressive eloquence. No clerical improver has tagged a religious moral on to it (or, if he has, it has not survived in the incomplete version which alone is extant) and the mood is somberly fatalistic. *The Ruin* is not incompatible in feeling with much of *Beowulf*, which has its own stern sense of fate, and we can see from it how in Anglo-Saxon poetry one kind of elegiac mood was the reverse of the medal whose obverse was heroic.

The Exeter book contains nearly a hundred Anglo-Saxon riddles, some of which seem to have been translated from Latin originals composed in England by clerics of the seventh and eighth century and some derived from the fourth- to fifth-century Latin writer Symphosius. This form of literary amusement has little appeal for the modern reader, though many of *The Riddles*—which are in regular Anglo-Saxon verse form—show considerable literary skill, particularly in descriptive passages. Their chief interest today lies in the incidental glimpses they give us of the daily life of Anglo-Saxon England and the folk beliefs of the time. Similarly, the so-called "Gnomic Verses," some of which are also in the Exeter Book, and some in a British Museum manuscript, with their generalizations about morals and experience and the properties of objects encountered in daily living, are of interest to the social historian as the only group of existing Anglo-Saxon poems which are not on the whole aristocratic in origin; they reflect the manners and opinions of the peasantry of the period.

Toward the end of the Anglo-Saxon period the old heroic note, so long unheard, re-emerges finely in two poems dealing with contemporary history. *The Battle of Brunanburh* appears in the *Anglo-Saxon Chronicle* under the date 937: it celebrates the victory of

Æthelstan of Wessex and Eadmund, his brother, against the combined forces of Olaf the Norseman, Constantine, king of Scots, and the Britons of Strathclyde. There is an important difference, however, between the heroic tone of this poem and that of the older Anglo-Saxon poetry. In the older heroic poetry, emphasis was laid on the individual hero, and his national origins were of little importance—he was one of the heroes of Germania and as such claimed the admiration of all the Germanic peoples without any national prejudice. But *The Battle of Brunanburh* shows strong patriotic sentiment. The victory is regarded as a victory of the English forces against Norse, Scots, and Welsh enemies, and though the heroism of Æthelstan and Eadmund is celebrated, the two princes appear not as heroes in their own right so much as champions of their nation. The *Battle of Maldon* appears in the *Anglo-Saxon Chronicle* under the date 991. It deals in the older epic manner with one of the many clashes between English and Danes that resulted from the latter's attacks on England, which culminated in the conquest of the country by Cnut (Canute) in 1012. The older heroic poems did not, of course, deal with historical events that had only just occurred, nor, as we have noted, did they show any trace of national patriotic feeling. Yet *The Battle of Maldon* is remarkably similar in spirit to the older heroic poetry. It is the story of a disastrous English defeat: Byrhtnoth, ealdorman of Essex, who led the English forces, fought and died in a recklessly courageous attempt to stem the Danes. The poem contains nine speeches, mostly of exhortation and encouragement to the English forces, delivered by seven different speakers; many of the English warriors are mentioned by name (though not one of the Danes is so singled out); the passionate loyalty of retainers to their chief is eloquently presented; and the tone of desperate courage against hopeless odds becomes more and more intense as the poem proceeds, to culminate after the death of Byrhtnoth in the final words of his old retainer Byrhtwold:

> Hige sceal þe heardra,   heorte þe cenre,
> mod sceal þe mare,   þe ure mægen lytlað.
> Her lið ure ealdor   eall forheawen,
> god on greote;   a mæg gnornian
> seðe nu fram þis wigplegan   wendan þenceð.
> Ic eom frod feores;   fram ic ne wille,
> ac ic me be healfe   minum hlaforde,
> be swa leofan men,   licgan þence.

> Thought shall be the harder, heart the keener,
> Courage shall be the more, as our might lessens.

Here lies our lord, all hewn down,
The good man in the dust; ever may he lament
Who now from this war-play thinks to turn.
I am old in years; from here I will not go,
But I by the side of my lord,
By the man so dear, purpose to lie.

And, in this high strain, Anglo-Saxon heroic poetry comes to an end.

The Anglo-Saxon invaders of Britain brought with them their own poetry, but there is no evidence of their having possessed any literary prose tradition. The development of Old English prose does not therefore go back to earlier Germanic origins, as the poetry does: it takes place wholly in England, and largely as a result of the Christianization of England. It is not surprising that prose developed later than poetry: that is the normal thing in the history of any literature, for the primal urge to artistic expression is bound to be poetic, while the proper maturing of the more utilitarian prose medium of communication follows the emergence of later political and cultural needs. With the Germanic peoples, the delay in the development of prose was emphasized by their contact with the old and mature Greco-Roman civilization, which supplied clerks ready to act as secretaries to their leaders and a sophisticated Greek or Latin prose more than capable of making any formal communications or keeping any legal or historical records which might be required. For the celebration of their own heroes and the perpetuation of their own legends, a native poetry was necessary and indeed inevitable, but the need for prose was only felt by barbarian chieftains after they had come into contact and had been deeply affected by the civilization they threatened; and that civilization could easily supply the need of which it made them aware.

There were exceptions to this generalization, but there can be little doubt that it applies to the Anglo-Saxons, or that English prose begins in the reign of King Alfred in an attempt by the King and his associates to bring within range of the people the most significant aspects of earlier thought. Latin was, of course, the language of the Christian Church, and an essential tool in clerical education; perhaps if England had been geographically closer to Rome, Latin might have stifled a native prose altogether, just as its prestige and availability had earlier hampered the development of a formal native prose among many of the Germanic peoples. But, as one of the most perceptive historians of early English prose has put it, "when Gregory the Great sent his missionaries to England, Latin civilization reached a land which was so remote from Rome that Latin could influence the native language without depressing it,"[6] and when the laws of Kent were amended to introduce new Christian notions, the new clauses were written not in Latin but in English.

King Alfred of Wessex, known in political history for his achievement in stemming the Danish conquest of England, the acceptance of his overlordship by—in the words of the *Anglo-Saxon Chronicle*— "all the English people except those who were under the power of the Danes" and the consequent advance of the peoples of the various Anglo-Saxon kingdoms toward an awareness of their political unity as Englishmen, and for his remarkable combination of the statesman, the military strategist, and the patriot, is even more important in the history of English education and the history of English literature. Throughout a reign troubled by military problems of desperate urgency, not all of which had been resolved by the time of his death in 899, he yet found the time and the energy to meditate on the means of bringing the fruits of Western culture to "all the free-born young men of England" and to see those means in large measure achieved. In his preface to his translation of the *Cura Pastoralis (Pastoral Care)* of Pope Gregory the Great he tells of his concern at the dearth of scholars in England at the time of his accession to the throne (in 871) and at the destruction of churches and books by the Danes, and his wonder why earlier English scholars had not translated any of those books into the vernacular; then he immediately proceeds to answer the last question by saying that those earlier scholars can never have supposed that a knowledge of the original languages should have declined to such a degree. But he realized that Christian culture had its roots in Hebrew, Greek, and Latin sources, and that if these were to be made available to the people an ambitious program of translation into the vernacular would have to be undertaken. "When I remembered how Latin learning has already decayed throughout England, though many can read English writing, I began, among many other varied and manifold cares of this kingdom, to translate into English the book which is called in Latin *Pastoralis* and in English 'Hierde-boc' (herd's book, i.e., shepherd's book, pastoral)."

Alfred's program of translation did not include direct translations from the original sources of Christian culture, but concentrated on later Latin works in which, as he believed, much of the ancient wisdom was distilled. Thus Gregory's *Cura Pastoralis*, a work describing the duties and responsibilities of a bishop which had come to be

<hr>

[6] R. W. Chambers, "The Continuity of English Prose," in *Harpsfield's Life of Sir Thomas More*, edited by Elsie Vaughan Hitchcock and R. W. Chambers, London, 1932. Page lix.

regarded as a manual of a parish priest's duties, came first on his list: he must have been attracted by Gregory's emphasis on the bishop's duty to teach the laity. Alfred was especially concerned with the training of teachers—who would all, of course, be clerics, and whose teaching would be religious—as his choice of this work indicates. All the free-born English youth should be able to read English, and those who wished to proceed to the priesthood would, after learning English, go on to Latin. English was necessary as a first step both for priest and layman.

The translation of the *Cura Pastoralis* was done by Alfred with the assistance of scholars who explained the meaning to him "sometimes word by word, sometimes sense by sense"; for Alfred was late in learning Latin and depended on a number of helpers of whom seven are known to us by name. It is on the whole a literal rendering, but it flows easily and there is little indication of the forcing of one language into the idiom of another such as we might expect in a pioneer translation. Alfred's next work was a translation of the *Historiae adversum Paganos* of the fifth-century Latin writer Paulus Orosius, a work written under the influence of St. Augustine in order to prove that the introduction of Christianity had not made the world worse than it had been before. Orosius chronicles the calamities of mankind from the Fall of man to the fall of Rome with an equal disregard for historical accuracy and literary grace, and it is a pity that this shoddy production was the only world history available to Alfred. Fortunately, Alfred treated his original rather freely, adding his own illustrations and omitting much propaganda; more important, he added two entirely new narratives, one told him by Ohthere, a Norwegian who had explored from his home within the Arctic Circle, sailing round the North Cape as far as the White Sea, the other told him by a voyager named Wulfstan who had sailed the Baltic from Schleswig to the mouth of the Vistula. These lively accounts of foreign lands and peoples, together with Alfred's additions to Orosius drawn from his own knowledge and experience, give this translation its present value. The voyages of Ohthere and Wulfstan are justly celebrated as among the high spots of Anglo-Saxon prose, and the prose is certainly Alfred's own.

The translation of Bede's *Historia Ecclesiastica* (*Ecclesiastical History of the English People*) associated with Alfred's name is a literal rendering of the Latin, perhaps not done by Alfred himself though certainly inspired by him. Alfred's two final translations were of more philosophical works. That of the *De Consolatione Philosophiae* (*The Consolation of Philosophy*) of Boethius, a Roman philosopher and statesman of the late fifth and early sixth centuries, made available in Anglo-Saxon one of the most popular philosophical works of the Dark and Middle Ages, later translated by Chaucer. It deals (in the form of a dialogue between the author and Philosophy) with the fundamental problems of God's government of the world, the nature of true happiness, good and evil, and the question of God's fore-knowledge of man's free will; though there is no specific reference to Christianity anywhere in the work and the general tone of the work derives from Greek and Roman ethical thought rather than from Christian teaching, its high idealism and, in particular, its reconciliation of God's perfection with the apparently imperfect state of His world, appealed to Christian thought. To the eighteenth-century Gibbon "such topics of consolation, so obvious, so vague, or so abstruse, are ineffectual to subdue the feelings of human nature," but the medieval mind found them more helpful. Alfred in his later years had left history and geography to meditate on profounder philosophical themes, and the work of Boethius—written in prison while the author was awaiting execution—had a particular appeal to a man and to an age familiar with sudden reversals of fortune and anxious to find a wider and a calmer perspective from which to contemplate human vicissitudes. Alfred's last work was a book of "Blossoms" derived for the most part from the *Soliloquies* of St. Augustine but with freely interspersed original comments and illustrations. In his preface Alfred compares himself in his literary endeavors to a man collecting wood in a vast forest which contains plenty of materials for all kinds of building. The analogy is apt enough, and expressed in a fine piece of Anglo-Saxon prose: it can serve as a summing up of Alfred's literary purposes.

Alfred's Laws, though of great importance to the political historian must, like the laws of other Anglo-Saxon kings and like Anglo-Saxon charters and similar nonliterary prose works, remain outside the purview of the historian of literature, even though they, like the charters, have considerable interest for the student of the development of English prose. The Laws, however, are prefaced by a translation of chapters 20 to 23 of Exodus, which tell of the giving of the law to Moses (including the Ten Commandments and other civil and criminal laws), followed by the passage from the fifteenth chapter of Acts describing the enactment of the council of Jerusalem and the relation of the Mosaic law to the new dispensation, which represent the earliest extant English biblical translations except for some literal renderings of the Psalms. Bede (who died in 735) was said to have translated the Gospel of St. John from Latin into English, and probably did translate the first six chapters, but the work has not survived.

It was probably in King Alfred's time that the great *Anglo-Saxon Chronicle* was begun, a series of annals which commence with an outline of English history from Julius Caesar's invasion to the middle of the fifth century and continues (in one of its seven manuscripts) to 1154. The different manuscripts, each of which was kept and continued at a different locality, diverge considerably after the beginning of the tenth century, often including material of especial local interest. The *Chronicle* includes some fine examples of prose narrative, one of the most notable being the story of Cynewulf and Cyneheard, occurring under the surprisingly early date of 755, which shows that at least one English writer of the middle of the eighth century had at his command a prose style comparable to that of the Icelandic prose sagas. The continuity of English prose from the Old English (or Anglo-Saxon) period to the Middle English period is demonstrated by the *Chronicle* more clearly than anywhere else, and its different manuscripts are of prime importance for the student of the English language. The level is far from consistent, dropping considerably in the middle of the tenth century (which is surprising, for that was a period of stability and prosperity) and flaring up into some vivid descriptions at the end of the tenth and the beginning of the eleventh centuries, when the second great wave of Danish invasions was tearing the country apart. The manuscript known as *D* gives a full and lively picture of the relations between England and Scandinavia in the reign of Edward the Confessor (1043–66) and a most important account of the Norman invasion and subsequent events, while another manuscript, *C*, which ends in 1066, gives a vivid account of the conflicts with the Danes in the reign of Ethelred the Unready (978–1016). The latest entry is in a manuscript that was continued at Peterborough; it is for the year 1154. By this time the English language had developed from the stage we call Anglo-Saxon or Old English into Middle English. By this time, too, as a result of the Norman Conquest and what followed, English as a literary language seemed about to disappear and English historical prose appeared to have come to an end. Until well into the fourteenth century, English, replaced at court by Norman French since 1066, seemed to be dwindling away into the rustic speech of a handful of "uplandish men." But, as we shall see, the tradition did not wholly dry up; it was to emerge again triumphant three hundred years after the Conquest; the English language eventually conquered the language of the Norman conquerors, and English prose rose to new life in the fifteenth century.

Alfred and the writers who kept up the *Anglo-Saxon Chronicle* were not the only writers of Anglo-Saxon prose. Alfred's associates were also responsible for translations, and we know that Bishop Wærferth of Worcester translated the *Dialogues* of Gregory the Great. The most notable of all Anglo-Saxon writers was Ælfric, abbot of Eynsham, the great English scholar of the Benedictine reformation of the tenth century, whose sermons in the vernacular (the first two series known as the *Catholic Homilies—Homiliae Catholicae—*and the third as *Lives of the Saints—Passiones Sanctum—*though their subject matter is not as clearly distinguished as these titles would suggest) with their careful balance and prose rhythm display a fine virtuosity. Ælfric also produced a somewhat abbreviated version in Anglo-Saxon of the first seven books of the Old Testament (the *Heptateuch*) done with sufficient skill to enable us to call him the first English Bible translator to have gone a considerable way toward achieving an appropriate literary prose style for biblical translation. Beside the carefully balanced sentences of Ælfric we can set the more fiery eloquence of his contemporary, Wulfstan, Archbishop of York from 1002 to 1023. His famous *Sermon to the English*, entitled in the manuscript *Sermo Lupi ad Anglos*, was delivered in 1014: in it Wulfstan paints a vivid picture of the horrors brought about by the Danish invasions—a picture of wrongdoing, betrayal, violence, crop failures, civil war, treachery, murder, immorality of every kind—and uses it as a means of hammering home to his audience the necessity of amendment if they are to avoid hellfire and earn "the glory and the joy that God has prepared for those that do His will on earth." A desperate sense of the imminence of doomsday pervades the whole sermon, from the opening statement that "this world is in haste and approaches its end" to the powerful "God help us!" of the conclusion. Wulfstan's prose, though he, like Ælfric, uses alliteration and antithesis, gives an impression of breathless passion, of eloquence breaking out through its own force, which is markedly different from Ælfric's finely chiseled urbanity.

The ravages of the Danes at the end of the ninth century had wrought havoc with the organization of the English church and, while Alfred's translations represented a remarkable attempt to improve the state of education, it was not until the middle and latter part of the tenth century that a real revival of religious learning took place in England. That revival was the work of the great churchman Dunstan who, after a life devoted to monastic reform, was translated to the See of Canterbury in 960; of Oswald of Worcester and Æthelwold of Winchester, who carried further the monastic revival begun by Dunstan; of Æthelwold's pupil Ælfric, who led the literary movement; and of Archbishop Wulfstan, Ælfric's friend for whom he wrote some of his famous "Pastoral Letters." If Ælfric and Wulfstan extended the range of effective Anglo-Saxon prose, it was not because they or any ecclesiastic of the time were primarily interested in vernacular literature, but rather because the vitality of the movement of which they were a part carried over into this field. To a tenth-century cleric, Latin was the language of learning and of literature, and concessions to the unlearned in the form of translations were achievements of minor importance. The main thing was to keep up the standard of Latin scholarship among the clergy. The most popular of Ælfric's works with the modern reader is a set of simple Latin dialogues (the *Colloquy*) intended to teach Latin to boys in a monastic school. These dialogues (between the teacher and a monk, the teacher and a plowman, the teacher and a shepherd, the teacher and a fisherman, etc.) interest us today because of the lively glimpses they give us of the daily life of the time; but for Ælfric they were means to a very important end.

Ælfric's *Colloquy* reminds us that with the triumph of Christianity all culture was ecclesiastical culture and all ecclesiastical culture was based on Latin. The Latin literature of the Anglo-Saxon period is much greater in bulk than that written in the vernacular, and the history of Anglo-Saxon learning is more extensive and in many ways more remarkable than the history of Anglo-Saxon literature. The story of the conversion of England and the development of its ecclesiastical institutions from the landing of Augustine in Kent in 597 through the Synod of Whitby to the tenth-century reformation, which includes the story of English Latin culture, the art of illuminating manuscripts and of handwriting—and, indeed, all the other arts, including architecture—is a rich and noble one. It would include the names of Aldhelm, "perhaps the most learned man of his day in Europe"; of Boniface, who lacked Aldhelm's over-elaboration of style but whose Latin writings have their own individual power and charm; of Benedict Biscop of Northumbria, who founded the two famous Benedictine monasteries of Wearmouth and Jarrow; and of Bede (673–735), Biscop's great pupil, who spent his life as a monk at Jarrow and is one of the really great scholars of England and of Europe, author of numerous works of Biblical interpretation, history, biography, and science; of Alcuin of York (735–804) who ended his career as adviser to Charlemagne and head of his palace school, thus playing an important part in the European cultural movement known as the Carolingian Renaissance; as well as of the tenth-century writers who have been already discussed. It would include the story of the relations between scholars who looked to Ireland and those who looked to Rome, and the special contributions of each, and it would tell of the part played by English church-

CHAPTER TWO

The Development of Middle English Prose and Verse

THE NORMAN CONQUEST of England in 1066 provides one of those convenient landmarks for the historian, whether political, social, or cultural, that divide up his subject almost too neatly. The temptation to take 1066 as the dividing line between the old Anglo-Saxon England and the new Anglo-Norman England is indeed difficult to resist, and of course it should not be altogether resisted. The Norman Conquest imposed a French-speaking ruling caste on England, with the result that Anglo-French developed as the literary language of the highest social classes and Anglo-Saxon (now rapidly developing into that stage of the English language known as Middle English) was for a period relegated to the lower classes. English, which remained the language of the vast majority of the people, eventually won out over French, and by the beginning of the fourteenth century its victory was clearly evident, but its re-establishment as a polite literary language after the period of Anglo-French ascendancy did not mean that it was starting altogether anew, without awareness of its Anglo-Saxon roots. The English which finally ousted French as the language of the literature of England was a language changed in many important respects—it had lost the Anglo-Saxon inflections and had greatly enriched its vocabulary from French—but it had not wholly lost touch with its traditions, and there is a greater continuity between Anglo-Saxon and Middle English literature than the casual reader of both might imagine. It is true that in English poetry the rhymed verse of French soon replaced the Anglo-Saxon alliterative tradition, though there was a remarkable revival of alliterative verse in the fourteenth century. And the English tradition in prose, which, after the achievements of the Alfredian translators and the homiletic tradition of Ælfric and Wulfstan, was much more advanced than anything in French prose, did not prevent French influence from making verse the medium of much Middle English historical and miscellaneous writing for which prose would have been (and, in the Anglo-Saxon period, was) the appropriate vehicle. Yet, though French influence brought rhyme instead of alliteration to English poetry and restricted the range of English prose, and though the French language affected both the vocabulary and the pronunciation of English, Middle English literature—English literature between the early twelfth and the late fifteenth centuries—is in many important respects the heir of its Anglo-Saxon ancestry, and the elements which distinguish it most sharply from Anglo-Saxon literature are those which might well have flowed into it in the normal course of international cultural influence. The influence of French literary methods and French literary attitudes was felt all over Europe, and would have been felt in England even if there had been no Norman Conquest. We are entering the period of French cultural domination of Europe, which is a much more significant phenomenon—even for English literature—than William the Conqueror's victory in 1066.

But if the long-term development of English literature was less affected by the Norman Conquest than might at first sight be imagined, there can be no doubt that the immediate effect of the Conquest was to disrupt the course of English[1] literature considerably. The position with regard to language was enough to ensure that. Even though modern scholars tend to regard as exaggerated the older view which held that French was the regular language of the upper classes for more than two and a half centuries after the Conquest, and stress the evidence that points to the use or at least the knowledge of English among the upper classes outside the immediate circle of the Court, the fact remains that for over two centuries the literature produced under courtly or aristocratic patronage was French both in tone and in language, while literature in English was either rough and popular (much of it oral, and so lost), or simply didactic, written by the lower clergy with the object of instructing the common people in biblical story and the duties required by their

[1] I am using the term "English" to refer to the whole field of literature discussed in this book, as I regard the Anglo-Saxon phase as an integral part of the English literary tradition. The logical term to use for Anglo-Saxon for anyone with this point of view would be "Old English," which gives us the neat tripartite division of the English language into Old English, Middle English, and Modern English, the common word "English" emphasizing the continuity. Many modern scholars do this, yet "Anglo-Saxon" remains the older-established and better-known term, and it seems pedantic to refer, for example, to the well-known *Anglo-Saxon Chronicle* as the *Old English Chronicle,* as is sometimes now done.

religion. The immediate form in which Anglo-Saxon alliterative verse survived was less technically subtle, more simply accentual, than the stricter form of the Anglo-Saxon period: it probably represented a popular oral tradition which was less likely to be affected by the displacement of polite English literature by French, and it was certainly a kind of verse which was more susceptible to the influence of the French rhymed couplet, toward which it moved. One might, indeed, distinguish two lines of development of the old Anglo-Saxon alliterative verse. One moves via this popular tradition toward the rhymed couplets of the French, the long alliterative line breaking into two, acquiring rhyme, and becoming metrically regular. The other somehow made contact with the purer and stricter alliterative tradition and emerged in the so-called "Alliterative Revival" of the fourteenth century, which produced, in western and northern parts of the country where national English feeling had remained strongest, some of the most interesting works in the whole of Middle English literature.

But if some aspects of the Anglo-Saxon verse tradition lingered on, the same cannot be said for the heroic note of Anglo-Saxon poetry. The Norman Conquest was itself the last of those many movements, migrations, invasions, and expeditions, which had ended the Roman Empire and brought a new Europe into being; by the beginning of the twelfth century this new Europe had defined its relation to the Roman past, had established itself as a Christian civilization, and had become sufficiently stable culturally to form its own norms of politeness both in life and in letters. The heroic age was gone, and new kinds of courtly sophistication replaced the heroic ideal in manners. There are, of course, links between the new Europe and the old, and we can trace the movement from the *chansons de geste,* with their sterner note of heroic endeavor—they include the verse tales of Charlemagne and his peers—to the Arthurian romances, with their stress on courtly behavior and new ideals of love and sentiment. Of these romances, more hereafter; at the moment we note merely that the old heroic note was dying away throughout Europe, because the new Europe of the Middle Ages was not a heroic society in the strict historical sense but a feudal society with its own conventions of service, honor, and obligation, its own kind of literary patronage, and its own social conditions breeding its own view of the relation between the sexes. The Norman Conquest did not bring this feudal organization to England; it had been developing in late Anglo-Saxon times; but it certainly hastened the process and, what is more important to the literary historian, it brought England more immedi-

ately into contact with continental civilization and especially with
the new flowering of French culture which was to change the pattern
of all medieval European literatures. Again, we must not imagine
that Anglo-Saxon England had been isolated from the continent, and
that it was not until 1066 that relations between England and the
continent developed. There were in fact powerful Norman influences
working in England in the generation before the Conquest, and the
Anglo-Saxon kingdoms, at the height of their prosperity, had many
and significant European contacts. But the Norman Conquest
brought a more immediate, a more active, and a more continuous
relationship with the continent, and, by imposing a French-speaking
ruling caste on England, brought the achievements of the new
French culture more rapidly and more forcibly to the attention of
Englishmen.

The story of English literature during the two centuries and a
half after the Norman Conquest is the story of what the late seventeenth-century critics were to call, with reference to the achievement
of their own poets, "the refinement of our numbers." Forced back to
its more popular elements, English literature soon began to rise again
slowly in the social scale, gradually acquiring an ease, a skill, and a
polish which would enable it to hold its own with French. The full
and triumphant achievement of this new ease and skill and polish—in
the work of Chaucer—coincides in date with the final re-establishment of English as the universal national language, the speech, both
written and spoken, of both Court and people. It was a very different
language now from that of *Beowulf* or of Ælfric, having come under
many influences in addition to undergoing those changes in pronunciation and word structure which any language undergoes with
the passing of time. But it was the legitimate descendant of its Anglo-
Saxon parent. The reader of English literature of this period is struck
by the number of different Middle English dialects: it was not until toward the end of the Middle English period that the East
Midland dialect became more or less the standard literary language.
The reason for the number of Middle English literary dialects
was that, as a result of the Conquest, Wessex lost its political and
cultural importance, and its dialect, West Saxon, which had established its supremacy as the literary language, therefore similarly lost
its prestige. With the Court and aristocratic circles using French,
there was no force making for the supremacy of any one Middle
English dialect over the others, so writers in English used the language of their own region. These regional dialects of Middle English
were the descendants of their Anglo-Saxon ancestors: the Northum-

brian dialect of Anglo-Saxon split up into Scots and Northern English; Mercian developed into East Midland and West Midland; West Saxon divided into the Southwestern and Central-Southern dialects; and Kentish became the basis of the dialects of the Southeast. Where there is no central standard of polite usage, a language will always split up into regional dialects, which is of course why a popular literature, developing independently of polite standards, will tend to use the language of its own region, as in American folk song to this day. This also explains why, for example, Scots, originally a branch of Northumbrian English and later, as a result of its use by the Middle Scots poets, a fully developed literary language in its own right, split up into regional dialects after the Middle Ages, when, as a result of increasing association with England, Scotland more and more adopted standard English as its literary language and thus lost its standard for polite Scots. Just as the eclipse of Wessex and the loss of the standardizing power of its language produced by the Norman Conquest and the emergence of French as the courtly language led Middle English to relapse into a series of dialects even as a written language, so the union of the crowns of England and Scotland in 1603 and the union of the parliaments of the two countries in 1707 made English the standard polite language of Scotland and split Scots up into the series of local dialects which it has remained until our own time, when the movement of contemporary poets to create a synthetic Scots literary language is at last trying to reverse this trend.

As French receded, even among the upper classes, and English moved slowly up in the social scale, the possibility of a new standard form of literary English grew steadily, until, by the end of the Middle English period, the dialect of London, now the dominant city of England, reigned supreme. The London dialect had originally been a Southern dialect, with its characteristics largely Southeastern, but by Chaucer's time it had become mainly East Midland in character, with the result that standard modern English derives from East Midland and not, as any one looking at the English literary scene about the year 1050 might have predicted, West Saxon.

The loss of Normandy by the English in 1204, and royal decrees in both England and France in 1224 making it illegal for any one to hold land in both countries, must have helped to make the descendants of the Normans in England consider themselves bound purely to England and encouraged the growth among them of the English language. Besides, it must be remembered that the Norman Conquest did not represent—as did the invasions of the Saxons and the

Danes—a national migration. The army brought to England by William, Duke of Normandy, consisted of no more than about six thousand men, and some of these were mercenaries who returned across the Channel after the subjugation of England was completed in 1070. William gave English estates to his followers and made them into a small ruling class which replaced the Anglo-Saxon nobility, but underneath, English life went on very much as usual. It is true that Henry II (1154–1189), the first of the Plantagenet kings, possessed vast realms in France, extending from the Channel to the Pyrenees (having inherited Normandy and Maine from his mother, and Anjou and Touraine from his father, and acquiring Poitou, Guienne, and Gascony by his marriage to Eleanor of Aquitaine, and Brittany through his son Geoffrey, who married Constance, heiress of that province), and throughout the late Middle English period English kings regarded themselves as the rightful kings of France (a claim which produced the Hundred Years War, which began in 1338[2]). But, though this intimate contact with France kept the influence of French culture very much alive in England, it could not prevent the steady rise of the English language until it became again, in the fourteenth century, the polite as well as the popular language of England; for the masses of Englishmen had spoken English all along.

The classic document on the rehabilitation of English in educated circles is a paragraph in John of Trevisa's translation of the *Polychronicon* of Ralph Higden. Higden, writing about 1350, had stated that ever since the Normans came to England Englishmen had been forced to leave their native language and do everything in French, and that the children of gentlemen were taught to speak French from infancy. Trevisa, translating Higden's work from the Latin in 1385, adds his own comment on Higden's statement:

Þys manere was moche y-vsed tofore þe furste moreyn, and ys seþthe somdel ychaunged. For Iohan Cornwal, a mayster of gramere, chayngede þe lore in gramerscole and construccion of Frensch into Englysch; and Richard Pencrych lurnede þat manere techyng of hym, and oþer men of Pencrych, so þat now, þe ȝer of oure Lord a þousand þre hondred foure score and fyue, of þe secunde kyng Richard after þe Conquest nyne, in all þe gramerscoles of Engelond children leueþ Frensch, and construeþ and lurneþ an Englysch . . .

[2] In spite of some impressive victories over the French, such as Crecy and Poitiers (1346 and 1356 respectively), the English never established their claim for any length of time; even Henry V, who after his victory at Agincourt in 1415 and his triumphant entry into Paris had himself named the heir to the French throne, never lived to be King of France, and in the following reign, that of Henry VI, the revival of French national feeling resulted in the driving out of the English. By 1453, when the Hundred Years War (which had been far from continuous since 1338) came to an end, the only French possession left to the English was the port of Calais.

This was the general custom before the first plague [the Black Death of 1349], but things have changed now. For John Cornwall, a school teacher, changed the method of teaching in school and made his pupils translate from French into English; and Richard Pencrych learned that way of teaching from him, as did other men of Pencrych, so that now, 1385 A.D., the ninth year of the reign of King Richard II, in all the grammar schools of England children have abandoned French and translate and do their lessons in English.

This sets the date of the change from French to English as the means of instruction in schools fairly precisely, and when we realize that formal educational methods are always conservative and are slow to reflect public opinion, we can see why the social and cultural rehabilitation of English can be said to have been achieved in the first half of the fourteenth century. English was introduced into the law courts in 1362,[3] and English was used for the first time in the opening of parliament in 1363; the work of Chaucer came in the immediately following decades. By this time, too, Anglo-French—the development of Norman French in England—was giving way in England to Parisian French, the standard French of France, which indicated that its knowledge was a polite accomplishment rather than a native endowment.

Besides French and English there was Latin, the learned language of Christian civilization. Latin had also, of course, been the learned language in Anglo-Saxon times, and it was only the dearth of good Latinists in England that led to the use of Anglo-Saxon in serious didactic literature (we saw earlier how King Alfred's program of translation was caused by his fear that Latin had declined throughout the country). This illustrates very clearly how ignorance—of a kind—can encourage the growth of a vernacular literature, a not uncommon phenomenon in the history of culture. Anglo-Saxon literary prose was among the best developed in Europe, and far more advanced than French prose; but had the Danish invasions not produced a decay of Latin learning, it would never have developed as it did. The ecclesiastical reforms introduced into England by the Normans restored Latin as the language of serious didactic works and thus did grave harm to the tradition of English literary prose—though, as we shall see, the tradition did survive, to re-emerge impressively later.

With the Latin literature of medieval England we are not concerned in this history, though no one who wishes to understand the

---

[3] At least, an Act of Parliament of that year ordered that all pleas should be conducted in English; but in fact French remained the language of the law courts for much longer.

literary culture of the Middle Ages can ignore it. Latin was not only the language of theological and didactic works; it was also the language of science, philosophy, history, and a great deal of poetry. Latin was also used for all official documents, and was the legal language of Norman England until it was replaced by Anglo-French in the thirteenth century. (Anglo-French remained the official legal language of England until 1731.) Perhaps the most interesting Latin prose works produced in England in the early Middle English period were the histories. Such Anglo-Latin historians as William of Malmesbury, whose histories of England show both learning and a critical judgment, and Matthew Paris, the greatest of the twelfth-century English historians, are of more interest to students of historiography than to those concerned primarily with literature, but the *Historia Regum Britanniae* of Geoffrey of Monmouth, written in the third decade of the twelfth century, provided a mine of material which was later to be fruitfully employed by poets and romancers. Geoffrey was a Welshman, and drew on old British traditions, including the Welsh historians Gildas and Nennius. He gives us a picture of the Anglo-Saxon invasions seen through the eyes of the retreating Britons, and his pages are filled with figures which were to become famous in imaginative literature. Here we first find the stories of Lear and Cymbeline and Gorboduc, and here, most important of all, we get the first full-dress story of the exploits of King Arthur. It is Arthur himself, rather than his knights, who keeps the center of the picture: we hear nothing yet of Lancelot or Tristan; but we have Uther Pendragon and Merlin; we have the treachery of Arthur's nephew Mordred and the disloyalty of Guanhumara (Guinevere), and we have the final bearing of the mortally wounded Arthur to Avalon. Arthur is a great hero to Geoffrey, rather than a great symbolic figure in the background, as he was later to become, and the knights by whom he is surrounded are loyal feudal retainers rather than epitomes of courtly virtues. Geoffrey has Arthur successful in war against enemies both at home and abroad, until, rejecting Rome's demand for tribute, he sets out to conquer Rome itself. But the disloyalty of Mordred and of Guinevere recalls him, and so the story goes to the last great battle and the journey to Avalon. Here is the outline of the story that so much later medieval literature was to use as a grand backcloth for innumerable individual incidents.

The *De Nugis Curialium* ("Courtiers' Trifles") of Walter Map is another twelfth-century Latin work likely to interest the reader of medieval English literature, though for very different reasons from those which lead him to Geoffrey of Monmouth. It is a lively collection of the most miscellaneous material, loosely organized in the form of a satire on contemporary abuses. It contains anecdotes, folk tales, pieces of invective, witty observations, amusing stories, and similar entertaining matter, and its existence is a reminder that medieval Latin was not the language only of solemn works. Walter Map was long credited with many of those lively Latin lyrics—satirical, amorous, irreverent, bacchanalian, and sometimes indecent—which belong to the medieval Goliardic tradition, the tradition of the wandering scholars, the rollicking secular protest against official Christendom's focusing on the next world. How many of these poems, if any, Map himself wrote is not known; but Goliardic poetry, with its secular moods and its frequent metrical skill, represents a chapter of European poetry of the greatest interest to anyone concerned with any of the European literatures. The movement from classical Latin quantitative verse to the rhymed accentual Latin verse of medieval hymns and of these Goliardic poems represents a major shift in the nature of the European ear for poetry, one might almost say, and it can be studied more happily than elsewhere in the fascinating literature of the wandering scholars. The clear voice of the disinterested lyrist comes to us from the Middle Ages more often than we realize in the Latin words of some impoverished but singing scholar:

> Musa venit carmine,
> dulce modulamine:
> pariter cantemus . . .

> The Muse comes with song,
> with sweet harmony.
> Let us sing, too.

There was also an important Anglo-French literature in England in the twelfth and thirteenth centuries. Much of it is religious and didactic—and we must never forget that by far the largest number of medieval works in any language are religious and didactic—of which only a few have any strictly literary interest, among them the allegorical poem *Le Chasteau d'Amour* by the brilliant and learned Robert Grosseteste, bishop of Lincoln, where praise of the Virgin and many aspects of Christian theology are presented through an elaborate allegory of a castle and its defenders. The lively and metrically interesting *Voyage of St. Brendan*, with its rich collection of marvelous adventures, is another Anglo-French poem of some literary interest today. There are also many Anglo-French chroniclers, among whom by far the most significant for the reader of English literature is Wace, whose translation of Geoffrey of Monmouth's *Historia Regum Britanniae*, in the middle of the twelfth century, represented an important stage in the transmission of the Arthurian legend. Wace's *Roman de Brut*, as his work is generally called, is more than a simple translation of Geoffrey of Monmouth; he also includes Arthurian stories from other sources, and is the first actually to mention the Round Table, though his references to it seem to indicate that it was already known to his readers. The *Roman de Brut* consists of fifteen thousand lines of verse, done with vivacity and a feeling for dramatic incident that strike the imagination more forcibly than the straightforward historical narrative of Geoffrey of Monmouth. It is with the translation of Wace's *Roman de Brut* by Layamon early in the thirteenth century that the Arthurian story first appears in English.

Works in French written in England during this period also include a number of romances, verse stories written purely for entertainment, and some shorter verse narratives, generally based on folklore and often dealing with the supernatural, to which the name Breton *lais* has long been given. The *lai* is of Celtic origin, and seems to have derived both from Welsh and Breton sources. (Brittany, it will be remembered, was settled by fugitives from Britain after the Anglo-Saxon invasions, so that the Bretons were very closely akin, both in speech and in traditions, to the Britons of Wales and Cornwall; they spoke almost the same Celtic tongue and cherished alike the Arthurian and other Celtic British legends.) The best known author of *lais* was Marie de France, who was apparently born in France but wrote in England and dedicated her *Lais* to King Henry II. Of the romances we shall speak in greater detail later; they represent one of the most important branches of medieval secular literature and require separate treatment.

Anglo-French literature, whether written in that form of French which, since King John's loss of Normandy in 1204, had been developing in its own way in England, or written in England in the French of Paris, was part of the wider stream of French literature which, partly because of the Norman Conquest but more fundamentally because of the extraordinary efflorescence of French literature in the twelfth century, swept into English literature in the Middle English period and moved it far away from the Anglo-Saxon heroic mold. We shall have to look more closely, therefore, at French literature and the techniques, attitudes, and subject matter which it introduced.

But what, meantime, was happening to the native Anglo-Saxon tradition? In poetry, there is little extant to show precisely what was happening in the late eleventh and early twelfth centuries. We have some fragments of religious and didactic poetry which are sufficient to indicate that the Anglo-Saxon alliterative line was continued, though in a looser and more popular form. The *Worcester Fragments* (so called because they consist of the remnants of a manuscript which had been cut up and pasted together to make the covers of a book in the library of Worcester Cathedral) preserve, in addition to portions of Ælfric's *Grammar* (in West Saxon), a short poem lamenting that the people are no longer taught in English, as they used to be in Anglo-Saxon times by the great Anglo-Saxon saints and scholars, but are left in ignorance by foreign teachers, so that both teachers and people are damned together.

> Nu is þeo leore forleten and þet folc is forloren.
> Nu beoþ oþre leoden þeo læraþ ure folc,
> And feole of þen lorþeines losiæþ and þet folc forþ mid.

> Now is this teaching abandoned and the people is lost.
> Now it is men of other languages that teach our people,
> And many of the teachers are damned and the people as well.

The language here is early Middle English, and probably represents a late twelfth century scribe (about 1180) transcribing into his own West Midland dialect a poem originally written in West Saxon soon after the Conquest. The language is, indeed, transitional between Anglo-Saxon and Middle English and is nearer to the language of Ælfric than to that of Chaucer. The verse form is still the Anglo-Saxon alliterative line, though looser than in classical Anglo-Saxon poetry. But neither this poem nor the fragmentary *Debate between the Body and the Soul* which follows it is of any general literary interest: their interest lies in their illustration of the development of the language and of the verse forms of the Anglo-Saxons in the twelfth century. The development can be traced further in much religious and didactic literature (including paraphrases of parts of the Bible), though there is little else that is so close to the Anglo-Saxon tradition. We soon begin to see the increasing influence of French models, an influence particularly noticeable where, as often happened, the Middle English work was itself a translation from the French.

A startling break with any tradition is the curious *Orrmulum*, written probably about the year 1200 by an Augustinian canon named Orm or Ormin. Orm's intention was to translate into English verse the Gospels that were read in the Mass during the whole year, but the verse he used employed neither the rhyme of the French nor

Anglo-Saxon alliteration, depending simply and wholly on strict syllabic regularity. It can be best illustrated by quoting the opening line:

> Þiss boc iss nemmnedd Orrmulum forrpi patt Ormm itt wrohhtë
> This book is called Orrmulum, because Orm made it.

This is the first of the ten thousand extant lines of the poem (fortunately, only about one-eighth of the whole survives), and each of the other lines is of exactly the same length, each has precisely the same metrical pattern, with fifteen syllables and a "feminine" ending, and there is nothing to vary the intolerable monotony. Orm's spelling is also original: it is a phonetic spelling, with a double consonant after every short vowel except when the vowel is in an open syllable. Whatever his reason for doing this (and it has been much debated) he produced a very odd-looking text, interesting to philologists but of more than usual tedium to the general reader. Orm's meter is not in itself unusual—if we divide his line into two we get the standard ballad measure:

> He turned his face unto the wall,
>   And death was with him dealing:
> "Adieu, adieu, my dear friends all,
>   And be kind to Barbara Allan."

Wordsworth was partial to it:

> And hark! how blithe the throstle sings!
> He, too, is no mean preacher:
> Come forth into the light of things,
> Let Nature be your Teacher.

But Wordsworth and the ballad writers at least had the variety of rhyme, and none of them ran to ten thousand lines.

Orm might have done better to accept the French rhyming fashion, which was now beginning to come into Middle English religious and didactic verse. The four-hundred line *Poema Morale* or *Moral Poem* is a late twelfth-century versified sermon written in the same meter as the *Orrmulum*, but with more flexibility and employing rhyme. Though hardly the most exciting of poems, the *Poema Morale* has a certain vigor and some signs of personal feeling that are wholly lacking in the *Orrmulum*. It deals with the usual medieval religious commonplaces—lost opportunities in this life, the Last Judgment, the horrors of Hell, the joys of Heaven, the call to repentance—but the note of earnest conviction which comes through saves it from being the purely mechanical rehearsal of commonplaces.

Once the Middle English writers had learned rhyme, nothing could stop them, and a didactic writer or long-winded romancer given his head in a clippety-clop meter was very hard to stop. Octosyllabic couplets could go on for ever:

> Men yhernes rimes for to here,
> And romans red on maneres sere,
> Of Allsaunder þe conquerour;
> Of Iuly Cesae þe emparour;
> O Grece and Troy the strang strijf;
> Þere many thosand lesis their lijf;
> O Brut that bern bald of hand,
> Þe first conquerour of Ingland;
> O Kyng Arthour þat was so rike,
> Quam none in hys time was like,
> O ferlys þat hys knythes fel,
> Þat aunters sere I here of tell,
> Als Wawan, Cai and oþer stabell,
> For to were þe ronde tabell;
> How Charles kyng and Rauland faght,
> Wit sarazins wald þai na saght;
> O Tristrem and hys leif Ysote,
> How he for here be-com a sote,
> O Ioneck and of Ysambrase,
> O Ydoine and of Amadase. . . .

This is the opening of the *Cursor Mundi,* an enormous poem of some thirty thousand lines which deals with all the important incidents of both Old and New Testament story and a great variety of moral and religious topics. The poem, which dates from the last quarter of the thirteenth century, is encyclopedic in scope, and is carried along through its varied subject matter by its author's determined and not unskillful rhyming. It is a good introduction to the medieval view of world history and of much else, and serves to remind us once again of the didactic purpose of so much medieval writing.

With properly varied rhymes and metrical skill—which took a long time to develop—the Middle English poet was able to achieve something far removed from anything possible to his Anglo-Saxon predecessor, and even the most stereotyped religious subject could be made fresh and moving with the proper lilt and the proper imagery. One of the earliest successful religious poems in Middle English is the twelfth-century *Love Rune* by Thomas of Hales. It urges the vanity and transience of earthly love and advocates instead the love of Christ. The traditional theme of *ubi sunt qui ante nos fuere?*—where are those who lived before us?—rings out with a new confidence:

> Hwer is Paris and Heleyne
>> Þat weren so bryht and feyre on bleo [face],
> Amadis and Ideyne,
>> Tristram, Yseude and alle þeo,
> Ector, wiþ his scarpe meyne,
>> And Cesar, riche of wordes feo [wealth]?
> Heo beoþ iglyden vt of þe reyne [world]
>> So þe schef is of þe cleo. [As the sheaf is from the hillside
>> *or* As the sheaf is (cut) by the reaping-hook.]

This sounds the true note of medieval plangency, a note sounded first (as far as the Middle Ages knew) by the late fifth- and early sixth-century Roman philosopher Boethius, one of the most popular writers in the Middle Ages, translated both by King Alfred and by Chaucer. Boethius had asked:

> Ubi nunc fidelis ossa Fabricii manent,
> quid Brutus aut rigidus Cato?

> Where now lie the bones of the faithful Fabricius,
> What now is Brutus or upright Cato?

King Alfred, in his rendering, substitutes for the remote classical character figures nearer home, and asks, "Where are now the bones of the famous and wise smith Wayland, and who knows where they be? . . ."

A late thirteenth-century English lyrist asked the same question:

> Were be they þat biforen us weren, [that were before us]
> Houndes ladden and havekes beren, [led hounds and carried hawks]
>> And hadden feld and wode? [field and forest]

And a century later, in France, Villon was to ask:

> Dictes moy où, n'en quel pays,
>> Est Flora, la belle Rommaine;
> Archipiada, ne Thaïs,
>> Qui fut sa cousine germaine;
>> Echo, parlant quant bruyt on maine
> Dessus rivière ou sus estan,
>> Qui beaulté ot trop plus qu'humaine?
> —Mais où sont les neiges d'antan?

A sense of transience of earthly life pressed hard on the Middle Ages, and medieval writers developed their own kind of cadence for its expression. It is equally far removed from Æschylus' stern sense of fate, from the chastened melancholy of Sophocles, and from the civilized, almost self-indulgent sadness of Virgil; nor has it anything of the thoughtful introspection of Matthew Arnold's "Dover Beach." It is perhaps a simpler note than any of these, and it comes impressively into medieval literature only after the development of rhyme and meter had made it possible for medieval poets to express it with that special kind of lyric lilt. Anglo-Saxon alliterative verse was an effective medium for the older heroic poetry; but new kinds of sensibility demanded a lighter and more flexible mode of expression. The new rhyme and meter that the French brought to Europe meant, as we have said, a change in the European ear, but that corresponded to a deeper change—a change in European sensibility.

The octosyllabic couplet, which English learned from French, is not always, even in the early Middle English period, handled by determined and long-winded didactic writers; apart from its use in romances, it is found in a variety of works. One of the earliest appearances of this verse form in English is one of the most successful —in the vivacious *The Owl and the Nightingale*, written probably around 1200, the first example in English of the *débat*, the contest in verse between two or more speakers. The verse debate had become a literary convention in both Latin and French, and could serve a great many different purposes. In *The Owl and the Nightingale* the two birds, who pursue their altercation with great spirit and with all the legal tricks of a twelfth-century lawsuit, presumably stand allegorically for two ways of life, the monastic and the secular, or for two kinds of poetry, the didactic and the amorous. The nightingale is the more sympathetic character to modern readers, but, though the conflict is unresolved by the end of the poem, the owl would appear to have won on points. But whatever the allegorical intention, it is clear that the author delighted in the dramatic quality of the poem and that his main interest lay in giving life and spirit to a conventional form. The narrative is handled with an accomplished ease, and the dialogue succeeds in painting with great vividness not only the characters of the two speakers (the respectable owl and the hedonistic nightingale) but also aspects of the daily life of the period.

But these exceptional instances of accomplished early Middle English poems must not be allowed to obscure the fact that the recovery of an English poetic style after the Norman Conquest was a slow business, and was not generally accomplished until the fourteenth century. There were individual successful poems before the fourteenth century, but no great English poet. The substitution of rhyme and meter for the Anglo-Saxon alliterative verse was not the result of a revolution in taste and attitude, such as some literary historians have seen in the Romantic Movement; it was a slow process of imitation of and adaptation from the French, with the English language itself continually growing in vocabulary and in flexibility until it reached the point where it could handle the new verse form with confidence and variety. Without the French element in Middle English vocabulary, the possibilities for rhyme would have been very restricted.

Some of the early Middle English poems we have quoted above will show how the native Anglo-Saxon tradition gave way to the new rhyming fashion; but the alliterative tradition was not altogether dead. We can see it; in its more popular form, in Layamon's *Brut,* a metrical history of Britain based on Wace's *Roman de Brut* and written some time in the late twelfth century. Layamon's verse lacks the careful parallelism of Anglo-Saxon verse as well as such Anglo-Saxon poetic devices as the "kenning," and his lines have become purely accentual in rhythm, but he uses alliteration and no rhyme. More impressive testimony to the survival and even development of the Anglo-Saxon alliterative tradition is the group of accomplished alliterative poems which suddenly appear in the fourteenth century. These include romances, religious poems, and satirical and allegorical works. In the last group is the well-known *Piers Plowman,* to be discussed later, and among the romances is the remarkable *Sir Gawain and the Green Knight,* one of the most brilliant of all Middle English allegorical tales of adventure and of the marvelous, written in alliterative blank verse each paragraph of which concludes with four short lines having alternate rhyme. Among the religious poems of the so-called "Alliterative Revival" are three which are found in the same manuscript as *Sir Gawain;* they are *Patience, Purity,* and *Pearl,* of which the first is a homily on the virtues of patience illustrated by an effective recounting of the story of Jonah, and the last is both an elegy on the poet's dead daughter and an allegory of Christian faith, one of the most interesting and skillful religious poems of the Middle Ages.

In prose, it is easier to trace the continuity of the Anglo-Saxon tradition. Its variety and liveliness had made Anglo-Saxon prose remarkable among European literatures of the period: translations, homilies, and didactic, devotional, and informative works of many kinds were to be found in prose, while in the *Anglo-Saxon Chronicle* a tradition of historical prose was maintained for centuries. Copying of Anglo-Saxon prose works went on assiduously in monasteries after the Conquest, and the *Chronicle* was continued: the last entry was made in the Peterborough Chronicle in the middle of the twelfth century, after a gap caused probably by the confusions of King Stephen's reign, and it is between the language of this final scribe and that of his predecessor who brought the narrative up to 1132 that scholars have drawn the necessarily somewhat arbitrary line between Anglo-Saxon (Old English) and Middle English. This was the end of the Anglo-Saxon tradition of historical prose, and England now loses its lead in the development of vernacular historical writing. The Norman clerics who took over the local and national administrative positions in England after the Conquest introduced Latin as the language of official communication and historical record, and English historical prose did not emerge again until the time of the Tudors. At the same time French influence was leading English writers to turn to rhymed verse rather than prose for historical and other kinds of writing which had been prose in Anglo-Saxon times, while the increase of dialectical differences in Middle English helped to make a standard literary prose impossible. As far as English historical prose was concerned, then—as with such other arts as manuscript illumination, metal work, and jewelry—the Norman Conquest put the clock back.

In homiletic and devotional prose, however, the tradition was not lost; in spite of handicaps, the work of instructing the people in the vernacular went on after the Conquest. Here the fall from supremacy of the West Saxon literary language in favor of different local dialects was less significant, for instruction of the common people could in any case be most effectively done in their own dialect. Thus the Anglo-Saxon homiletic tradition—carrying on the work of Ælfric with modernizing of and additions to his sermons—continued to flourish, and English religious prose prospered side by side with the new French verse renderings of similar literature. This was especially true in the west of England; in the southeast French seems to have predominated even in this field early in the thirteenth century, but the mass of homiletic literature in the West Midland dialect of this period carried English religious prose safely through the danger period to provide continuity with the prose of Tudor times. The fact that Wulfstan, bishop of Worcester, retained his see after the Conquest until his death in 1095 must have helped to encourage this vernacular prose tradition in the west; it is significant that after his death his biography was written in English by Coleman, a Worcester monk.

The sermons, translations, saints' lives, and other devotional and didactic works in which this prose tradition manifests itself are of little literary interest, though they are of importance to the philologist and to the historian of thought and society. The earliest writings of this kind after the Conquest are those known as the *Katherine Group,* and include the lives of three virgin saints, Katherine, Margaret, and Juliana, a treatise pointing out the discomforts of marriage and the advantages of virginity, and a prose homily in which Wit, the informed master, and Will, the foolish mistress, appear struggling (amid a great number of allegorical figures) for control of the soul. These works are written in a conscious literary prose, with use (especially in the three saints' lives) of alliteration and deliberate rhythmic effects. They were addressed to a female audience, as was the *Ancren Riwle,* a manual of instruction intended for three young girls who had decided to become anchoresses. In addition to the usual devotional and didactic material, the *Ancren Riwle* contains much lively incidental material by way of illustration, and the author's use of proverb, anecdote, character sketch, and realistic detail, as well as his numerous references to matters of daily life—domestic affairs, farming, travel, sport, among other aspects—makes the work an important and interesting historical document as well as providing it with a human interest which the modern reader appreciates so much more than the conventional didactic element. It was written probably about 1200 in the West Midland dialect, and its influence and popularity were enormous. Its influence on the religious prose of the thirteenth and fourteenth centuries was largely instrumental in ensuring the transmission of the prose tradition of the Anglo-Saxon homilies to such writers as Richard Rolle of Hampole, the fourteenth-century mystical and devotional writer, and his follower Walter Hilton. Rolle is important both for the movement of devotional piety, with its ascetic bias and lyrical development of personal feeling in religious matters, which he founded, and for the clarity and cogency of his prose (which is in the northern dialect of Yorkshire). There is a modern ring to Rolle's prose style, partly because he tends to reduce the inflections as in modern English, but more significantly because of the simple directness of his word order. His rhymed verse is technically less distinguished. Of Rolle's followers, Walter Hilton (who died in 1396) is the most interesting, and his prose work *The Scale of Perfection,* which debates the respective claims of the active and the contemplative life, is another important document in the history of English prose style. How unreadable fourteenth-century religious treatises could be when devoid of any personal inspiration or stylistic grace can be seen in Michael of Northgate's *Ayenbyte of Inwyt* (*Prick of Conscience*) a translation of a thirteenth-century didactic work done with an infuriating mechanical dullness, not even accurately, and not always intelligibly. (This is the work whose title haunts Stephen Dedalus in Joyce's *Ulysses,* symbolizing his feeling of guilt with reference to his mother.) Its importance has been magnified by philologists, to whom it is a great treasure, for it is written in the pure Kentish dialect of Canterbury and its date is known precisely, a note at the end of the manuscript making clear that it was finished on October 27, 1340.

Contemporary with Walter Hilton is John Wyclif, a very different figure from any member of the Rolle group, for Rolle was a contemplative mystic by temperament and sought to withdraw from the world, while Wyclif, controversialist, philosopher, politician, and reformer, was with his followers responsible not only for attacks on some important claims and practices of the Church but also for the first complete translation of the Bible into English. The Wyclif Bible was certainly not all translated by Wyclif; but it was done under his inspiration. Nicholas of Hereford seems to have done part of the earlier of the two versions (finished between 1382 and 1384) and John Purvey the later (finished soon after 1388). The translation is done from the Latin text of the Vulgate and it has little grace or life, though the later version is better in this respect than the earlier. The Wyclifite versions have neither the strength nor the idiomatic flow of Rolle's prose, and scholars today are inclined to put Rolle and Hilton far above Wyclif, both among those responsible for the continuity of English prose from Anglo-Saxon to modern times and as pioneers of English prose style. They helped to keep a standard of English prose alive until the late fifteenth century, when the increasing use of English prose in both secular and religious writing meant that the danger was over, and henceforth the development of English prose, however uneven, was part of the natural progress of the language and its literature.

One of the most striking differences between Middle English and Anglo-Saxon literature lies in the realm of verse narrative. The replacement of the older heroic poetry by the verse romance marks a significant change in taste and sensibility. Heroic poetry is sterner in mood, more realistic in treatment, and claims to deal with the exploits of heroes who have had some real place in history; the romance is more frankly escapist and the marvelous is introduced for its own sake. Fighting in heroic poetry is a grim affair, engaged in for some specific purpose, and even the most valiant hero is liable to lose if he fights against heavy odds; in the romance, characters fight on principle, as it were, or as a matter of fashion, often without any specific object; the outcome depends more on the character of the fighter than on the odds against which he is fighting, and the whole thing is done ritualistically, as a stylized sport rather than a desperate necessity. The transition between heroic poetry and medieval romance can be seen in the French *chansons de geste,* of which the *Chanson de Roland* is the best known example. These poems are really short heroic epics, and it is not improbable that similar poems, dealing with Germanic heroes, existed in Anglo-Saxon England: perhaps *The Battle of Brunanburh* and *The Battle of Maldon* are lone survivors of this sort of thing. But the *chansons de geste* are also early romances as well as late heroic poems, for they already show something of the interest in idealized character and in purely imaginative elaboration which was to be the mark of the fully developed romance. This transitional kind of poetry flourished in France from the ninth to the twelfth centuries.

These heroic tales of action, the *chansons de geste,* were mostly produced in northern France; it was from the south, especially Provence, that the new elements of sentiment and courtly love came to produce a wholly new kind of romantic story. Provence had already developed, in the lyric poetry of the troubadours, a remarkable new literary form. The rise of Provençal language and literature in the tenth and eleventh centuries represents one of the most profound—and still one of the most mysterious—movements in European culture. In the tenth century the Provençal dialect—French in its southern form, the *langue d'oc*—began to prevail over others as the literary language of southern Europe. This was one of the results of the breakdown of Latin under the influence of the languages of the barbarians, and the process was fraught with the most far-reaching consequences. About 1100 a host of Provençal poets arose with remarkable suddenness, producing sophisticated love lyrics different in both tone and technique from anything hitherto known in Europe. The meter was regular and syllabic, and rhyme was used. The transition from classical Latin quantitative metrics to rhymed verse can be traced in late Latin hymns; it is one of the most fascinating stories in literary history; but it is no direct part of the history of English literature. The point that chiefly concerns the historian of English literature in dealing with the Middle English period is that English literature, like most of the

European literatures at this time, was in the French cultural orbit and that therefore what French literature had become by this time is directly relevant to any account of what was happening in English.

One might distinguish between the narrative romance of action, unaffected by the courtly and sentimental ideals of the south, and the romance as it was modified by the new Provençal sophistication. The former, the product of the *trouvères* (northern equivalent of the troubadours, professional minstrels who went around entertaining in the halls of the great houses), was written in the northern dialect of France, or *langue d'oil*, and, as we have seen, bore some resemblance to the earlier heroic poetry. Influenced by the southern love lyric, it bred the characteristic medieval form of literary entertainment, the romance in which loyalty to one's king is no greater force than loyalty to one's lady; where both love and war are ritualized by elaborate techniques of service; where the devoted knight overcomes fabulous obstacles by virtue of the strictness of his honor and the strength of his passion. We shall discuss later the ideal of courtly love which so affected the tone of medieval romance and indeed had an incalculable effect on all subsequent love literature; let us first look at the subject matter of these works.

The late twelfth-century *trouvère* Jean Bodel, in an often quoted couplet, divided the subject matter of medieval romance into three categories, the "Matter of France," the "Matter of Britain," and the "Matter of Rome the Great." The first of these groups was the earliest to be developed; it deals with the activities of Charlemagne and his knights, and its tone is nearer that of heroic poetry; it finds its greatest expression in the *Chanson de Roland*, which tells a desperate story of a courageous fight against hopeless odds, ending with the hero's death. As the cycle grew, the interest turned more and more away from the character of Charlemagne to concentrate on the exploits of individual members of the group of warriors that surrounded him, just as in the Arthurian cycle of romance the interest shifted from Arthur to his knights. The driving moral force behind the earlier romances of the "Matter of France" cycle is the sense of Christendom pushing back the infidel Saracen invaders of Europe, and it has been suggested that these romances were encouraged or even produced by monks of the monasteries on the pilgrim routes who thought in this way to identify their founder with one of Charlemagne's heroes and so attract patronage. Other romances in this group are concerned with the struggle of individual heroes against the Emperor's tyranny, or indeed with any kind of adventure which in the process of time became attached to the name of Charlemagne or one of his heroes. The "Matter of Britain" is concerned with the Arthurian stories, which we have seen beginning in Geoffrey of Monmouth and Layamon's *Brut*. But both Geoffrey and Layamon conceived themselves to be writing history, not romance; the Arthurian romances derive rather from the French Arthurian legends which were common long before Geoffrey wrote his history. The stories of a historical Romano-British or Cambro-British leader of his people against the Anglo-Saxon invaders may well have been handed down in Wales to be carried thence to Brittany by Welshmen who emigrated there in the ninth century, and it was from the Breton legends rather than from the English chroniclers that most of the later Arthurian romances seem to have sprung. These romances, dealing with the adventures of individual knights of the Round Table, are far removed in tone from the *Chanson de Roland:* they have lost the old heroic note completely and treat with extraordinary elaboration the practice and ideals of courtly love. The "Matter of Rome the Great" represented another great popular kind of subject matter—the ancient classical world, as seen through medieval eyes. This is not the world of Homer or of Pericles or of Virgil, but a curiously medievalized ancient world derived from sources and traditions far removed from what we would today consider the mainstream of classical culture. The story of Troy, which so haunted the medieval imagination, they got not from Homer but from the fourth-century Latin writer Dictys Cretensis (Dictys of Crete) and the somewhat later Dares Phrygius (Dares of Phrygia), who claimed to have been actually at the siege and told the story as eyewitnesses, Dictys on the Grecian side and Dares on the Trojan. If the *Aeneid* was the original source of the Troy story as the Middle Ages knew it,[4] it was the work of Dictys and Dares which developed the tradition, to be worked up in the late twelfth-century French romance, the *Roman de Troie* by Benoit de Saint Maure. A century after the *Roman de Troie*, came the *Historia Destructionis Troiae* by Guido delle Colonne, a full Latin version of the same material. The major figure in the development of the medieval Troy tradition is Benoit de Saint Maure, whose work first brings the material together to make it accessible to later medieval story; here we get not only a

[4] Virgil was known in the Middle Ages, though popularly as a "wizard" rather than a great poet. The *Aeneid* was made the basis of a French romance, the *Roman d'Eneas*. But the Troy story, as the Middle Ages knew it, was Benoit's, not Virgil's. Virgil's Dido, like the Medea of Ovid's *Metamorphoses* and other heroines from Ovid's *Heroides,* were treated as basic romantic love stories by the medieval courtly love poets.

full treatment of the Trojan war which is to be the standard medieval way of looking at it, but also the story of Troilus and Cressida, to be used so effectively by later English writers.

The "Matter of Rome" included not only stories of the siege of Troy, but other stories of the ancient world, of Thebes, of Alexander the Great, and of Julius Caesar among others. The medieval view of the civilization of Greece and Rome can be clearly seen in the "Matter of Rome" romances. Greece, of course, was more remote, and was seen less as a period of history than a group of legends concerning Greek historical and mythological figures who were conceived of as feudal lords with their retainers: we can see this very clearly in Chaucer's Knight's Tale. As far as the Trojan war was concerned, medieval Europe was on the side of Troy; indeed, many countries of Western Europe traced their origins from Trojan ancestors. Rome (also founded by a Trojan) was closer to them: its language was the international learned language of their day; its organization had enabled Christianity to establish itself throughout Europe once the Emperor himself had been converted; its roads and aqueducts were often still in use and still admired. It was the Roman Empire, not the earlier Republic, that the Middle Ages admired: Dante put Brutus and Cassius,[5] who conspired against the potential founder of the empire, in the lowest circle of Hell; for the Roman Empire was the divinely ordained machinery through which Christianity would come to Europe, and the term "Holy Roman Empire," in spite of the fact that the political entity so designated may have been neither holy nor Roman nor an empire, had real meaning to medieval minds in terms of historical continuity between the Christian and the Roman world. Yet with all this there was no real historical knowledge or historical perspective, no sense at all of different stages and kinds of civilization, no ability to conceive a radically different political or economic organization than their own. "Duke" Theseus, even to Chaucer, was essentially a medieval feudal lord. The medieval mind playing with the fragments of a lost classical civilization is a fascinating aspect of the history of culture.

The French romances dealing with the "Matter of Britain" and the "Matter of Rome" combined adventure and sentiment, the latter deriving from the elaborate conventions of courtly love which began in the love lyrics of Provence. The idea of courtly love proved to be one of the most far-reaching and one of the most revolutionary in

---

[5] With the revival of interest in the Stoic tradition in the Renaissance, it was the Republic rather than the Empire that was admired. Contrast Shakespeare's attitude to Brutus with Dante's, and note also Milton's attitude to Roman history.

the history of European sensibility; it spread rapidly throughout Europe, penetrating both lyrical and narrative literature from the Mediterranean to the North Sea, wherever the spirit of the Romance literatures touched. Hitherto, love between the sexes had been regarded simply as physical passion, or as a form of affection (but lower than that between man and man), or as a kind of madness, or as a combination of any of these three elements. In the poetry of the troubadours a new conception of love first appears. Love is service, like that of a slave to his master except that it is not based on outside compulsion. The knight serves the lady of his choice, suffers any and every kind of indignity for her sake, thinks only of her, commends himself to her when he goes into battle, and in referring to her uses language that is scarcely, if at all, distinguishable from that used in religious poems with reference to the Virgin Mary (and indeed there is a clear reciprocal influence between the cult of the Virgin Mary and the courtly love tradition). The slightest favor the lady chooses to bestow upon her servant is sufficient reward for the greatest hardship he may undergo for her sake. He is her humble vassal, and she is his liege lady. He must be loyal to her for life, however she may treat him. However desperate he is, however hopeless of winning his lady's favor, however he may sigh and moan because of unrequited love, he must never think of ceasing to be the servant of her whom he has originally chosen, for it is better to be in love than to have no liege lady to serve. Love is, as it were, its own reward, and though a more concrete reward is desired and sometimes obtained, the lover must not swerve in his allegiance if it does not come. This is not a relation between husband and wife: indeed, throughout most of this literature it is taken as a matter of course that a husband cannot be the lover of his own wife. That is a role to be taken by someone else. The courtly love tradition implies, in fact, an idealization of adultery, and if modern romantic love is automatically linked to marriage that is because the sixteenth- and seventeenth-century poets deliberately grafted the idea of courtly love onto the domestic ideal of married happiness. The concept of falling in love, wooing, and marrying, which has been one of the staple themes of fiction for two centuries, represents a modification of the medieval courtly love tradition while deriving from that tradition. In medieval courtly love, when a poet offers love to a lady he does not bother about her husband at all: his real rival is anyone who seeks to be a lover of the lady in the same way as himself. The lover's conduct must conform at all points to a strict code of honor: in addition to the service of his lady he must dedicate himself to the cause of women in a general sense, always ready to defend them, always prepared to succor damsels in distress. The rules of knightly behavior were carefully defined, and involved many subtle points of conduct: by these rules every lover was bound. There were, in theory if not in practice, "Courts of Love," which adjudicated on subtle points of honor and the proper conduct in love affairs.

The origins of this influential new conception of love between the sexes must be sought partly in social conditions, partly in the way in which such Latin writers on love as Ovid were interpreted in the Middle Ages, partly in a religious attitude which shifted attention from woman as Eve, the origin of all our human woes, to woman as the Virgin Mary, the pattern of ideal maidenhood. One must remember that feudal civilization (especially on the continent, where central government was generally less effective than in England) tended to resolve itself into separate islands of social life, the lord of the manor living with his lady in a little nucleus of civilization of which he was the guardian. Among his retainers and hangers-on there would be a great variety of male types who, while far above the land-tilling peasantry who supported the whole group by their labor outside the walls of the castle or manor, were nevertheless inferior to the lord of the manor and his lady: adventurers, landless knights, squires, pages, would look up to their master and mistress as their feudal superiors. The lady would become the source and arbiter of courtesy within the community, superior in rank to all except the lord himself, and, if he were away at the Crusades or on some other adventure, superior to all without exception. Thus service and courtesy were her rights anyway, and if any of the men of the community were to love her, the love would have to be expressed in a context of service and courtesy. Perhaps the genealogy of the courtly poet also throws some light on the ideals of humility and service so bound up with the new romantic attitude. Before the real troubadour poetry began, it was the common practice for the lord to have about him for his personal entertainment minstrels, *jongleurs,* at first merely primitive mummers or acrobats. When the new Provençal poetry began to develop, these humble entertainers— who were socially among the lowest of the castle servants—often took on the function of court poet, ceasing to be mere *jongleurs* and becoming troubadours. And though the troubadours rapidly rose in the social scale until they included in their number many of the lords themselves, it is not fantastic to see in the stress on service in courtly love poetry some trace of the humble position of the original troubadours, who were merely glorified clowns. Marriage, of course, would be out of the question between the lady and either the troubadour or one of her husband's male followers. An even more cogent reason for courtly love remaining outside marriage was that in feudal times marriage was so bound up with the inheritance and transmission of property that questions of love could not be allowed to enter into it. Lordship of land being the very basis of the system, anything connected with the disposal or acquisition of estates was a purely business matter into which sentiment must not intrude. Nor was the teaching of medieval religion calculated to drive the new conception of love into legal channels. Romantic passion in the relation between the sexes was not regarded by religion as a virtue under any circumstances, and there was no encouragement by the Church to graft the new feeling onto any conventional view of domestic happiness. From every point of view the difference between courtly love and the relations between man and wife was emphasized. The lady was mistress (in a literal sense) but never wife, and often had to be courted secretly (this explains much that is otherwise puzzling in the relations between Troilus and Criseyde in Chaucer's poem). The courtly lover did not even *wish* to marry his lady, though he sought a consummation of his love outside marriage. Marriage, the idea often seems to have been, would spoil everything. It was only later that the romantic ideal of love was linked with marriage and the passion was regarded as virtuous provided that it had marriage in view.

It is clear, therefore, that this conception of courtly love that swept over Europe and penetrated its literature was one that originated among the aristocracy and had little relation to the everyday lives of humbler men and women. It was, at its simplest, a conventionalization of the attitude of the high-placed feudal servant to his lord's wife, and if the lord himself was away at the Crusades there was all the more scope for the courtly lover. How far this attitude was a mere convention and how far it had a realistic basis is very difficult to say. Sometimes the whole business was nothing but a polite game, but we know that life often imitates art and the emotional pattern laid down in a literary convention is often spontaneously followed in real experience. There must have been something real behind it all. Of course to some the convention was just an opportunity to discourse subtly on the psychology of love, and it is to be noted that the psychological treatment of romantic love, so common in European literature, begins with the medieval allegories of courtly love.

This, then, was the kind of sentiment with which the medieval French romances surrounded their action. Such romances were produced in England as well as in France, for, as we have seen, French was the language of the English upper class from the Conquest until the fourteenth century, and during this period the "polite" literature of England was French, either imported or domestically produced. The translations of French romances into English give us an interesting indication of the difference in social polish between the audience for works in the French language in England and that for works written in English. The English translators were adapting a sophisticated, sentimental French literature for a much less sophisticated audience, who were more interested in the story than in the refined speculations about love and honor so characteristic of the courtly love tradition. The French romances combined sentiment with adventure; the English translators as a rule left out the sentiment and stuck to the adventure. The English romances were thus on the whole shorter, cruder, and more of a straight "story" than the French. Such a popular French romancer as the twelfth-century Chrétien de Troyes, who specialized in what a later age was to call "the language of the heart," in the psychology of courtly love, never achieved the popularity among the English that he had in France and Germany. The one English romance known to have been translated from Chrétien is the early fifteenth century *Ywain and Gawain* (a characteristic "Matter of Britain" story, telling of the adventures of a knight called Ywain who marries the widow of a conquered foe, is separated from her, and after many valorous deeds becomes reunited with her; with Gawain serving as a foil to Ywain and the figure of Arthur presiding dimly in the background). This was condensed from the much longer *Ywain, ou le Chevalier au Lion* of Chrétien; the long speeches, designed to illustrate the psychology of the speaker and the courtly conventions under which both thought and action develops, are cut in the translation. Those in England who were courtly and sophisticated enough to appreciate the finer points of courtesy and psychology, expected their literature to be in French: the English translations were for their ruder compatriots.

We must see these English romances against the larger European background to understand what they really were. The "Matter of France," with its echoes of the conflict between Christian and Saracen in Europe, attracting to itself and to its presiding figure Charlemagne folk legends and miscellaneous tales of adventure, providing one great focus for the medieval imagination; the "Matter of Britain," deriving originally from Celtic traditions of Arthur in Wales and Strathclyde and Cornwall and Brittany, providing a mold into which new notions of courtesy and honor could be poured, a strange symbolic fusion of Christian ideals, feudal convention, erotic fashion, and a deep underlying sense of change and fate; the "Matter of Rome," showing how the ancient classical world came by devious ways into the medieval imagination, with its sense of a lost world of heroes, the doom of Troy, the pathos of Dido, the grandeur of Alexander, the dignity of Theseus—to see all this, to understand the materials with which the medieval romancer worked, is to get closer to the minds of medieval people than any political or philosophical history could take us. The English romancer was part of this world of medieval romance, and if he often abbreviated and simplified his French originals because he was writing for a less courtly audience (and it is audience rather than readers, for these romances would as a rule be read or recited aloud to a group), this does not mean that he thought of himself as in any way living in a different world than that of fellow romancers, either in France or in England, who wrote in French. It is perhaps misleading to look at surviving English romance and conclude that that gives a representative picture of what the English produced in that field during the Middle Ages. There is little really interesting "Matter of France" material surviving in English, for example, but we know that the Charlemagne cycle was popular in England, for one of the earliest of the surviving manuscripts of the *Chanson de Roland* (and the best) was written in England, and there are references in contemporary literature to the popularity of these romances. The oldest surviving English romance dealing with "Matter of France" is the dull *Otuel*, dating from the first half of the fourteenth century; it is one of those deriving from a French group dealing with Roland's warfare against the Saracens and deals with a duel fought between Roland and the Saracen Otuel. The subject was popular and was treated more than once in English romance. More popular still was the story of Firumbras, Saracen king of Alexandria, and the combat between him and Roland; the late fourteenth-century *Sir Firumbras* is one of a number dealing with this material. Most interesting of the relatively few surviving English Charlemagne romances is the northern *Raif Coilyear*, written in Scotland and possessing a distinct Scottish background. This romance is a late example of its kind, composed in the last quarter of the fifteenth century and extant in a unique printed version of 1572. It is written in the popular thirteen-line stanza, of which the first nine lines are long, with anything from five to seven stresses, and the last four are shorter with three or four stresses. The versification is rough, jogging along with little polish, but the story has humor and vivacity and immense gusto. The story is a widespread folk tale which has been grafted on to the Charlemagne background: it tells of how Charlemagne seeks shelter in the forest hut of a collier, who entertains him rudely but lavishly without being aware of his identity; meeting him later at the palace, the collier learns who his guest was and is knighted by him.

The surviving English "Matter of Britain" romances are a more varied and more interesting lot, and at least three of them—the alliterative *Morte Arthure;* the romance entitled *Le Morte Arthure* which deals with the Maid of Ascolot, the discovery of the love of Lancelot and Guinevere, the combat between Lancelot and Arthur, and the passing of Arthur; and *Sir Gawain and the Green Knight*—having impressive qualities as literature, especially the last, which is one of the great literary productions of the Middle Ages. The ramifications of the Arthur story, with the development of its different phases, is the subject for a book in itself; all we can note here is that the romances can be grouped into those that deal with the whole story of Arthur's life (of which the alliterative *Morte Arthure* is easily the finest); those concerned with Arthur's youth, which is involved with the character of Merlin (e.g., *Arthur and Merlin*); those that deal with Gawain, who is the true hero of Middle English Arthurian romance, the only one to become the hero of a whole cycle of romances, eleven in all, of which *Sir Gawain and the Green Knight* is the most remarkable and *Golagrus and Gawain* and *Ywain and Gawain* are able and interesting; those that deal with Lancelot, never as popular a figure in the English romances as in the French, where he is the hero of an immense and widely popular prose romance, though he is the hero of the admirable late fourteenth-century English romance *Le Morte Arthure;* those that deal with the Holy Grail, an aspect of the Arthur story not much handled in English before Malory, though *Joseph of Arimathie*, one of the two English romances which do handle it, is historically interesting as being one of the earliest alliterative poems in Middle English; and the Perceval legend, a popular and widespread folk tale which became grafted on to the Arthurian story in the twelfth century, represented in English by a single romance, *Sir Percyvelle of Galles*, though more fully treated by the French romancers who developed him from a type of the simple innocent to the ideal and perfect knight who eventually attains the Grail (it is this Perceval who is Wagner's Parsifal). Finally, there is the story of Tristram, or Tristan, which in later times became perhaps the most popular of all the

Arthurian stories. The love of Tristram and Isoude (Iseult) is older in its origins than that of Lancelot and Guinevere and is another of those independent stories which eventually became associated with the Arthurian cycle; it is represented in English by a single northern romance, Sir Tristram, written at the end of the thirteenth century.

Of the origins of the stories of the different knights, Gawain, Lancelot, Tristram, and others, much has been written, and there has been much discussion, too, about the obscure origins and complicated development of the Grail legend; but we must pass these matters by and concentrate on the literature as we have it. And the Arthurian romance literature in English is remarkable enough. Its greatest document, as we have remarked, is Sir Gawain and the Green Knight, one of four notable poems written in the Northwest Midland dialect in the late fourteenth century and presumably by the same author.[6] The 2,530 lines of this poem are arranged in stanzas of unequal length, each of which contains a number of long alliterative lines followed by five short lines rhyming alternately (ababa), the first having one stress and the remaining four having each three. There is real technical accomplishment in the handling of this difficult stanza; the author also has great skill in setting a scene and a lyrical feeling in showing the movement of the seasons reflected in the changing face of nature. The story opens with the appearance at Arthur's court of the strange and menacing Green Knight, who asks for a volunteer from among the Knights of the Round Table to strike him a blow with the heavy axe he would provide, on the understanding that a year and a day later the knight would come and receive a similar blow from him. The knights are amazed and silent, and Arthur himself is driven to volunteer, but Gawain, model of courtesy, nobility, and courage, steps in and gives the blow. He strikes off the Green Knight's head, but the Knight simply picks his head up and rides off, telling Gawain to keep his bargain and appear at the Green Chapel a year and a day later to suffer a similar blow. A year passes, and we see the earth changing from winter to spring, then to summer, then to autumn, with angry winds and leaves falling from the tree, and finally to winter again. In the New Year Gawain sets out to look for the Green Chapel. On the way he seeks shelter at a castle and is handsomely entertained there by the lord and lady. Each morning the lord goes off to hunt, and his hunting is described with lively detail; Gawain stays in the castle, and is tempted by the lady who wants him to make love to her. He has a difficult time retaining his perfect courtesy and at the

6 See p. 46.

same time repulsing her advances; but he goes no further than allowing her to kiss him. Gawain and the lord have promised to exchange with each other whatever they gain during the day, and in accordance with this bargain the lord gives Gawain the animals he has killed in the hunt and Gawain gives the lord the kisses. But on the last day the lady presses Gawain to accept a memento of her, and he accepts a green girdle which she says will give him invulnerability, which he will require in his encounter with the Green Knight. He says nothing of this girdle to the lord. Then Gawain leaves to find the Green Chapel, which turns out to be a grassy mound nearby. He meets the Green Knight, who strikes him with his huge axe, but deflects the blow as Gawain flinches. He taunts Gawain for flinching, and Gawain replies that he will not flinch again. He strikes a second time, Gawain remaining steady, but again he turns away the blow. The third time the axe lands, but only wounds Gawain slightly on one side of the neck. Gawain now says that he has fulfilled his bargain and demands a chance at a fair fight, but the Green Knight good-naturedly laughs at his ferocity and reveals himself as the lord of the castle; the slight wound on Gawain's neck is for the girdle which he took from his lady in order to preserve his life. Gawain, humiliated, admits his weakness and reproaches himself bitterly, but the Green Knight absolves him and tells him to keep the girdle. On his return to Arthur's court Gawain tells the whole story, not as a heroic exploit but as an example of moral failure, and Arthur comforts him and all the knights agree to wear a green belt for Gawain's sake.

The story clearly has deep roots in folklore and is capable of many kinds of allegorical interpretation. But it interests the reader today for the grace and liveliness with which the narrative is presented, for the technical skill of the versification, for the simple moving way in which the ideal of courage and courtesy is illustrated in Gawain's behavior, for the charm and conviction of Gawain's conversation with the lady and the genial humor of the Green Knight's last conversation with Gawain, for the brilliant detail of the hunting scenes, and above all for the feeling for nature and the movement of the seasons, embodied perhaps best of all in the description of the chill winter morning when Gawain leaves the castle to keep his appointment at the Green Chapel. It is a civilized and sophisticated work, and it shows what an unusually accomplished English romancer could make out of one of the Arthurian stories when the particular tradition represented by that story had reached just the proper stage. A story of marvels is interpreted in the light of a high ideal of physical and moral courage. The Gawain we see here is the true heroic Gawain, before he was ousted from his supremacy by Lancelot, who in later Arthurian romance completely replaced Gawain (even in England, where Gawain remained the great hero longer than in France) as the central heroic figure of the Arthurian cycle. The Gawain of Malory, as of Tennyson, is no longer the model of virtue, courtesy, and courage but an altogether debased figure. *Sir Gawain and the Green Knight* splendidly preserves the older, heroic Gawain, and does so in a typical Arthurian context, with Arthur presiding over his knights at Camelot at Christmas time and the spotlight on the individual adventure of one of them. In it the English romance achieves full literary stature. Elements from Anglo-Saxon, Norman, and French combine in a remarkable way: apparently the Anglo-Saxon alliterative tradition survived in modified form in the north, while the Arthurian legends were centered in the West, so a Northwestern poet, as the author of *Sir Gawain* appears to have been, was in a good position for uniting Anglo-Saxon and Celtic traditions. The vigor of the Anglo-Saxon, the polish of the French, and the magical folk strain of the Celtic combine successfully in the poem. Only Chaucer among medieval poets could achieve this kind of synthesis.

Jean Bodel's third category, the "Matter of Rome the Great," must be stretched to include a very miscellaneous collection of stories. There are lives of Alexander in both verse and prose, poems on the siege of Troy (of which the fourteenth-century West Midland alliterative poem, *The Gest Historiale of the Destruction of Troy* is the liveliest), verse accounts of the destruction of Jerusalem, and of course Chaucer's Knight's Tale. Apart from the last of these, which is a special case, an elaborate and polished verse narrative by a master, these romances are more important for the light they throw on the medieval imagination than for any special literary achievement. More important for English literature was a fourth category of which Jean Bodel says nothing, for it is peculiarly English. This is a group of romances drawing their material from English history; stories of these English heroes must have come down orally, and eventually reached the Anglo-French romancers who turned them into French verse narratives. Only after they had been rendered in French did they appear in English, sometimes as translations and sometimes as renderings of the version currently popular in England. (Evidently the English romancers did not feel that a popular oral tradition about an English hero was worth the dignity of being turned into a written romance unless it had already attracted the

Anglo-French romancers: this seems to be the only explanation of the fact that, English though these stories are in origin and subject, only those of them which have French originals or parallels appear in English romance.) On the analogy of Jean Bodel's classification, the subject matter of these romances has been called the "Matter of England," and this is a convenient enough term. That part of the "Matter of England" which achieved permanence in written romance must have represented but a small portion of the oral legends celebrating popular English heroes such as Athelstan, Offa, Earl Godwin, Eadric the Wild, and Hereward the Wake: we know of these oral traditions because they are referred to by the historians William of Malmsbury and Henry of Huntingdon.

Some of the most popular of the "Matter of England" subjects dealt with in English romance seem to derive from traditions associated with the Viking raids on England. *King Horn,* the earliest of the extant romances in the English group, tells the story of Horn, son of the king of Sudene, who after his father's death at the hands of pirates is set adrift and comes ashore at Westerness, where Rimenhild the king's daughter falls in love with him. Horn, after living with the king's household, eventually departs to prove his knighthood and returns after destroying a pirate crew. King Aylmar of Westerness finds Horn and his daughter embracing, and banishes Horn, who goes to Ireland where he does knightly deeds. He returns in disguise to Westerness in time to prevent Rimenhild's marriage to another prince, and, after further complications which almost duplicate earlier parts of the story, Horn slays his rival, regains his father's kingdom, and makes Rimenhild his queen. The poem is interesting for its meter; it is in short rhyming couplets which perhaps show the old alliterative line giving way before French influence or may be more directly related to contemporary French and Anglo-French verse. The short rhyming lines give the story rapidity of movement, and a certain declamatory tone which indicates that it was intended to be spoken. The audience envisaged is clearly a simple one; the tale is essentially naïve, with the interest deriving wholly from the sequence of incidents and the shifts in the fortunes of the protagonists. *King Horn* is a good example of the way in which the English romancers left out the courtly elements of the French; the love element is not dwelt on, and the emphasis is on action and adventure. The story trots on from incident to incident:

> He fond bi þe stronde,
> Ariued on his londe,
> Schipes fiftene,

Wiþ sarazins kene.
He axede what isoȝte
Oþer to londe broȝte.
A Payn hit of herde
And hym wel sone answarede,
"Þi lond folk we schulle slon
And alle at Crist luue vpon,
And þe selue riȝt anon;
Ne schaltu todai henne gon."

This simple movement of verse narrative is a pretty fair sample of the way the ordinary folk of thirteenth-century England liked to have their stories told. The story itself, with its folk elements of the returned exile and the reuniting of lovers, shows how a legend originally deriving from history can be overlaid by folk material to become an unsophisticated romance. There is also an early fourteenth-century North Midland version of the story in twelve-line stanzas, known as *Horn Childe*, and there are several ballad versions.

Another "Matter of England" romance which apparently derives from events of the Viking period but which also has been overlaid with much folk material (indeed, the central plot is a common folk tale which, as so often happens, became attached to a particular hero late in its history) is *Havelok the Dane*, one of the most successful of the simple tales of adventure in Middle English verse narrative. The story opens with the death of King Athelwold and the appointment of Earl Godrich as guardian of his infant daughter Goldeboru; but Godrich seizes power himself and imprisons Goldeboru. Then we are taken to Denmark, where Earl Goddard plays a similar role to that of Godrich. Having been appointed guardian of the children of King Birkebayn, Havelok and his two sisters, Goddard takes over the kingdom himself, kills the daughters, and hands Havelok over to Grim the fisherman with orders that he is to be drowned. But Grim, made aware by a supernatural sign of Havelok's royal birth, saves Havelok, and with his wife takes him and his own five children to England, where he founds the town of Grimsby. Havelok eventually takes a job as scullion to Earl Godrich's cook, and impresses everybody by his beauty, physique, and skill at games and in arms. Godrich, thinking that Havelok is "some churl's son and no more," plans to marry him to Goldeboru, and thus confirm his own possession of the throne. He forces the reluctant pair to marry, and they return to Grimsby, where Goldeboru learns from a mysterious light issuing from Havelok's mouth that he is really of noble blood and, at the same time, an angel's voice announces Havelok's royal parentage and glorious future: this cheers her immensely and at once puts the relation between the pair on a proper footing. Further adventures bring them to Denmark where Havelok destroys Goddard and regains his ancestral throne before returning to England to make an end of Godrich and gain the English crown as well.

The story moves along in rapid octosyllabic couplets: like *King Horn* it concentrates on the physical adventures and plays down the love interest. The scenes describing Havelok's activities as a scullion have a lively realism, and there are accounts of popular sports and a sense of the ordinary people of England at work which give this romance a special interest and vitality. A brief quotation may give some indication of the speed and vigor of the narrative: this is from the section describing Havelok's life as a scullion:

Þet oþer day he kepte ok	[second kept watch for also]
Swiþe yerne þe erles kok,	[very eagerly]
Til þat he saw him onþe brigge,	
And bi him mani fishes ligge.	[lying]
Þe erles mete havede he bouht	
Of Cornwaile, and kalde oft:	[called]
'Bermen, bermen, hider swiþe!'	[quickly]
Havelok it herde, and was ful bliþe	
Þat he herde 'bermen' calle;	
Alle made he hem dun falle	[them]
Þat in his gate yeden and stode	[way went stood]
Wel sixtene laddes gode. . . .	

In addition to the romances of these four "matters," there are a number of miscellaneous romances dealing with independent subjects. The mid-thirteenth-century *Floris and Blancheflour* is a pleasing rendering in rhymed couplets of a popular legend of eastern origin. It is a story of love triumphant, with Floris following his Blancheflour to the harem of the Emir of Babylon, who in the end is so moved by the tribulations of the lovers that he forgives them and has them married. The plot is one of many that came into Europe from the East through the Crusades bringing a special kind of imagination with them. The thirteenth century, when Welsh, Norman, and Anglo-Saxon traditions mingled in England, when Bretons and French influenced each other's storytelling, when mental traffic between east and west had been stimulated by the Crusades and by the journeys of merchants and scholars and pilgrims who took advantage of the relatively long period of internal peace in Western Europe, was a great century of literary cross-fertilization. *Floris and Blancheflour* is a product of such cross-fertilization, and brings a refreshing change from the constant fighting and courtly love-making of the typical romance and from the treatment of the Saracens as conventional infidels which we get in most of the "Matter of France" romances—for Floris is a Saracen (though he becomes a Christian in the end), Blancheflour is the daughter of a French widow carried off to Spain by a Saracen king, Floris' father, and the whole setting of the romance is Saracen. Another of the unclassified medieval romances is the fresh and charming *Sir Orfeo*, which shows a different kind of cross-fertilization: here the classical story of Orpheus and Eurydice has been treated as a Breton *lai* and in the process has been changed into a light-hearted fairy story far removed in tone from the stern Greek myth of Hades. *Sir Orfeo* was probably translated from a French original in the South or South Midlands of England soon after 1300. The story trips along in four-stressed rhyming couplets, simple without being dull, naïve in tone but with the incidents well manipulated and the story well constructed. The setting is medieval, of course, with nothing Greek about it: it is a minstrel tale of a rescue from fairyland through the power of music; Sir Orfeo regains his Dame Herodis—there is nothing about his not looking back—and the story ends happily. W. P. Ker has said of *Sir Orfeo* that "one may refer to it as a standard, to show what can be done in the medieval art of narrative, with the simplest elements and smallest amount of decoration."

There are other unclassifiable Middle English romances on a great variety of themes, some dealing with the patience and constancy of an abused woman, some dealing with stock courtly situations, some combining history and folklore in one way or another. The fourteenth-century *Ipomadon* is an especially interesting example of those dealing with stock courtly situations: a translation of an Anglo-French romance, it provides all the standard material of the typical French romantic story—the noble knight falling in love with a lady he has never seen, the faithful service, the analysis of emotion, the tournaments, disguises, all the physical and psychological goings-on that the medieval audience so delighted in; and the English translator has cut less of the passages of sentiment than he usually did. There are two verse versions and one in prose; the earlier of the two verse renderings is by far the better, though unlike the later, it substitutes for the French rhyming couplets one of the favorite and most wearisome of the English romancer's stanzas—the twelve-line stanza with *rime couée* or tail rhyme, whose monotony Chaucer illustrated (in a six-line stanza of exactly the same kind) in his parody of *Sir Thopas*:

Yborn he was in fer contree,
In Flaundres, al biyonde the see,
At Poperyng, in the place.
His fader was a man ful free,
And lord he was of that contree,
As it was Goddes grace.

The verse forms of the English romances are not always the happiest for narrative; they vary from short rhyming couplets to the complicated stanza of *Sir Gawain and the Green Knight*. There was clearly a lot of experiment in versification going on among the English romancers. They were learning how to rhyme in English in the French manner and trying out different kinds of stanzas. The simple, lively trot of *Havelok* or *Sir Orfeo* represents favorably the level of metrical competence in couplets. Sometimes the handling of stanzas is reasonably adroit, but the stanza itself is not suitable for narrative verse. And all the time Middle English verse is learning to become as supple and assured and polished as the French: with Chaucer it more than achieves this.

CHAPTER THREE

Middle English Literature: Fabliau, Lyric, Dream Allegory, Ballad

THE COURTLY French romance, as we have seen, drew its ideals partly from feudal notions of service and honor, sometimes (as in many of the Arthurian stories) oddly combined with more specifically Christian virtues; and when it was rendered into English much of the courtliness was lost and interest centered on the physical adventures. Not all medieval French narrative was "polite," however; from France also came a type of short narrative poem, realistic, humorous, often coarse, known as the *fabliau*, and *fabliau* and romance existed side by side. The *fabliau* is associated with the new middle classes who slowly grew in importance as the feudal system developed only to decay. If romance begins in France as the entertainment of a feudal aristocracy, *fabliau* is the product of the class which was eventually to destroy feudalism. The development of a money economy out of a natural economy, hastened both by the commutation of different kinds of feudal service to money-payments and the growth of towns with their trading communities, gradually took away the very basis of the feudal system by encouraging the growth of a class which had no place in it. This new class, town dwellers who carried on commercial activity of one kind or another, traders and artisans who no longer lived on the land but who obtained their food and their raw materials by selling to the peasants the goods they manufactured, were less impressed by courtly notions of love and honor than the more conservative feudal landowners; realistic, iconoclastic, priding themselves on knowing life as it really is and on refusing to look at it through the rose-colored spectacles of

68

sentimental idealists, they sponsored a boisterous, satirical kind of narrative which was, as it were, the antitype of the idealizing vision of courtly knight or pious churchman.

This middle-class challenge of the knightly ideal was but one phase of a significant movement in the history of European culture. The heroic age, reflected in Germanic epic, had given way to the feudal age, with its own concept of the hero; when a more commercial civilization develops, the whole possibility of heroism in the modern world is re-examined. We are approaching Don Quixote, the knightly hero as fool, and Don Quixote, who though a fool is also in an oblique way admirable, is a sign on the road which in England comes at last to Robinson Crusoe, the hero as prudential merchant who, even when cast away on a desert island, spends his time recreating as best he can the urban business world he left behind him. When prudence and self-interest become the chief motive power of the hero, a reaction sets in, led by those who deplore the loss of the "crowded hour of glorious life." Prudential morality is examined ironically (as in Fielding or Thackeray) or is reluctantly conceded to be a condition of progress by a novelist such as Scott who in his best novels weighs the competing claims of commercial progress and heroic tradition, of Baillie Nicol Jarvie and Rob Roy, to conclude that while the future lies with the former the latter is more attractive and its loss a bitter price to pay for material advancement. The fate of the hero in English literature will emerge more clearly in subsequent pages of this history; here we pause to remark only that the *fabliau* represents the first real challenge in European literature to the notion of heroic idealism as a way of life, and that challenge can be traced in its influential course from Cervantes to Evelyn Waugh.

Fabliaux are found in France in the twelfth and thirteenth centuries but are rare in England before 1400; they apparently originated in Northern France. There are many types: some are indecent stories of town life whose only point is their indecency; others are humorous, satiric tales of intrigue; others again, like the *Roman de Renart* cycle, are animal stories, also generally humorous and satiric in tone. Some are made into awful warnings or otherwise turned into *exempla*, "examples," for the use of preachers; the *Gesta Romanorum*, of which we have an early fifteenth-century English version, is a collection of such *exempla*, moralized tales for the enlivening of sermons (such as Chaucer's Pardoner's Tale). In Middle English literature, strangely enough, there are very few individual *fabliaux*, though French literature abounds in them. The only English *fabliau* that has survived by itself is *Dame Sirith*, a low tale of how a merchant's wife is persuaded by a trick to allow a clerk to make love to her in her husband's absence. Yet reference to (and warnings against) such stories in contemporary religious literature make it clear that they were common in medieval England; presumably, however, being a popular rather than a courtly form of literature, they were not often written down. The clergy would have had no interest in them, except in their moralized form, and the clergy were the guardians of the written word throughout the Middle Ages. We do find the *fabliau*, however, in Chaucer, who puts stories of this kind into the mouths of the Merchant, the Miller, the Reeve, the Shipman, and the Summoner in his *Canterbury Tales*.

Another popular medieval literary form—indeed, a popular form in most ages and civilizations—is the fable, which came to the Middle Ages from both Greek and Indian sources. The fable is a short story in which animals, acting more or less as human beings, behave in such a way as to illustrate a simple moral. Beast tales represent a very widespread kind of popular literature, and the fable develops out of the beast tale in much the same way as the *exemplum* develops out of the *fabliau*. In spite of the popularity of the fable in medieval England, especially in the twelfth and thirteenth centuries, no Middle English collection of fables exists. Books of fables in French and Latin survive, but there are only a handful of extant English fables from before Chaucer, and each of these is found as part of a longer work (two, "The Owl and the Falcon" and "The Fox and the Cat," in *The Owl and the Nightingale*). Beast tales were also adapted for satirical purposes: by having animals act as men it was easy to satirize human follies and vices, the presentation of men as animals being itself an implicit criticism of man's claim to superiority over the brutes. These stories about animals varied considerably in tone: some are substantially *fabliaux* with the characters animals instead of men, others are more purely satires, others again are simply entertaining stories about the cunning or resourcefulness or misadventures of animals.

A whole cycle of the beast stories developed, with Reynard the Fox as the principal hero (or villain); one of the most popular of these collections was the French *Roman de Renart*, of which no Middle English translation (if it was made) has survived. Indeed, there are only three Middle English extant representatives of that cycle of animal tales sometimes called the "beast epic," and these are *The Fox and the Wolf*, the sofar unpublished *Fox and Geese*, and Chaucer's *Nun's Priest's Tale*, though it seems fairly certain that there were other such stories which have not survived. The coarse, satirical tone of so many of these animal stories cannot have made them welcome in monastic libraries, the true custodians of literature in the Middle Ages. *The Fox and the Wolf* is a lively, humorous tale in rhymed octosyllabic couplets, with spirited dialogue, shrewd characterization and a general lightness of touch: the story appears to have been translated from the French; it is in the *Roman de Renart* and was told again in the *Fables* of the fifteenth-century Scottish poet Robert Henryson.

A rather different kind of interest in animals shows itself in the medieval bestiary, a literary form which probably originated in Egypt in the second century A. D. and comes from the Greek through the Latin into medieval literature. The bestiary is a series of accounts of animals, of their qualities and of the legends associated with them, with a moral application made at the end; first there is the description, then the "significacio" or moral meaning. In the Middle English Bestiary, the lion, eagle, adder, ant, hart, fox, spider, mermaid, elephant, turtledove, panther, and dove are dealt with in seven hundred rather crude rhyming lines of varying length. The work is of little interest as literature, but it provides an interesting window onto the medieval mind, with its mixture of pseudoscientific description, wonder, and moralizing, and it provided a storehouse of animal lore which continued to be used in literature long after the bestiary was forgotten.

More congenial to the modern mind, and more readily appreciated by the modern reader, is Middle English lyrical poetry, much of which reaches across the ages with a freshness and directness that sometimes positively startle:

> Fowler in þe frith,
> Þe fisses in þe flod,
> And I mon waxe wod.   [must grow mad]
> Mulch sorw I walke with
> For beste of bon and blod.

This passionate stanza survives in a manuscript with its musical annotation, reminding us that so much early lyric poetry, like the ballads, was meant to be sung. The tone of Middle English lyrics, even when it is one of sorrow or complaint as in the poem just quoted, is far removed from the more meditative elegiac strain of these few Anglo-Saxon poems which can perhaps be called lyrical—*The Wanderer* or *The Seafarer,* for example. Whether the Anglo-Saxons had any body of short lyrical poems is doubtful; none has survived at any rate. And when we realize how accidental has been the preservation of those secular Middle English lyrics which we have—often scribbled by a bored clerk on the margin or a blank leaf of a manuscript dealing with some quite different subject—we can see how dangerous it is to generalize from extant Middle English literature. On a blank leaf of a manuscript in the Bodleian Library, Oxford, some one noted down a tantalizing little rhyme, to be worked up by W. B. Yeats many centuries later:

> Icham of Irlaunde,
> Ant of the holy londe
> Of Irlande.
> Gode sire, pray ich þe,
> For of saynte charite,
> Come ant daunce wyt me
> In Irlaunde.

And on the same blank page we find another fragment:

> Maiden in the mor lay,
> In the mor lay,
> Seuenyst fulle, seuenist fulle,
> Maiden in the mor lay,
> In the mor lay,
> Seuenistes fulle ant a day.

> Welle was hire mete;
> Wat was hire mete?
> Þe primerole ant the,—
> Þe primerole ant the,—
> Welle was hire mete;
> Wat was hire mete?—
> The primerole ant the violet. . . .

Much of the Middle English secular lyric that we have consists of casually preserved scraps.

There is no extant English lyric poetry from before the twelfth century. The first record that we have of a Middle English lyric is found in the *Historia Eliensis* of the twelfth-century chronicler Thomas of Ely, who tells us that when Canute (died 1035) was rowing near the Isle of Ely he heard the monks singing and, pleased with their singing, he himself composed a song in English of which the Chronicler gives the first four lines:

> Merie sungen the Munekes binnen Ely.
> Tha Cnut ching reu ther by.
> Roweth cnites noer the land.
> And here we thes Muneches sæng.

> Merrily sang the monks of Ely
> When King Canute rowed thereby.

"Row, knights, near the land
And hear we the singing of these monks."

The chronicler adds that this and "other verses which follow are to this day sung publicly in dances and remembered in proverbs." This proves at least that there was a song of this kind known in the twelfth century and regarded then as a *carole* (a song with a refrain sung by a chain of dancers, with a leader singing the stanzas and the whole group joining in the refrain), though it does not prove that Canute was in fact the first English lyrist. Whether the *carole* existed in Anglo-Saxon England we cannot tell; it was certainly popular in England soon after the Conquest, presumably as a result of French influence. Giraldus Cambrensis, writing his *Gemma Ecclesiastica* (a series of saints' lives) at the end of the twelfth century, tells the story of a company of dancers singing and dancing all night in a churchyard in Worcestershire with the result that the following morning the priest, unable to get the refrain of their song out of his head, intoned at Mass not *Dominus vobiscum* but "*Swete lemman, dhin are*" ("Sweet mistress, have mercy").

The *carole* comes at the end of a long tradition of development which cannot be certainly traced, even in French literature. Its ancestry may well include pre-Christian seasonal celebrations, communal work songs sung to the rhythms of spinning or threshing or rowing among other activities, or the danced folk song arising from pure play and recreation. Its movement from folk art to the professional craftsmanship of the minstrel brought with it not only sophistication of technique but some significant shifts in attitude—for example, folk love poetry tends to give the woman's view, while the love lyrics of the *trouvères* present the courtly love attitude of the man languishing for love of the woman. What begins as a spontaneous accompaniment to work or play, largely feminine in inspiration (for the women would do most of the work for which rhythmic singing was a suitable accompaniment, as in the Hebridean wauking songs today), develops into the careful product of a conscious art predominantly masculine in origin and point of view.

We get our first glimpse of written French poetry when this process has just been completed. The new development is recent enough for it still to bear marks of its origin (the woman's point of view for example, being preserved in that species of *chanson d'aventure* where the *trouvère* reports what he has overheard a woman singing), yet the process of sophistication is sufficiently far advanced for the new ideas of courtly love to provide most of the conventions. The courtly love lyric from Provence traveled northward through France to reach England at last and influence English poetry. This French influence intermingled with that of Latin hymns, which were written in that accentual Latin verse which derived orginally from popular songs and soldier songs of Rome. The goliardic poems of the "wandering scholars" show clearly how these influences could come together as well as how the technique of rhymed accentual Latin verse influenced both French and English versification.

As so often in medieval literature, we can see the whole picture more clearly in France than in England. There, in addition to the sophisticated lyric of courtly love, we find varieties of lyric of a more popular kind representing a development halfway between the folk song and the fully professional composition. There is the *chanson d'aventure*, where the poet tells of what happened to him when he went abroad one morning; there is the *aube*, song of lovers parting at dawn; the *chanson de mal mariée* gives a woman's complaint against married life overheard by the poet (another example of the older folk point of view—the woman's—surviving in these more popular though no longer folk lyrics); the *chanson de carole*, dance song with refrain, both popular and courtly varieties; and other kinds. The more popular kinds of poetry cannot always be sharply distinguished from the more courtly, but different layers of sophistication can be traced.

It is not until well into the thirteenth century that we find any significant number of English lyrics, though their quality makes it clear that the tradition of lyrical poetry in English had by this time been well established and confirms other evidence that much has been lost. The well-known "Sumer is icumen in" is found in a manuscript of about 1240, together with a fairly elaborate musical setting: the refrain indicates the *carole* ancestry of the poem, while the theme was a common one in medieval Europe:

> Sumer is icumen in,
>   Lhude sing cuccu!
> Growe sed and blowe med
>   And spring þe wde nu.
> Sing cuccu! . . .

The hailing of spring is often—as in the French lyric—the prelude to the description of the woes of the lover whose mistress is cold to him, but the welcome of spring for its own sake is also an important theme, an expression of genuine excitement at the return of the growing season after the bleak medieval winter without adequate heat or light or food. Joy in spring was no mere convention in the Middle Ages, when men had not yet learned to make themselves an artificial summer indoors or found a way of feeding cattle adequately

during the winter. Darkness, cold, isolation, a diet at best of salt
meat—these were the accompaniments of the medieval winter, and
we must bear them in mind when we read such poems as:

> Lenten ys come wiþ loue to toune,
> Wiþ blosmen and wiþ briddes roune,
>   Þat al þis blisse bryngeþ.
> Dayeseȝes in þis dales,
> Notes suete of nyhtegales,
>   Vch foul song singeþ.
> Þe þrestelcoc him þreteþ oo,
> Away is huere wynter wo,
>   When wonderoue springeþ.
> Þis foules singeþ ferly fele,   [wondrous many]
> Ant wlyteþ on huere wynter wele,   [warble]
>   Þat al þe wode ryngeþ.

This joyful hail to spring is found in the great Harleian Manuscript
2253 in the British Museum, in which much of the best extant Middle
English lyric poetry has been preserved. The manuscript was probably written at Leominster and dates from the first quarter of the
fourteenth century. It contains a fine variety of lyrical poems. The
nightingale, spring, and love make their usual conjunction in one
typical poem:

> When the nyhtegale singes the wodes waxen grene,
> Lef and gras and blosme springes in Averil, I wene,
> And love is to myn herte gone with one spere so kene, . . .

Or a similar theme treated with greater metrical dexterity:

> Between March and Averil,
>   When spray beginneth to spring,
> The little fowl hath their wil
>   On their lud to sing.   [in their own language?]
> I live in love-longing
>   For semlokest of alle thing;   [fairest]
> He may me blisse bringe—
>   Icham in her baundoun.   [I am at her disposal]
> (Refrain)
> An hendy hap ichabbe yhent;   [gracious got]
> Ichot from heaven it is me sent;   [I know]
> From alle wymmen my love is lent
>   And light on Alysoun.

Another of the Harleian poems has the refrain:

> Blow, northerne wynd,
> sent thou me my suetyng!

> blow, northerne wynd,
> blou! blou! blou!

A rather unexpected poem is a swinging, humorous lyric addressed to the man in the moon, the only one of its kind among surviving medieval lyrical poetry.

The political lyric was another medieval form, written chiefly in Latin or French in England before the fourteenth century. When it does appear in English it clearly owes the usual debt to Latin hymns and French lyrics as far as versification goes, but its inspiration is, naturally, purely native. The only political poem in English which has survived in complete form (it also is in Harley 2253) is the "Song of Lewes," a mocking poem addressed by the triumphant followers of Simon de Montfort after the battle of Lewes (1264) to Richard, Earl of Cornwall, the king's brother, who is regarded as a trickster responsible for misleading Edward, the king's son; it has a narrative basis, with the catchy refrain:

> Richard, thah thou be ever trichard,   [trickster]
> Tricchen shalt thou nevermore!   [deceive]

In the fourteenth century, popular interest in social and political matters is reflected in an increasing number of political songs and poems, of which perhaps the most impressive, and certainly the briefest, is the grim little couplet summing up the year 1390–91 and explaining more eloquently than any historian why men turned against Richard II:

> The ax was sharpe, the stokke was harde,
> In the xiiii yere of Kyng Richarde.

We know, too, the couplet which the radical priest John Ball used in preaching his equalitarian doctrine at the time of the Peasants' Revolt in 1381:

> When Adam dalf, and Eve span,   [delved (dug)]
> Who was then the gentleman?

The fourteenth century also produced the patriotic versifier Laurence Minot, who illustrated the growing national feeling of England in his political poems attacking the French and the Scots and celebrating English victories over them. Secular literature is expanding its scope, reflecting an increasing number of aspects of the life and thought of the time. Between the purely conventional courtly love lyrics and the simple and heartfelt political pieces can be found every stage of sophistication; the fourteenth-century lyric has become capable of handling a relatively wide range of subjects with varying degrees of stylization and polish. Spring and love are still the dominant themes—and with the sweep of the Petrarchan tradition over Europe is to be confirmed as a dominant theme for another three hundred years—among secular lyrics, but there is also "occasional" poetry, springing from particular events or situations.

But of course the commonest theme among surviving Middle English lyrics—especially among those of the earlier Middle English period—is religious, for religious poems would be most likely to have been transcribed and preserved in an age when clerics were in charge of both activities. The relation between the Middle English religious lyric and the medieval Latin hymn can be seen most clearly in those "macaronic" poems where Latin and English are used together.

> Of on that is so fayr and briȝt
>   *velud maris stella,*
> Briȝter than the dayis liȝt,
>   *parens et puella,*
> Ic crie to the, thu se to me,
> Leuedy, preye thi sone for me,
>   *tam pia,*
> That ic mote come to the,
>   *Maria.*

Sometimes the words of an actual hymn are worked into a macaronic poem:

> *Ave maris stella,*
>   The sterre on the see,
> *Dei mater alma,*
>   Blessed mot sche be!
> *Atque semper virgo,*
>   Pray thy sone for me.
> *Felix celi porta,*
>   That I may come to thee.

But secular themes and techniques soon begin to influence religious poetry, and the folk tradition, too, is employed for religious themes, as in many Christmas carols and in songs of Mary and the holy child:

> This endris night I saw a sight,   [other]
>   A maid a cradell kepe,
> And ever she song and said among
>   'Lullay, my child, and slepe.'

The medieval religious lyric ranges from the simply moral to the devotional and even mystical, and between these extremes we can find many kinds of use of religious material, including the merely descriptive and anecdotal. In later phases of English literature we distinguish between the religious poem (as we get it, say, in John Donne or George Herbert) and the hymn (such as those of Isaac Watts), the former being a personal handling of religious experience so as to produce a complex and highly individual lyrical poem while the latter, intended for the singing of a congregation, reflects a communal emotion and is both less complex and less individual. Something of the same distinction may be drawn in the Middle English religious lyric, though by no means so definitely. The picture is complicated by the continuous clerical attempt to turn secular emotion into religious, an attempt which was part of the Church's perpetual warfare against "songis of lecherie, of batailis and of lesyngis." Some time in the fourteenth century, Bishop Richard de Ledrede composed Latin songs for the minor clergy of his cathedral "ne guttura eorum et ora deo sanctificata polluantur cantilenis teatralibus turpibus et secularibus" ("so that they should not pollute their throats and mouths, sanctified to God, with disgraceful and secular minstrel songs") and they were set to the tunes of well-known secular lyrics. The most extreme case of the deliberate adaptation of secular poetry to religious purposes is the Scottish *Gude and Godlie Ballatis* of the mid-sixteenth century, in which even such an unpromising poem as "John come kiss me now" is given a religious meaning by having John represent man and the wooer God: though these are Protestant poems, with a strong anti-Papal bias, they represent in an extreme form something that was happening right through the Middle Ages. Clearly something similar has happened to this poem:

> The shepard upon a hill he satt;
>   He had on him his tabard and his hat,   [short coat]
> His tarbox, his pipe, and his flagat;   [flagon]
> His name was called Joly Joly Wat,
>   For he was a gud herdes boy.
>   Ut hoy!
> For in his pipe he made so much joy.

> The shepherd upon a hill was laid;
> His dog to his girdell was taid;
> He had not slept but a litill braid,   [time]
> But 'Gloria in excelsis' was to him said.
>   Ut hoy!
> For in his pipe he made so much joy. . . .

Sometimes, elements from Christian story are treated in a dramatic fashion which reminds one of the ballads, as in the famous thirteenth-century *Judas,* which some have seen as the earliest extant English ballad:

. . . In him com ur Lord gon, as is postles seten at mete:
"Wou sitte ye, postles, ant wi nule ye ete?

Wou sitte ye, postles, ant wi nule ye ete?
Ic am iboust ant isold today for oure mete."

Up stod him Iudas: "Lord, am I that?
I nas never o the stude ther me The evel spec."   [place]

Dramatic in a more subdued way is the Crucifixion dialogue preserved in MS Harley 2253:

> "Stond wel, moder, under rode,
> Byholt thy sone with glade mode,
>   Blythe moder myht thou be!"
> "Sone, hou shulde Y blithe stonde?
> Y se thin fet, Y se thin honde
>   Nayled to the harde tre." . . .

The note of simple devotion is effectively sounded in some of the
lyrics on the Virgin:

> I sing of a mayden
>   that is makeles   [peerless]
> King of all kynges
>   to here sone che ches.   [chose]
>
> He cam also stylle
>   ther his moder was,
> As dew in Aprylle
>   that fallyt on the gras.
>
> He cam also stylle
>   to his moderes bowr,
> As dew in Aprylle
>   that fallyt on the flour. . . .

Lyrics in praise of Mary, or describing her sorrows, or invoking
her, are common in the fourteenth century; carols in the modern
sense of Christmas carols range from pagan celebrations of the holly
and the ivy and the boar's head to awed celebrations of the Nativity;
there are religious poems where a secular *chanson d'aventure* has
been adapted to a religious context, as in one with the Latin refrain, "Quia amore langueo"; there is occasionally a deft treatment of
the theme of original sin and the Christian scheme of redemption, as
in this remarkable little piece:

> Adam lay i-bowndyn,
>   bowndyn in a bond,
> Fowre thowsand wynter

> thowt he not to long;
> And al was for an appil,
> 　an appil that he tok,
> As clerkis fyndyn wretyn
> 　in here book,
> Ne hadde the appil take ben,
> 　the appil taken ben,
> Ne hadde never our lady
> 　a ben hevene qwen.
> Blyssid be the tyme
> 　that appil take was,
> Therfore we mown syngyn
> 　*Deo gracias.*

This is a skillfully compact account of what modern critics call "the paradox of the fortunate fall," rendered in terms of lyric simplicity, very different in tone but similar in general idea to the view Milton expresses in *Paradise Lost,* where Adam, after hearing of the Christian plan of redemption from Michael, exclaims:

> O goodness infinite, goodness immense!
> That all this good of evil shall produce,
> And evil turn to good; . . .

In the medieval religious lyric Christian themes mingle in many different ways with themes deriving from a variety of other traditions; there are, as in the secular lyric, varying degrees of sophistication, of technical accomplishment, and individual sensibility. These lyrics illustrate, sometimes with startling clarity, some of the ways in which religion entered men's imagination in the Middle Ages. Sometimes, in coalescing with pre-Christian material which reached back into a dimly remembered world of symbolism, a poem can achieve an unexpected effect, as in the Corpus Christi poem found in an early sixteenth-century manuscript commonplace book in the library of Balliol College, Oxford:

> He bare hym up, he bare hym down,
> He bare hym into an orchard brown.
>
> In that orchard there was a hall,
> That was hanged with purpill and pall.
>
> And in that hall ther was a bede,
> Hit was hanged with gold so rede.
>
> And in that bed ther lythe a knyght,
> His wounde bledying day and nyght.

By that bedes side ther kneleth a may,
And she wepeth both night and day.

And by that beddes side ther stondeth a ston,
Corpus Christi written thereon.

This is essentially a folk song, of which, interestingly enough, versions have been found in modern times in the oral traditions of both Britain and America; its meaning went far deeper than either the compiler of the Balliol manuscript or the modern folk singer could have known. The central symbolism of the poem appears to derive from the Grail legend: Joseph of Arimathea bore Christ's blood, which he had collected in the Grail, to Avalon ("He bare hym up"); the wounded knight is the Maimed Knight, the keeper of the Grail, whose hall is the Castle of the Grail; and so on. Behind this lies a pre-Christian symbolism. The whole poem is based on the same set of symbolic meanings which T. S. Eliot employed in *The Waste Land*. Thus the medieval poet, mingling themes of different origins and at different levels, was often working with richer materials than he guessed. The Christian tradition, as mediated through sermons, Church worship, and the pictures on stained-glass windows; the classical world, obliquely reflected through late Latin writers and a mass of legends and traditions; memories, folk notions, and fragments of pre-Christian paganism changed in strange ways in the process of oral transmission—these helped to condition the mind and the imagination of the Middle English poet and to give unexpected overtones of meaning to his poetry.

If the medieval writer sometimes dealt with materials of whose symbolic significance he was unaware, he also dealt often in conscious and deliberate allegory whose meaning he knew perfectly well. Indeed, as has often been pointed out, the medieval mind worked naturally in allegory in a way that we seem to have lost, and produced a body of allegorical writing which is of central importance in European literature. The origins of the medieval allegorical mode are complex. Allegorical interpretation of parts of Scripture had already a long history in both Jewish and Christian biblical commentary; late Latin poetry tended to use the old Roman gods as personifications of abstract qualities and psychological situations; and the new introspective tendency that Christianity encouraged induced men to objectify their mental and spiritual struggles by personifying their desires and aims, the appetites and qualities that produced them. By the time courtly love appears on the scene the allegorical mode is ready to be its medium, and so at length we have the allegorical romance, the most artificial and in many respects the most influential and tenacious of the different kinds of literature produced in the Middle Ages. Of the three major kinds of literature we consider in this and the previous chapter—the narrative romance, the lyric, and the allegorical romance—the allegorical romance was the last to appear, and the only one which underwent no development from popular to sophisticated. This was essentially a "polite" literature from the beginning: or, if it was not very "polite" in its earliest, germinal stages, it was at least learned.

The most noteworthy allegorical romance of the Middle Ages, the most elaborate specimen of its kind and the most influential on subsequent literature, for which it proved an inexhaustible quarry, is the *Roman de la Rose,* of which the first part (over four thousand lines in short couplets) was composed by Guillaume de Lorris about 1227, and the second, over twenty-two thousand lines, was written by Jean de Meun in the years 1268-77. Guillaume de Lorris' share represents the true allegory of courtly love, where the new psychology of love-making is treated with great subtlety and effectiveness. Qualities of the heroine, such as shame, fear, kindliness, courtesy, etc., are personified, and the hero's encounter with the lady in her different moods—in some of which she encourages and in others of which she repels his suit—is described as an attempt to obtain the "rose" (standing for the lady's love) which is enclosed within a hedge in a garden which is the scene of the action. In his attempt, the hero is aided by such personified qualities as the heroine's natural kindliness and courtesy (*bialacoil,* "fair welcome") and hindered by, for example, fear and shame. The whole background of the story is courtly life, a life of leisure and good breeding, where there is nothing to do but dance and sing and make love.

The story as Guillaume de Lorris planned it is unfinished, and the conclusion written by Jean de Meun about forty years later is quite different in aim and nature. Jean's bulky work is quite formless beside the well-constructed earlier portion, and it shows little ability to handle the allegorical method with effectiveness. The allegory in the first part is done with real skill and finesse; but Jean is a clumsier and more realistic writer, and the fine allegorical fabric of Guillaume de Lorris comes to pieces in his hands. His purpose is not to tell a subtle love story so much as to produce a piece of work which is at once didactic, philosophic, satiric, scientific, religious, and lots of other things besides. There is a strong satiric strain in his writing which is quite absent from the earlier part of the poem: Jean sometimes gives the impression that he is utterly contemptuous of the courtly love tradition and takes every opportunity to leave the story and digress at inordinate length on philosophic, satiric, or mythological subjects.

We see in his attitude something of the temper of the rising class of realistic writers which the new bourgeois element was producing at this time. Polite, courtly literature is no longer sufficient to satisfy the reading (or listening) public, even with the alternative of simple narrative romances of wonder and marvelous action. There is growing up a taste for something different both from the sentimental, sophisticated love story and the simple tale of derring-do. Jean de Meun is still working within the courtly tradition, but he is out of sympathy with it. He has more learning and philosophy, more of a serious didactic purpose, than the typical *fabliau* writer shows; yet in many ways he has something of the same temper and illustrates the same movement from a courtly to a bourgeois tradition.

The influence of the *Roman de la Rose*, especially of the first part, was enormous. The poem was translated all over Europe, and its characters and conventions are to be met with again and again throughout later literature. In England it was translated, at least in part, by Chaucer. The scene at the beginning of the *Roman de la Rose* is a riverbank outside a walled garden, and the hero enters the garden through a wicket gate: this scene becomes a stock property in later medieval literature. The story is told by the narrator in the form of a dream, from which he awakes at the conclusion, and this dream form is copied by later writers. The story opens on a May morning, with the birds singing and nature looking her best. The May morning, the wandering into the country, the falling asleep and dreaming, the garden—these are the characteristic features of this type of literature, known as the dream allegory. The dream allegory is literature produced for a leisured audience, an upper-class audience cut off from the simple routines of labor that formed so important a part of the life of the peasant and the yeoman and cut off likewise from many of the oral folk traditions that simpler folk perpetuated in their daily work. Even more than the sophisticated French narrative romance of courtly love, the dream allegory represented a literature of self-conscious sensibility. The influence of the *Roman de la Rose* is relatively late in coming into English literature: it is seen in Chaucer and in the poets that follow him.

The dream allegory is sometimes used for very different purposes from those which either of the authors of the *Roman de la Rose* had in mind. The late fourteenth-century poem *The Pearl,* an elegy in some twelve hundred lines arranged in groups of twelve-line stanzas, is cast in the form of a dream: the poet falls asleep in an arbor on an August (not the usual May) morning and has the dream which forms the substance of the poem. *The Pearl* has little else in common with the *Roman de la Rose,* however. Using both rhyme and alliteration, it is the product of that alliterative revival (or survival) which produced also *Sir Gawain and the Green Knight, Patience,* and *Cleanness*; because, in addition, all four poems are of the same date and are in the same West Midland dialect, they are sometimes assigned to the same author, though this is mere conjecture. In mood, tone, and emotional effect *The Pearl* stands alone. The poet is lamenting the loss of a little girl, who died before she was two years old. Looking in vain for his "precious pearl without a spot," he falls asleep and in a marvelous dream finds himself in a land of great beauty with a bright river running by. He cannot cross the river, but sees on the other side, where the country is even more beautiful, a shining maiden dressed in white with ornaments of pearl. She is the lost child, and he is speechless with wonder and fear. She speaks to him, however, and explains her position in the New Jerusalem. The poet attempts to cross the river to be with her, but she warns him that this cannot yet be: since Adam's fall the river can only be crossed in death. He grieves at this, but is told to be patient and resign himself to God's will and mercy. She then tells him much about the means of salvation, answering his questions in detail, and finally he sees her in a procession of virgin brides of Christ, led by the Lamb. In an ecstasy of joy and longing the poet again attempts to cross the river to be with this glorious vision, but he awakes to find himself again in the arbor, sad yet resigned to the will of God. The poet shows real dexterity in handling a difficult rhyme scheme and in arranging a complex pattern in the poem as a whole; but the most arresting quality is the richness of color and the profusion of imagery, combined with a wide emotional range which enables him to domicile theology in elegy and sometimes in wonder. *The Pearl* stands alone in Middle English religious poetry for its sustained emotional quality and technical mastery of versification. *Patience* and *Cleanness* (i.e., purity), which discuss these moral virtues and illustrate them by retelling appropriate biblical stories, are technically accomplished but lack the special kind of sensibility which makes *The Pearl* so impressive.

All this while, the English language was being exercised, developing its literary potentialities, and English writers were learning to handle their tongue with cunning and flexibility. With Chaucer, the rehabilitation of English as a literary language seems to be complete: here is a master who can handle it in verse as the ablest French poets handled their language. But before we leave the great army of anonymous medieval writers to dwell on the first great known poet of Middle English, something must be said about another kind of anonymous literature which was to have such a great effect on English writing centuries later—the ballad. The ballads, which are orally transmitted narrative poems dealing either with themes common to international folk song or with themes derived from the romances, or with popular class heroes, or with historical or semihistorical events, date, in most of the versions which we now have, from the sixteenth and seventeenth centuries and later; but there can be no doubt that the ballad flourished in the late Middle Ages, even though, being still at this stage a purely oral literature, it was not likely to be written down and so has not survived in its earlier forms. Oral transmission is the very essence of balladry; whatever the origin of the ballad—and the older view that it was the spontaneous communal creation of "the folk" is not now maintained in its primal simplicity —their original life was that of sung poems which were sometimes improved and sometimes corrupted by generations of singers. Nevertheless, the great majority of the ballads which we have are not medieval, and some of them deal with specific historical events which took place in the sixteenth century and later. The Robin Hood ballads date from long after the period to which they are supposed to refer and have little if any historical basis: Robin Hood is a yeoman hero, the hero of a class, not a historical figure: there is evidence of the existence of "rymes of Robin Hood" in the fourteenth century, but of the Robin Hood ballads that we have, two are of the fifteenth century and the others are known only in sixteenth-century texts. We have, in fact, not more than a total of fourteen ballads surviving in manuscripts or printed texts earlier than 1600. In the seventeenth century, broadsides and songbooks make many more available. From the mid-eighteenth century onward, interest in the recording and collecting of ballads proceeds apace, but the early collectors freely altered and "improved" the texts which they got from oral recitation or written sources. The dating of ballads is therefore not easy: we can say in general that ballads were known in the fourteenth century and popular in the fifteenth, while the sixteenth and early seventeenth century was the period productive of most of the ballads of which we have record. The ballad, indeed, is not so primitive a literary form as used to be thought: it is far removed from the heroic epic, which celebrates a hero of the whole race; it is the product of a settled group and deals with the affairs of that group. There is no trace of the ballad anywhere in Europe until after the great migrations had long been completed, and if we look at the ballad picture in Germany, France, Spain, and Scandinavia as well as Britain, we can see that the ballad, as a rule, develops in the late Middle Ages.

Some of the most impressive ballads deal with folk themes common to many nations; these generally deal with a single situation involving revenge or jealousy or a return from the grave or simply the finality of loss. "Lamkin" is a good example of the first, "The Twa Sisters." of the second, "The Wife of Usher's Well" of the third, and "The Unquiet Grave" with its plaintive opening—

> The wind doth blow today, my love,
>   And a few small drops of rain;
> I never had but one true-love,
>   In cold grave she was lain—

of the fourth. Or the ballad might create an atmosphere of violence or tragedy or horror for its own sake, as in the well-known "Lord Randal" and "Edward," or deal with deception, betrayed lovers, or the testing of love. Some deal with the supernatural, with transformations and witchcraft and the intrusion into human affairs of the world of faery: in "Tam Lin," for example, the hero has been carried off by the fairies and is redeemed when the heroine, following his instructions, holds him fast throughout a series of terrifying transformations (this old folk theme is found in the *Odyssey*, when Menelaus gets information from Proteus, the old man of the sea, by holding fast to him throughout his many transformations). Another important category of ballads deals with historical events, either real events in national history or recollections of local events which have often been modified by some folk theme. "The Battle of Otterburn" and "Chevy Chase" represent the former and "Sir Patrick Spens," the latter.

The ballads are often thought of as peculiarly Scottish, because the enthusiasm of Scottish collectors gathered so many Scottish examples; but, in fact, they have been found in all parts of England as well as elsewhere in Europe. (The popularity of Scott's *Minstrelsy of the Scottish Border* accounts similarly for the belief that most Scottish ballads come from the Borders: the majority, in fact, come from Aberdeenshire.) Some of the best extant ballads deal with events in Scottish history, real or imagined, but what makes them ballads is the treatment rather than the provenance. The ballads are narrative poems which, completely suppressing the personality of the narrator, tell a story dramatically by moving—often without any specific indication of the transition—from one incident to the next:

> The king sits in Dunfermline toun,
>   Drinking the blood-red wine:
> O whare will I get a guid sailor
>   To sail this ship of mine?

> Up and spak an eldern knicht,
>   Sat at the king's richt knee:
> "Sir Patrick Spens is the best sailor
>   That sails upon the sea."
>
> The king has written a braid letter,
>   And signed it with his hand,
> And sent it to Sir Patrick Spens
>   Was walking on the sand. . . .

In these last two lines the sudden shift to a picture of Sir Patrick Spens walking on the sand—comparable, as Mr. M. J. C. Hodgart has pointed out, to the motion picture technique of "montage"—is characteristic of the ballad method. In the dialogue in "Lord Randal" and "Edward" the lack of background explanation enhances immeasurably the dramatic effect.

Other devices used in the ballads to increase dramatic effect include "incremental repetition," that is, the repetition of one line from the preceding stanza with an addition leading closer to the climax:

> In and come her father dear,
>   Canny cam he stepping in;
> Says, "Haud your tongue, my dochter dear,
>   What need ye mak sic heavy mene?   [moan]
>
> "Haud your tongue, my dochter dear,
>   Let all your mourning be;
> I'll carry the dead corpse to the clay,
>   And I'll come back and comfort thee."

The repetition of the questions in "Lord Randal" shows the same sort of thing worked up to an extraordinary pitch of tension. Repetitions often have something of an incantatory effect in the ballads:

> They hadna been a week from her,
>   A week but barely ane,
> When word came back to the carline wife
>   That her three sons were gane.
>
> They hadna been a week from her,
>   A week but barely three,
> When word came to the carline wife
>   That her sons she'd never see.

The stanza is generally the simple "ballad meter" of alternate four- and three-stressed lines, though sometimes (as in "Lord Randal") all the lines are four-stressed: the music of the ballads, where it is known, is a better guide to the stresses than some of the printed texts. Many of the extant ballads are pretty rough affairs, others have been unduly refined by such collectors as Bishop Percy or Scott; but ballads are by nature subject to change, and there is no point in being puritanically censorious either about popular corruptions or literary polishing—both fates are part of the destiny of the ballad. The uncanny power of the best of them remains something to wonder at; the mixture of simplicity and cunning, of elementary verse form and mastery of some subtle effects of rhythm and expression, is of a kind we rarely get in "art" poetry. And, like some of the lyrics we discussed earlier, only more continuously and arrestingly, they can make contact with deep-seated folk themes with quiet power. The second stanza of "The Wife of Usher's Well" is a good example of this controlled suggestiveness:

> It fell about the Martinmass,
>   When nights are lang and mirk,
> The carlin wife's three sons came hame,
>   And their hats were o the birk.

> It neither grew in syke nor ditch,   [stream]
>   Nor yet in ony sheugh;   [trench]
> But at the gates o Paradise,
>   That birk grew fair eneugh.

It is not enough to explain the *frisson* that the reader gets from that simple statement about the birk to say that it is an oblique way of saying that the returned sons were in fact dead, or to explain the magical or other significance of the birk (the earliest of English trees to come out in full spring green): the touch of quiet horror derives from the balladist's having made contact with some deep stratum of human fear. The ballad at its best can do this with extraordinary effect. Though its development belongs to the later Middle Ages and not earlier, it is the last literary species to draw nourishment from what might be called the anthropological past: it was this element in it that stirred the imagination of later poets such as Coleridge (not Wordsworth, who looked to the printed broadside ballad, a much cruder affair) and so helped to fertilize Romantic and later poetry.

CHAPTER FOUR

Chaucer, Gower,
Piers Plowman

GEOFFREY CHAUCER, who was born in the early 1340's and died in 1400, marks the brilliant culmination of Middle English literature. He had the metrical craftsmanship to handle English with a subtlety, a flexibility, and a polish which made it at once the equal, as a literary language, of French or Italian; he had the European consciousness, too, to enable him to render in English the dominant themes and attitudes of European literature and at the same time the English national consciousness to allow him to present the English scene as it had never been presented before. He had the relaxed, quizzical attitude that let him contemplate the varieties of human nature with a combination of sympathy, irony, and amusement, together with the good fortune to have opportunities of knowing men in all ranks of society; he was trained in the courtly life, the diplomatic life, and the urban life of affairs; his visits to France and Italy on Government service gave him an opportunity of coming into direct contact with French and Italian men of letters and enriching his knowledge of the literature of those countries. He was, in fact, fitted by both natural genius and the circumstances of his life to become the most technically accomplished, the most widely ranging, and the most universally appealing of medieval English writers, and indeed one of the most skillful and attractive of English writers of any period. With Chaucer, the English language and English literature grew up. The gradual process of recovery and refinement which the English language had been undergoing since it emerged after the Conquest in rough popular renderings of French romances was now complete. It was a happy accident that the man who had the technical brilliance in the metrical handling of language also had the breadth of view, the knowledge, the interests, the experience of life, and largeness of sympathy to enable him, in the latter part of his poetic career, to embody his great secular vision of his fellow men in brilliant literary form. He used the intellectual and imaginative resources of the Middle Ages, not, as Dante did, to present a great concrete embodiment of the moral and theological universe in which medieval man lived, but to bring alive, with vividness and cunning, the psychological and social world of his time, which turns out to be also the world of our own and every other time.

Chaucer—to whom, it must be remembered, French was a language as familiar as English—early absorbed the courtly love tradition as represented by the somewhat overstylized French poets of his own time. He knew and drew on the poetry of Guillaume de Machaut, Jean Froissart, and Eustace Deschamps, and he was thoroughly familiar with (and, at least in part, translated) the *Romance of the Rose*, the source of so much fourteenth-century French poetry and especially of Machaut's sophisticated exercises in the conventions of courtly love. The dream allegory had by now become the standard method of entering into a poem. The waking dream, where the sleeper wanders into a garden on a May morning, gay with blossoming flowers and the singing of birds, and there encounters the characters who tell him their love affairs or lament their misfortunes in love or act out their story, derives from the *Romance of the Rose*, but is now treated with a sophistication, a formal manipulation of standard properties, with heraldic colors and shapes and a highly wrought surface finish, of which neither the fresh vision of Guillaume de Lorris nor the encyclopedic and more cynical mind of Jean de Meun was capable. Guillaume's brightly pictured characters dancing in the garden and Jean's learned misogynistic digressions mingle in Chaucer's early poetry, presented in narrative frameworks and with picturesque detail which owe a considerable amount to Machaut and others. But the debt is simply an indication that Chaucer is working in a European tradition. As he developed, he was to draw on more and more aspects of that tradition and to make a more and more specifically English use of it. His visits to Italy in 1372–73 and in 1378, brought him into contact with the work of Dante, Boccaccio, and Petrarch, and this widened and deepened his literary resources and encouraged him to seek wider fields than the formal garden of Guillaume de Lorris. And all the time his career as courtier, man of affairs, and civil servant (for Chaucer was a bourgeois with courtly connections and thus had the freedom of at least two social worlds) brought him into contact with people of all ranks and professions to provide increasing opportunities for his clear-eyed observation of his fellow men.

Chaucer was thus brought up on the Rose tradition and on later French developments of it before moving to the deeper seriousness of Italian poetry. The ritual dance of an idealized courtly life, with its emphasis on "gentilesse" and "franchise" (nobility and generosity of character), gives way to larger concern with the fundamentals of human character and behavior and this, in turn, moves into contemplation (both delighted and ironical) of the foibles, vanities, absurdities, pretensions, villainies, the color, vitality, and exuberance, the everyday virtues and vices, of men as he knew them. But it would be a gross simplification of Chaucer's literary career to trace it merely from an imitative formalism through a greater seriousness and flexibility to subtle and realistic psychological observation, conventionally symbolized by reference to his "French," "Italian," and "English" periods. From an early stage he was free of a wider world of books than is suggested by any of these categories. What the Middle Ages knew of the classical world—its history, its mythology, its literature —Chaucer knew; what it knew of astronomy, astrology, medicine, theology, philosophy, he knew as well as a layman could; and it is not the least testimony to his genius that his poetry gives us the richest picture in English of how the ancient world of Greece and Rome appeared to the medieval imagination, its curiously transmuted image mingling with patristic thought, scholastic categories, and popular beliefs to produce an attitude to man and the world which is still an important part of the Western tradition. If the *Romance of the Rose* and the poetry of Machaut and Froissart and Deschamps were important to him, so were Virgil's *Aeneid*, Ovid's *Heroides* and *Metamorphoses*, Lucan's *Pharsalia*, Statius' *Thebaid*, Boethius' *De Consolatione Philosophiae* (which he translated), Macrobius' commentary on the *Somnium Scipionis* of Cicero, the Troy stories of Dares Phrygius and Dictys Cretensis and of later writers, Pope Innocent III's *De Contemptu Mundi* (which he apparently also translated), and much patristic literature, to say nothing of the Vulgate, the Latin liturgy of the Church, vast numbers of medieval romances, and a miscellaneous assortment of medieval scientific, religious, historical, and entertaining works. This assorted reading blended in his mind, as it did in the minds of his contemporaries, to produce a world of the imagination in which "Pluto and his queene, Proserpina, and al hire fayerye" can meet in a walled garden made by a merchant—a garden

So fair . . .
That he that wroot the Romance of the Rose
Ne koude of it the beautes wel devyse—

and quote to each other "Jhesus, filius Syrak" (author of Ecclesiasticus) and "this Jew, this Salmon" (i.e., King Solomon). Classical myth

transposed into the key of medieval folklore and seen against a background of biblical story and in an ethical context which includes the
courtly notion of "gentilesse," Christian ideals of virtue, and a robust
acceptance of human weakness and absurdity in the *fabliau* tradition—this is typical of Chaucer and of the civilization for which he
spoke. In this sense Chaucer is fourteenth century, and his work
gives us a vivid insight into the fourteenth-century world; but in his
art he transcended the bounds of his time, so that he illuminates his
background rather than allows his background (if we have learned
it) to illuminate him. We need make no historical allowances for
Chaucer at all, for he fully justifies his picture of the world by the literary uses to which he puts it. He is perhaps the first English poet
known by name for whom this claim can be made unreservedly.

Chaucer's first narrative poem, *The Book of the Duchess,* is in the
dream allegory convention and draws considerably on Machaut. It
was written at the end of 1369 on the death of Blanche, Duchess of
Lancaster, to celebrate the dead woman and console the bereaved
Duke: in a dream the poet sees "a man in blak" in a wood, who tells
him of his courtship of his beautiful lady and ends by revealing that
his present mourning is for her death. This ingenious adaptation of
the dream allegory for the twin purposes of eulogy and elegy is already straining out of its conventional framework: the interest lies
less in the celebration of the dead duchess than in the life given to
the poem by the current of psychological curiosity that runs through
it. The octosyllabic couplets move easily enough, though without the
combination of control and variety that characterizes Chaucer's maturer verse, and they begin by presenting a picture of the poet suffering from insomnia, reading the story of Ceyx and Alcione (in
Ovid) to while away his sleepless night. He tells the story, with
speed and economy, lingering only on an occasional detail that will
add vividness, as when Juno's messenger comes to Morpheus, the
god of sleep:

> This messenger com fleynge faste
> And cried, "O, ho! awake anoon!"
> Hit was for noght; there herde hym non.
> "Awake!" quod he, "whoo ys lyth there?"
> And blew his horn ryght in here eere,
> And cried "Awaketh!" wonder hye.

Having told the story, he goes on to describe how he settled down to
sleep, hoping that "thilke Morpheus, /Or hys goddesse, dame Juno /
Or som wight elles, I ne roghte who" would send him sleep, and
offering Morpheus a feather bed "Yif he wol make me slepe a lyte."

He finally falls asleep, and dreams that he wakes to find himself in bed on a May morning with the birds singing sweetly. The windows of his room attract his attention:

> For holly al the story of Troye
> Was in the glasynge ywroght thus,
> Of Ector and of kyng Priamus,
> Of Achilles and Lamedon,
> And eke of Medea and of Jason,
> Of Paris, Eleyne, and of Lavyne.
> And alle the walles with colours fyne
> Were peynted, both text and glose,
> Of al the Romaunce of the Rose.

This is the world in which the poem moves. The poet goes outside, into a wood, and finds a hunt in progress. On inquiring from a huntsman who is hunting here, he is told:

> "Syr, th'emperour Octovyen,"

an answer which seems somehow appropriate in the trancelike atmosphere of the dream, with its stylized, heraldic scenery. The hunt is forgotten when the poet comes upon the black knight, whose lamentations leave the poet rather stupidly puzzled as to their cause. Chaucer—and this was to be a frequent device with him—makes himself out to be somewhat obtuse, and even when the knight goes on to a description of his courtship of his lady he does not realize that it is the loss of the lady that now causes his grief. After the account of his wooing and winning his love, done with a grave and formal beauty in spite of its use of the conventional courtly love properties, the poet asks where the lady is now, and the knight falls into lamentation again. Still the poet is puzzled.

> "Allas, sir, how?   what may that be?"
> "She ys ded!"   "Nay!"   "Yis, be my trouthe!"
> "Is that youre los?   Be God, hyt ys routhe!"

At this moment the hunt returns, the nearby castle bell strikes twelve, and the poet awakes to find the book with the story of Ceyx and Alcione by his side. Chaucer has succeeded in infusing some slight element of psychological and dramatic liveliness into this formal, visionary elegy. But the world of the poem is trancelike and its forms and colors heraldic.

With *The House of Fame*, which is probably Chaucer's next work, we move out of the world of trance, though the framework is still the dream. The influence of Dante's *Divina Commedia* is clear in the

second and third of the three parts, but the mood of the poem is far
from Dantesque. Book I opens with a discussion of dreams (a subject on which Chaucer was much given to speculation) and proceeds
to describe a dream in which he found himself in a temple of glass—
"Hyt was of Venus redely, /The temple"—on whose walls was engraved the story of the *Aeneid*, with special emphasis (as always in
the medieval treatment of the *Aeneid*) on the Dido episode, which
Chaucer tells in a hundred and forty lines; this leads him to give a
conventional list of faithless lovers (Ovidian in origin) before continuing the story up to Aeneas' marriage with Lavinia. The incidents
are presented as a series of pictures, introduced by t..e formula "Tho
saugh I" ("Then saw I"). Coming out of the temple doors he sees a
golden eagle shining in the sky. At the opening of Book II the eagle,
having descended, seizes the poet in its claws and bears him aloft.
With this, the mood of the poem changes from the visionary to the
lively, humorous and colloquial. The poet describes his fright, the
eagle's reassuring words and subsequent conversation. The eagle
explains to Chaucer that he is taking him to the House of Fame, for
the poet is a dull fellow who knows nothing of his neighbors. There
he will learn of love tidings and of all the jealousies, fears, and hypoc-
risies of men. The eagle lectures the unhappy man (whom he addresses familiarly as "Geffrey") on acoustics, explaining how all
speech eventually reaches the House of Fame, and prides himself on
his ability to explain difficult scientific matters simply to an ignorant
man. The poet replies in placatory monosyllables. Nothing can stop
the flow of the eagle's didactic talk, which continues until he lands
the poet on the steep slope below the House of Fame. Book III, beginning with an invocation to "God of science and of lyght" imitated
from Book I of Dante's *Paradiso*, goes on to describe the poet's difficult ascent to the House of Fame, which was situated on a high rock
of clear ice. The names of many famous people were engraved on
this rock, but some letters of every name had melted away. On the
other side he saw names of famous persons of antiquity, and they
were still as fresh as ever. The castle itself is made of beryl stone,
and Chaucer's account of what he saw there is a crowded collection
of deliberately incongruous detail, presented with an air of naïve
wonder. In the hall he saw statues of Josephus, Statius, Homer,
Dares Phrygius, Dictys Critensis, Guido della Colonne, Geoffrey of
Monmouth, Virgil, Ovid ("Venus clerk"), · Lucan, Claudian (who
wrote the *De Raptu Proserpinae*), among others; and then a large
company of people swarmed in, beseeching the Goddess of Fame to
grant them her favor:

> And somme of hem she graunted sone,
> And somme she werned wel and faire,
> And some she graunted the contraire
> Of her axyng outterly.
> But thus I seye yow, trewely,
> What her cause was, y nyste.   [I know not]

Another group ask for good fame and get the reverse; a third ask for it and receive it; a fourth group of well-doers do not wish for fame, and receive the oblivion they seek; a fifth group with a similar request receive immortal fame; a sixth group, of idlers, seek the good fame of active heroes and receive it; a seventh, in a similar position, are refused it; a group of people guilty of treachery ask for good fame and are denied it; finally, a group of cheerful and self-satisfied evildoers ask for fame as evildoers, which is granted them. All this is done with sounding of trumpets, crying of heralds, and much lively ceremonial. Chaucer, though he is still in the world of medieval dream allegory, is beginning to enjoy himself in a new way.

After Fame has disposed of the final group, a man turns to the poet and asks:

> Frend, what is thy name?
> Artow come hider to han fame?

Chaucer hastily disclaims any such intention, and says he is there to learn some new tidings. The man takes him out of the House of Fame to the House of Rumor, a building of twigs more strangely wrought than the famous Labyrinth built by Daedalus. This cagelike building, full of holes to let the sound out, seethes with the noise of rumors of all kinds. As the poet wonders at the strange place, he sees his eagle perched on a stone nearby—

> And I gan streghte to hym gon,
> And seyde thus: "Y preye the
> That thou a while abide me,
> For Goddis love, and lete me seen
> What wondres in this place been . . ."
>   "Petre! that is myn entente,"
> Quod he to me.

"Precisely why I am here," in fact, and the eagle takes him up to a window, where he hears people reporting gossip to each other. Each man tells his neighbor, and so the tidings grow and spread until they go out by the holes in the house, to come to Fame, who determines their future duration. The poem ends abruptly, unfinished, with the poet's discerning a man who

> seemed for to be
> A man of gret auctorite.

With these words the poem ends. Presumably, the man of great authority was to announce some important tidings, which may or may not have been the nominal *raison d'être* of the poem.

A strange mélange of a poem. The dream and the allegorical figures belong to a hackneyed enough convention, but the poem strikes notes that had not before been struck in English. The conversation of the eagle in Book II, with its quizzical humor, the poet laughing both at himself and at the loquacious and self-important bird, and some of the detail of action and conversation in the crowded Book III, let a fresh wind into the medieval garden of poetry. Echoes of Dante add occasional overtones of high seriousness, but the comic tone predominates, even though the poet touches now and again on some of the most profound of human problems. The versification has a sureness and flexibility that *The Book of the Duchess* lacks, while the handling of dialogue would itself justify the claim that *The House of Fame* is one of the important transitional poems in English, pointing forward to far-reaching developments in the presentation of character and conversation in fiction:

> With that this egle gan to crye,   [began]
> "Lat be," quod he, "thy fantasye!
> Wilt thou lere of sterres aught?"   [learn]
> "Nay, certeynly," quod y, "ryght naught."
> "And why?" "For y am now to old."
> "Elles I wolde the have told,"
> Quod he, "the sterres names, lo,
> And al the hevenes sygnes therto,
> And which they ben." "No fors," quod y.
> "Yis, pardee!" quod he; "wostow why? . . ."

The Parliament of Fowls is probably Chaucer's next major poem. It, too, is in the dream convention, but elements from both Dante and Boccaccio now enrich the style and the content. The verse form is the seven-line stanza (rhyming *ababbcc*), known as "rhyme royal" because of its later use by James I of Scotland in his *King's Quair* (if James I really was the author), and Chaucer handles it with a poise and a liquid flow of language that is something new in Middle English:

> The lyf so short, the craft so long to lerne,
> Th'assay so hard, so sharp and conquerynge,
> The dredful joye, alwey that slit so yerne:
> Al this mene I by Love, that my felynge

> Astonyeth with his wonderful werkynge
> So sore iwis, that when I on hym thynke,
> Nat wot I wel wher that I flete or synke.

He goes on to say—and this is typical of Chaucer's combination of gravity with irony—that he himself knows love not from experience but from books. He had been reading, he says, the *Somnium Scipionis* (as interpreted by Macrobius), which he proceeds to summarize, after a comment on the significance of old books which gives us a vivid insight into Chaucer's attitude toward his reading:

> For out of olde feldes, as men seyth,
> Cometh al this newe corn from yer to yere,
> And out of olde bokes, in good feyth,
> Cometh al this newe science that men lere.

Old books and personal observation—"experience" and "auctoritee" to use Chaucer's terms—are the two sources of knowledge and understanding, and for Chaucer character was largely determined by the use an individual makes of each. For the Wife of Bath, experience was to be enough—

> Experience, though noon auctoritee
> Were in this world, is right ynough for me;

enough at least to tell her all she needed to know about marriage, though the lady was not averse to reinforcing her conclusions with copious reference to authorities. In Chaucer's own literary career the relation between literary sources and personal observation keeps shifting. It is not that he moves from the former to the latter—no writer moves simply from literature to life, however much more simply derivative his earlier work may be than his later—but he finds more original and richer ways of combining the two elements and allowing each to illuminate the other. Like *The House of Fame, The Parliament of Fowls* imposes the author's personality on conventional material. A graver utterance from Dante and picturesque descriptions from Boccaccio's *Teseide* (which he was to draw on more extensively in the Knight's Tale) are part of the new literary materials he assimilates in the *Parliament,* which in its narrative outline and its theme are wholly conventional.

After reading the *Somnium Scipionis,* the poet goes to bed, as daylight is failing:

> The day gan faylen, and the derke nyght,
> That reveth bestes from here besynesse,
> Berafte me my bok for lak of lyght . . .

This echoes Dante's

> Lo giorno se n'andava, a l'aere bruno
> toglieva li animai che sono in terra
> dalle fatiche loro,

and there are several other such echoes throughout the poem. They are all subdued to the mood of the poem, and the mood itself is deftly modulated through several different keys. Sleep produces its dream in which, after a Dantesque journey with Scipio Africanus as his guide ("Can not I seyn if that the cause were /For I hadde red of Affrican byforn, /That made me to mete [dream] that he stod there"), he comes to a garden by a river, with the usual birds singing, and the usual allegorical characters disporting themselves. Cupid, Pleasaunce, Curteysie, Delyt, Gentilesse, Beute, Youthe, Flaterye, Desyr, and others. It is yet another picture of the ubiquitous garden of the Rose tradition, but described freshly enough for all that. He sees the temple of Venus, too, with its appropriate characters, and comes at last to a beautiful soft green place, where the goddess Nature, on a hill of flowers, was presiding over a great congress of birds. This was Saint Valentine's Day, and the birds had assembled to choose their mates in accordance with Nature's rule. Three noble eagles claim the hand of the beautiful formel eagle perched on the goddess's wrist, and each of the three (in descending order of rank) claims the formel eagle as his bride in proper courtly-love terms. Then the mass of birds take up the debate: many of them have little patience with the niceties of courtly love, the goose in particular laughing at the notion of constancy to a beloved who does not love in return—

> But she wol love hym, lat hym love another.

The sparrow hawk in turn scorns the goose's vulgar attitude. "Lo, here a parfit resoun of a goos!" he exclaims contemptuously. The turtledove defends constancy, and the argument grows into a magnificent hubbub until Nature silences them all and gives her verdict, that after waiting a year the formel eagle should make her choice. Then the birds sing a roundel for Saint Valentine's Day, "to don to Nature honour and plesaunce" before flying away, and the poet wakes.

The Parliament of Fowls is thus a poem in celebration of Saint Valentine's Day, using the convention of the dream allegory and the *demande d'amour*. It may also have been prompted by some specific royal courtship, and scholars have spilt much ink in debating which one. But any contemporary reference is irrelevant to the true significance of the poem, which is a deftly handled "occasional" piece, showing Chaucer's growing mastery of his medium, his ability to impose his own tone on conventional material. The mood shifts easily from one of quiet gravity through an occasional flash of irony to a lively and humorous realism, to end on a note of happy celebration.

Troilus and Criseyde, written probably in the middle 1380's, is a major work in which the full genius of Chaucer as metrical technician, as storyteller, and as student of human character is triumphantly displayed. It is in a sense the first real novel in English: it tells a love story with a delicacy of psychological awareness, a brilliant handling of detail, a firm sense of structure, and a mastery of controlled digression. The verse—which is the rhyme royal stanza again—adapts itself easily to the changing demands of the narrative, and in its liquid flow seems to increase the sense of fate and inevitability which hangs over the action throughout. Its immediate source is Boccaccio's *Il Filostrato*, but, while taking the main action and many specific incidents from Boccaccio, he expands the simple, highly-colored, fast-moving Italian story of love and betrayal into a multidimensional work, subtler in psychology, more varied in detail, and richer in moral overtones. Behind the *Filostrato* lies the curious and characteristically medieval transmutation of a couple of minor Homeric characters, who originally have no connection with each other at all, into the familiar story of Troilus' love for Cressida, his winning of her, and her eventual desertion of him for the Greek Diomede. Homer's Briseis and Chryseis were Trojan captives whose disposal helped to produce the wrath of Achilles. Dares Phrygius— whose importance for the medieval view of the Troy story we have noted—gives brief character sketches of Troilus, Diomede, and Briseis, but does not bring them together in a story. Benoit de Sainte-Maure's *Roman de Troie* makes Briseida the daughter of Calchas, the Trojan seer who deserted to the Greeks on foreseeing their ultimate victory, and makes Troilus in love with her, but the only part of the story he dwells on is the winning of her love by Diomede after she has been sent to join her father among the Greeks. Guido della Colonne in his *Historia Trojana* follows Benoit. Briseis and Chryseis eventually coalesce as Criseida (later Cressida), and Boccaccio is the first to tell the story of Troilus and Cressida now so familiar. Boccaccio dedicates his poem to the lady whom he loves and who has left him, as a memorial "of your worth and of my sadness," and it has a personal, lyrical, youthful tone throughout. He first introduces Pandarus, whom he makes the brother of Criseida and contemporary of Troilus, a young man who brings his sister and his friend together out of his friendship for the latter. Chaucer's Pandare is Boccaccio's Pandaro in function but not in character or behavior: he is Criseyde's uncle as well as Troilus' friend, evidently an older man, much given to quoting proverbs and precedents: a shrewd, good-natured, worldly-wise, affectionate man who shows infinite resource in bringing the lovers together but who is helpless in the face of the final tragedy. Chaucer's Troilus is the parfit, gentil knight, not substantially different from Boccaccio's Troilo. But Chaucer's Criseyde is drawn with a psychological subtlety that makes her into a wholly new character: she is the first truly complex heroine in post-classical European literature.

This development of a story which grew up within the framework of the Troy story throws interesting light not only on the medieval perspective on the classical world but also on Chaucer's methods and on the way in which his imagination worked. The Middle Ages had not the sense of literary property that we now have, and there was nothing improper in Chaucer's taking Boccaccio's story as a basis for his own—he had done that sort of thing before and was to do it again. On that story Chaucer brought to bear both "experience" and "auctoritee," his own knowledge of human nature, and his wide reading. The conception of the wheel of fortune, ever turning so that the individual is now up, now down, and the whole problem of fate and free will as discussed by Boethius, pervade the poem. Boethius is more than once paraphrased at length; Dante, Petrarch, and Ovid are drawn on for lines or images or situations; indeed, a whole world of reading is domiciled in the richly textured narrative. And Chaucer's own insight and humor and irony and sympathy play over all.

The Trojan war is the background. A medievalized Troy is presented to us in varied detail, with the classical properties somehow made to fit a medieval way of life; sallies out from the city walls against the besieging Greeks are daily occurrences, a constant opportunity for the performance of knightly deeds. We see Troilus first, the gay young knight scornful of love, and then Criseyde, the demure young widow, standing in the temple at a religious festival in her black habit. Troilus sees her there and is suddenly smitten— he has fallen in love in church, as it were. Criseyde is the very perfection of womanhood:

> She nas nat with the leste of hire stature,
> But alle hire lymes so wel answerynge
> Weren to wommanhood, that creature
> Was nevere lasse mannyssh in semynge.
> And ek the pure wise of hire mevynge

> Shewed wel that men myght in hire gesse
> Honour, estat, and wommanly noblesse.
>
> To Troilus right wonder wel with alle
> Gan for to like hire mevynge and hire chere,
> Which somdel deignous was, for she let falle
> Hire look a lite aside in swich manere,
> Ascaunces, "What! may I nat stonden here?" . . .

Troilus at once feels all the woes of the courtly lover. He automatically assumes that his beloved is unattainable, infinitely superior to him in every way. The cheerful, bustling, proverb-quoting Pandare finds him lamenting in bed, and after much vivid talk—it is remarkable how Chaucer can give the very accent of conversation in verse—gets his secret from him. When it turns out that Troilus is in love, and with Pandare's niece, Pandare has no doubt that all can be managed. This is courtly love, and it must be secret and outside marriage, free from scandal and the breath of wicked tongues (the contradiction at the heart of the courtly love notion, that love is supremely honorable yet the lady's reputation is injured if it be known, comes out clearly in the poem). More is involved than the winning of Criseyde's love: she must first be brought to lay aside her fears for her reputation and be reassured that everything can be done with discretion.

Those fears are particularly strong in Criseyde's case, for she is in a difficult position as well as fearful by nature. Her father is a traitor who has deserted to the other side, and she therefore must be especially careful in her behavior. Pandare has his work cut out. Meanwhile Troilus, reassured by Pandare, rouses himself and performs deeds of great valor against the Greeks. For courtly love ennobles the character and makes the heart more brave and generous:

> For he bicom the frendlieste wighte,
> The gentilest, and ek the mooste fre,
> The thriftiest and oon the beste knyght,
> That in his tyme was or myghte be.
> Dede were his japes and his cruelte,
> His heighe port and his manere estraunge,
> And ecch of tho gan for a very chaunge.

Book II opens on a note of hope. Echoing the opening of the *Purgatorio,* Chaucer begins:

> Owt of thise blake wawes for to saylle,
> O wynd, o wynd, the weder gynneth clere; . . .

This book is taken up with the maneuverings of Pandare. He visits his niece and, after a bantering conversation to put her in a good mood, he begins to warm up to his news, eventually rousing her to such a pitch of suspense that she can hardly wait to hear it. He then tells her of Troilus' love, saying that he asks only that she take pity on the young man and be nice to him, else he will die of love. And if Troilus dies, Pandare will die too. She reacts unfavorably at first. She is afraid of scandal. She is afraid of losing her independent way of life as a widow. She is afraid, it appears, of committing herself to any such relationship because it will mean adventuring out of her accustomed and comfortable single existence. But she is interested and, in spite of herself, excited. "Kan he wel speke of love?" she eventually asks her uncle, who then "a litel gan to smyle," for he knew the first round was won. And when Troilus, fresh from a victorious encounter with the Greeks, rides by her window amid the cheers of the crowd, she looks out and sees his handsome and knightly figure and his modest bearing

> And leet it so softe in hire herte synke,
> That to hireself she seyde, "Who yaf me drynke?"

But the siege is far from over. With a subtle combination of real reluctance and concern for appearances, both of which cover a genuine excitement about Troilus, she concedes little at first, and has to have her defenses broken down one by one. The story of this breaking down—too long to be satisfactorily summarized—is a brilliant piece of psychological fiction. The question of the genuineness of Criseyde's reluctance can still arouse heated argument among the critics, which is sufficient testimony to Chaucer's skill in character drawing. Criseyde is, in fact, the first character in English literature whose character is argued over as though she were a real person. First she is persuaded to receive—and to answer—a letter from Troilus. Then Pandare, by an ingenious device, brings them together briefly, but long enough to allow Troilus to offer and Criseyde to accept him with the ambiguous proviso "myn honour sauf." Finally, Pandare invites Criseyde to dinner when rain is expected; the heavy rain prevents her from going home and he gives her a bed in his house. Of course Troilus is there—he is supposed to have arrived suddenly, out of his wits because he has heard that Criseyde has been having an affair with someone else. Pandare brings Troilus to Criseyde's bedside and he explains his fears; she reproaches him for them so violently that he faints; Pandare heaves him into Criseyde's bed and after further maneuvering leaves him to be restored by Criseyde. Criseyde is now caught—or is it Troilus?

Pandare is gone, taking the candle with him, with the remark that it isn't good for sick folks' eyes. And Criseyde—when Troilus calls on her to yield at last, she answers passionately in his arms:

> Ne hadde I er now, my swete herte deere,
> Ben yold, ywis, I were now nought heere!

And a night of passion follows, described by Chaucer vividly but not coarsely. His account of the lovers' wonder in each other is done with a fine psychological realism. The morning follows, and the *aubade,* the song of lovers reluctantly parting at dawn. Thus Troilus and Criseyde become lovers, and continue to love secretly and happily until Fortune's wheel turns again.

This brings us to the beginning of Book IV, which tells of the exchange of prisoners and the decision to send Criseyde to her father, in the Greek camp, in return for Antenor. The distress of the lovers, Troilus' bitter speculations on fate, their final night together with their railings on fate and vows of eternal constancy take up most of the book. Troilus proposes that they steal away together, but Criseyde dismisses the plan as dangerous and impracticable. She fears scandal. She promises that she will contrive to get back to Troy on the tenth day after her departure. But of course she does not come, and the fifth book moves from Troilus to Criseyde showing the state of mind of each. Criseyde is led to the Greek camp by Diomede, handsome, self-confident, unscrupulous, an experienced lady's man. He lays siege to her at once, and she, fearful among strangers, glad to have his protection to fall back on, unable to face the dangers of the return to Troy, and taking the line of least resistance, accepts him as her lover. In Troy the line of least resistance had been to remain in her single wedded state; in the Greek camp, friendless and bewildered, acceptance of Diomede is the easy way. For all her good qualities, she was "slydynge of corage"; she lacked will power. She repulses Diomede's first attempt with a "not yet," which already shows that the game is up. And when she yielded to him she said to herself pathetically:

> But syn I se ther is no bettre way,
> And that to late is now for me to rewe,
> To Diomede algate I wol be trwe.

As for Chaucer:

> Ne me ne list this sely womman chyde
> Forther than the storye wol devyse.
> Hire name, allas! is punysshed so wide,
> That for hire gilt it ought ynough suffise.

> And if I myghte excuse hire anywise,
> For she so sory was for hire untrouthe,
> I wis, I wolde excuse hire yet for routhe.

Troilus waits for her return in vain. The picture of him waiting day after day, until dusk, at the city gates, making excuses for her delay, thinking he sees her in the distance only to find that it is "a fare-carte" (traveling cart), is one of the most poignant and perfectly wrought things in English literature. At last he writes, and receives a loving but suspiciously evasive answer; and finally he finds on a cloak taken from Diomede in fight the brooch that he himself had given to Criseyde, and he knows for certain what he had for some time suspected. With nothing to live for he becomes bold and cruel in battle, and is eventually slain by Achilles. The poem concludes with a picture of Troilus' spirit looking down from above at this tiny world, and laughing at the shabby human scene with its distracting emotions.

> Swych fyn hath, lo, this Troilus for love!   [such end]
> Swych fyn hath all his grete worthynesse! . . .
> Swych fyn hath false worldes brotelnesse! . . .

The end of the poem is religious, an appeal from human love to divine love, with a sonorous devotional stanza from the *Paradiso* to conclude.

The literary greatness and historical significance of *Troilus and Criseyde* lie in the way Chaucer has presented and enriched the narrative. It has more dimensions than anything that had hitherto appeared in English. Some of the most important effects are lost in a summary—the touches of humorous realism in the conversation of Pandare, particularly in his talk with his niece; the flashes of amused or ironic perception; the subtle discernment of character in all its phases; the moral and philosophical overtones; the adroit use of his reading to achieve these overtones; and the flow and flexibility of the steadily moving verse. The English prose novel was well advanced before anything comparable was to appear in English literature.

In *The Legend of Good Women* Chaucer returns to the love-vision for his framework. This unfinished work is a somewhat tiresome collection of accounts of loving and faithful women—including Cleopatra, Medea, Lucrece, Ariadne, Philomela, and others—which Chaucer explains was required of him as a penance by the god of love for having written heresies against love's law, and particularly for having drawn the character of a faithless woman in *Troilus and Criseyde*. The legends themselves, constructed on the analogy of that common medieval form, the legendary or collection of saints' lives, seem to have been written without any great enthusiasm, and there is nothing in them approaching the art of the *Troilus*. But the prologue to *The Legend of Good Women*—which exists in two interestingly different versions—has a charm and liveliness that the body of the work lacks. It opens with a sprightly discussion of the relation between book knowledge and experience:

> A thousand tymes have I herd men telle
> That ther ys joy in hevene and peyne in helle,
> And I accorde wel that it ys so;
> But, natheles, yet wot I wel also
> That ther nis noon dwellyng in this contree,
> That eyther hath in hevene or helle ybe,
> Ne may of hit noon other weyes witen,
> But as he hath herd seyd, or founde it writen; . . .

We must trust old books in matters of which nobody has direct experience; the poet himself reverences them

> So hertely, that ther is game noon
> That fro my bokes maketh me to goon,
> But yt be seldom on the holyday,
> Save, certeynly, whan that the month of May
> Is comen, and that I here the foules synge,
> And that the floures gynnen for to sprynge,
> Farewel my bok, and my devocioun!

And then Chaucer turns to a description of the conventional May morning of the Rose tradition; but it is done with a freshness and a sprightly charm that raises it far above most of the hundreds of other such descriptions in medieval literature. This freshness and sense of personal delight in the world of growing things which we find in the prologue is all the more remarkable when we consider that not only is the setting conventional, but the theme which he goes on to elaborate—the worship of the daisy—is itself bound up with a literary fashion of his time and the passage celebrating the daisy is based on a poem by Deschamps. By his choice of images, by the limpid flow of the couplets, by his cunning distribution of pauses and emphasis, Chaucer gives new life and conviction to this traditional material. The appearance in the meadow of the god of love and his queen Alceste occurs in the dream which he has after falling asleep in the open. The god reproaches him for his heresies against love, Alceste defends him and seeks to soften her lord's anger, and the result is that he is given the penance of writing the stories of faithful women betrayed by false men. The task, however, was one which Chaucer's genius had outgrown.

He must have been already thinking of the plan of *The Canterbury Tales,* that magnificent unfinished *opus* in which he finally drew the various strands of his genius together. What more perfect wedding of "auctoritee" and "experience," of books and life, than a collection of true-to-life pilgrims drawn from every class of contemporary Englishman who, to while away the hours of journeying, tell tales drawn from whatever literary or folk source seems most appropriate to the individual character? Some of the tales had been written before the plan to link them through the pilgrimage device had been thought of: the Second Nun's Tale, for example (the legend of Saint Cecilia) is early, as are the "tragedies" used in the Monk's Tale, and the Knight's Tale, a reworking of Boccaccio's *Teseide* probably done about the same time as the *Troilus.* The *General Prologue,* which establishes the characters and sets the scene, probably dates from the late 1380's; and the whole scheme—two stories from each pilgrim on the outward journey, and two each again on the return— was far from complete when Chaucer died. But the real purpose of the scheme was to give Chaucer the opportunity of welding his observation of men with his literary knowledge, and that purpose could be achieved without the completion of the total plan. The scheme was thus not so much a literary form in itself as a device for giving new life to other literary forms.

A group of linked tales told by different people was not unknown in earlier medieval literature, and scholars have come up with various parallels, of which perhaps the closest is the *Novelle* of Giovanni Sercambi, where the setting is also a pilgrimage, though the author himself (one of the pilgrims) tells all the tales. It is doubtful whether Chaucer knew Boccaccio's *Decameron.* But Chaucer's work is unique in its individualizing of the narrators and in the whole sense of the contemporary social scene which he brings to the reader. He brings together at the Tabard Inn at Southwark representatives of every class in the England of his day (except, it should be noted, the very highest and the very lowest; there is no one higher than the Knight or lower than the Plowman, who was a tenant farmer and not a tied laborer). Each pilgrim is at once a fully realized individual and a representative of his class or his profession. They are on holiday, not at their daily labors, so that they are more relaxed and self-revealing than they would otherwise be. Further, only on a pilgrimage could such a heterogeneous collection of people of different social status be brought together. The characters move between the inn and the shrine, the two places where different classes are likely to mingle. But their daily lives, their normal habits of thinking, their prejudices, professional bias, most familiar ideas, and personal idiosyncrasies come out in their conversation and their behavior. They are more than a framework: their conduct affects and is affected by the telling of the tales.

The *Prologue*, which describes them one by one, takes up the details that would strike the eye of a fellow traveler. There is a deliberately contrived disorder in the way in which the facts about each character are brought to our attention. For example, he describes the Cook's skill in boiling, roasting, grilling, and frying, then remarks

> But greet harm was it, as it thoughte me,
> That on his shyne a mormal hadde he.   [growth]
> For blankmanger, that made he with the beste.

The afterthought about the "blankmanger" (an elaborate creamed dish) gives an air of absolute naturalness to the description, and this air of innocent observation—the author as fellow pilgrim naïvely noting what he sees or learns about the others in the casual order which occurs to him—can be put to most effective ironic uses when Chaucer so desires. It is worth noting, too, how more than once he begins a new description on the second line of a couplet. Thus the first line of the Shipman's description follows immediately on the last line of the description of the Cook:

> . . . For blankmanger, that made he with the beste.
> A Shipman was ther, wonynge fer by weste;
> For aught I woot, he was of Dertemouthe. . . .

This again gives an air of naturalness and spontaneity. A good example of both these devices is in the description of the Monk, followed by that of the Friar. The account of the Monk concludes:

> Now certainly he was a fair prelaat;
> He was nat pale as a forpyned goost.
> A fat swan loved he best of any roost.
> His palfrey was as broun as is a berye.
> A Frere ther was, a wantowne and a merye, . . .

The color of the Monk's horse comes in casually at the end of his description, as though the author had just noticed it, and then the Friar is introduced in the same couplet.

Chaucer's naïveté as observer is assumed for purposes of irony. Nothing could be more perfectly done than the description of the Prioress: it is mere innocent observation, it seems, until we discover that the details add up to an amused picture of a nun whose real interest in life was to affect genteel behavior:

> Ther was also a Nonne, a Prioresse,
> That of her smylyng was ful symple and coy;
> Hire gretteste ooth was but by Seinte Loy;
> And she was cleped madame Eglentyne.
> Ful weel she soong the service dyvyne,
> Entuned in hir nose ful semely,
> And Frenssh she spak ful faire and fetisly,
> After the scole of Stratford atte Bowe,
> For Frenssh of Parys was to hire unknowe.
> At mete wel ytaught was she with alle;
> She leet no morsel from hir lippes falle,
> Ne wette hir fyngres in hir sauce depe;
> Wel koude she carie a morsel and wel kepe
> That no drope ne fille upon hire brest.
> In curteisie was set ful muchel hir lest.
> Hir over-lippe wyped she so clene
> That in hir coppe ther was no ferthyng sene
> Of grece, when she dronken hadde hir draughte.
> Ful semely after hir mete she raughte. . . .

Only the Knight, the poor Parson, and the Plowman are treated without any touch of irony at all, as almost ideal figures, and it is significant that they are all something like anachronisms by Chaucer's time. The Knight represents the highest ideals of chivalry and courtesy; the poor Parson's genuinely Christian behavior is implicitly contrasted with that of the other representatives of the church; and the Plowman, honest, hardworking, goodhearted, would be hard to find in the age of the Peasants' Revolt and the Statute of Laborers. These perhaps nostalgic portraits represent Chaucer's oblique comment on the troubles of his time, which he never overtly discusses. It is worth remembering—what would not be guessed from a study of Chaucer's writings—that the period in which he lived was a time of rapid change and even of confusion. The growing tendency for the commutation of labor service for money-payment combined with the results of the Black Death to cause the decay of villeinage and to increase the independence of the laborers, who, left small in number by the ravages of the plague, were able to set their own price on their labor. In vain the governing class tried to stop the rise in laborers' wages by statutes of laborers. The clock could not be put back, and the results of the Black Death in depopulating the countryside put the laborers in an extremely favorable position. Villeins slipped away from the land to which they were legally bound, to offer their services to the highest bidder. With harvests rotting for lack of workers, landowners were forced to pay in wages what was asked. In addition to the unrest produced by this problem, there were many other causes for general dissatisfaction in the last years of Edward III's reign and the beginning of Richard II's. England was being governed by a selfish and corrupt clique; France was slipping away from her control and her supremacy at sea being steadily destroyed; the glory of Crecy and Poiters had departed and—worst of all—the country was being taxed almost out of existence in a vain endeavor to win back the lost power and glory. English commerce depended largely on the maintenance of English sea-power, and the revival of French might by land and sea was more than a military question. Amid this general discontent the Peasants' Revolt broke out in 1381. Change was in the air, and to a contemporary it might well have seemed to be decay. Chivalry had become a farce. Every kind of magnificence was to be seen in the state of the small minority who wielded the power, while disease and misery prevailed throughout the countryside. The State had grown lopsided. When the Black Prince took Limoges in 1370 he massacred all the citizens, including hundreds of women and children, yet he treated the few knights who were in the town with exaggerated kindness and courtesy. In 1377 the Black Prince died, but the spirit exemplified in his action of 1370 prevailed now more than ever. The practice of knighthood had degenerated into a stupid pageantry: the old order was breaking up, with all the usual symptoms produced by the working of unrecognized forces. And in the Church, too, corruption was reaping an unpleasant harvest. Wyclif was a portentous symbol, and the connection of the priest John Ball with the rebellious peasants, however much Wyclif may have disapproved, was no accident.

Against such a background the characters of the Knight, the Parson, and the Plowman seem like nostalgic idealizations, and perhaps Chaucer meant them as such. For the rest, he takes men as he finds them, obtaining that kind of amusement in the ironic yet sympathetic observation of his fellows which yields itself only to the artist's vision. The social and economic background, with its confusions and upheavals, is transmuted through human character into individual examples of self-interest or rascality, portrayed with that relish for human behavior and human weakness that we find so often in Shakespeare. But we must not, as some critics have tended to do, play down Chaucer's irony. A high proportion of his pilgrims are rascals, and Chaucer knows that they are. Nor can we ignore his clear attack on corruption in the Church, though here again the attack is done obliquely through the presentation of individual characters. The Monk and the Friar and the Summoner are amusing enough characters as Chaucer describes them, but the behavior of the latter two, brilliantly presented and magnificently comic though it is, is the behavior of petty blackguards, while the Pardoner, perhaps Chaucer's greatest masterpiece of character drawing, implies a whole world of moral hypocrisy. Chaucer's point of view is secular throughout—in spite of evidence of his genuine religious feeling and of the famous "Retraction" which follows the Parson's Tale in the manuscripts—and he is intrigued rather than shocked by the weaknesses of human nature. But irony always has moral implications, and Chaucer in *The Canterbury Tales* was not an ironist for nothing.

Attempts have been made to identify some of the pilgrims with historical characters, but even if this could be done it adds nothing to our view of Chaucer's achievement. He gives us a collection of individuals who also represent the different social and professional strata of the England of his day. The Church, with its many representatives (for the Church was the dominant profession in the Middle Ages); the Knight and his son the Squire representing the upper classes (but not the high aristocracy); the Merchant represents the well-to-do middle classes, and the five members of trade guilds, also middle class; the Franklin, a nonaristocratic landowner; the Yeoman, independent but lower down in the social scale; professional men such as the Sergeant of the Law and the Doctor of Physic; executive or managerial characters such as the Manciple (who purchased provisions for an inn of court) and the Reeve (assistant manager of an estate); and so on down to the Plowman. Almost all have more characteristics than their representative capacities demand. The tales they tell, and the incidents in which they become involved, are for the most part suited to both their occupations and their characters, though Chaucer did not have time to fit all the tales to suitable tellers. These tales together give an almost complete conspectus of medieval literary forms, including the courtly romance (Knight's Tale), the *fabliau* (Miller's and Reeve's Tales), the Breton lay (Franklin's Tale), the saint's legend (the Second Nun's and Prioress' Tales), the preacher's *exemplum* (Pardoner's Tale), the beast fable (Nun's Priest's Tale), the sermon (Parson's Tale), and so on.

The Knight's Tale is a shorter and more rapidly moving version of Boccaccio's *Teseide,* one of the stories quarried by the Middle Ages out of the material about Thebes found in Statius' *Thebaid* and the *Roman de Thèbes.* In this tale of Palamon and Arcite and their joint love for Emily, Chaucer's narrative art is seen working with supreme efficiency. The rhymed decasyllabic couplets move smoothly and flexibly forward; incident is handled with vigor and vividness; highly colored picturesque details are brought in to provide appropriate pauses in the narrative; an undertone of gravity is properly subdued to the surface polish of the tale; glimpses of irony peep out occasionally to lighten a potentially tragic incident; and, altogether, the world of the chivalric romance lives here with a brightness and a charm rarely found in other examples of the species. The characters are not highly individualized, for the world of chivalric action and courtly love does not demand such individualization; but everybody has the characteristics necessary to take him through his assigned part with dignity and spirit. The Knight's Tale has not the depth or the modernity of the *Troilus:* it is a formal and graceful exercise in a medieval mode, perfectly executed.

The formal courtesy and gravity of the ending of the Knight's Tale—

> Thus endeth Palamon and Emelye;
> And God save al this faire compaignye!—

is followed by the drunken Miller's insistence on telling his tale next. This is Chaucer at his liveliest and most characteristic:

> Our Hooste saugh that he was dronke of ale,
> And seyde, "Abyd, Robyn, my leeve brother;
> Som bettre man shal telle us first another.
> Abyd, and lat us werken thriftily."
>   "By Goddes soule," quod he, "that wol nat I;
> For I wol speke, or elles go my wey."
> Oure Hooste answerde, "Tel on, a devil wey!
> Thou art a fool; thy wit is overcome."
>   "Now herkneth," quod the Millere, "alle and some.
> But first I make a protestacioun
> That I am dronke, I knowe it by my soun;
> And therfore if that I mysspeke or seye,
> Wyte it the ale of Southwerk, I you preye.
> For I wol telle a legende and a lyf
> Both of a carpenter and of his wyf,
> How that a clerk hath set the wrightes cappe."

The Reeve (whose duties apparently also involved carpentering) took offence, and protested violently at the Miller's "lewed dronken harlotrye:"

> It is a synne and eek a greet folye
> To apeyren any man, or hym defame,   [injure]
> And eek to bryngen wyves in swich fame.
> Thou mayst ynogh of others thynges seyn."

But the Miller persists, and tells his coarse and rollicking *fabliau* about a credulous carpenter and his pretty wife, who cuckolded him with an ingenious and personable young clerk. The company laugh,

and "Osewold the Reeve" who "was of carpenteris craft" felt somewhat annoyed. He could requite the Miller with a bawdy story of
"bleryng of a proud milleres ye," but he is getting old, and his days
of play are over. With a sudden yet wholly appropriate change of
mood Chaucer has the Reeve burst into an eloquent self-pitying
account of his growing old, using the images appropriate to his
daily work:

> . . . For sikerly, whan I was bore, anon
> Deeth drough the tappe of lyf and leet it gon;
> And ever sithe hath so the tappe yronne
> Til that almoost al empty is the tonne. . . .

But he finds the energy to requite the Miller with another coarse tale
of the *fabliau* variety, of how a crooked miller had his wife and
daughter seduced by a couple of Cambridge students. His conclusion
shows his satisfaction:

> And God, that sitteth heighe in magestee,
> Save al this compaignye, grete and smale!
> Thus have I quyt the Millere in my tale.

The Reeve's tale sends the Cook into roars of laughter, and he begins
a tale of his own, evidently in similar vein, as far as we can tell from
the sixty lines of it that alone are extant.

The Man of Law's Tale comes in the manuscripts after the unfinished Cook's Tale, preceded by "the wordes of the Hoost to the
compaignye" and followed by further talk: it is clearly a separate
fragment of the whole work. This tale is in quite different vein from
that of the Miller's or the Reeve's. Told in rhyme royal, it is a symbolic story of the manifold misfortunes of Constance, daughter of a
Roman Emperor, and her final delivery from woe after a series of
tribulations sufficient (as in the case of patient Griselda of the Clerk's
Tale) to drive most people out of their minds. The whole thing has
the dream quality of so much medieval pseudo-history (its source is
Nicholas Trivet's *Anglo-Norman Chronicle*), and may well be an
earlier work. The characters are figures in a tapestry, and while the
tale has a certain formal beauty it lacks complexity and life.

Another fragment contains the Wife of Bath's Prologue and Tale,
the Friar's Tale, and the Summoner's Tale. The Wife of Bath's Prologue is one of the high points of *The Canterbury Tales*. The character creates herself as she talks, strong-willed, opinionated, highly
sexed, frank, humorous, and masterful. Her account of her five husbands, her defense of human frailty and arguments against chastity
as a practicable ideal, the gusto and vigor and uninhibited relish of

her talk, present a character at once highly individualized and the first of a type that has had many successors in English fiction. In spite of her appeal to "experience" rather than "auctoritee," she can quote authorities with the best. For the antifeminist arguments which the Wife puts into the mouth of one of her former husbands, as well as for aspects of the Wife's own character, Chaucer drew on a great variety of sources, including the second part of *The Romance of the Rose,* Deschamps' *Miroir de Mariage,* Jerome's *Epistola Adversus Jovinianum* and Walter Map's *Epistola Valerii ad Rufinum de non Ducenda Uxore (Valerius' Letter to Rufinus about not Marrying a Wife)*: seldom has such a variety of material—which includes the most important antifeminist literature known to the Middle Ages —been so perfectly welded into a splendid original character portrait.

The Wife of Bath is concerned not only to defend the active use of sex in marriage—

> I wol bistowe the flour of al myn age
> In the actes and in fruyt of mariage—

but also to insist that married happiness is only possible if the husband yields the "maistrye" to the wife, and her tale, based on a story found in both literary and folk tradition, is designed to prove her point. It is the story of the "loathly lady" who turns out to be young and beautiful when the husband, whom she has acquired by doing him a service which he has promised to repay in any way she asks, promises to put himself under her "wise governance." The tale, told in decasyllabic couplets, combines magic with touches of shrewd realism, and a tone of romantic delicacy emerges at the end. This is perfectly in character, for the Wife of Bath believed in love and romance, though on her own terms.

The Wife of Bath's Tale is the first of a series of stories which deal with the question of "maistrye" in marriage. The theme is not pursued immediately, for the Friar and the Summoner, who have been spoiling for a quarrel since they interrupted the Wife of Bath's autobiographical discourse with mutually offensive remarks, proceed to tell their stories at each other's expense as soon as the Wife's tale has been concluded. Both stories are little masterpieces and show a brilliant handling of detail. The Friar tells of a rascally Summoner who meets the devil in the disguise of a yeoman and whose dishonest behavior finally puts him into the devil's power, so that he is carried off to Hell. The Summoner replies with a coarse story of a grasping Friar whose rapacity lands him in a comically humiliating situation. The picture given in this tale of the Friar's visit to a sick man, his hypocritical words of comfort and advice, his infuriatingly patronizing sententiousness, is one of the finest pieces of realistic etching Chaucer ever did. The dramatic exchanges between the Friar and the Summoner before and between the tales provide a setting and a "human interest" that make the whole episode a work of art in itself.

The Clerk's Tale, which begins another fragment, takes up the marriage question again. He tells of patient Griselda, a tapestry tale like the Man of Law's, presented in rhyme royal, based (as the Clerk acknowledges) on a Latin story by Petrarch, which is itself a rendering of a story from Boccaccio's *Decameron*. This picture of wifely meekness and obedience carried to an outrageous extreme is too much for Chaucer himself, who intervenes at the end with his own comment:

> Grisilde is deed, and eek hire pacience,
> And bothe atones buried in Ytaille;
> For which I crie in open audience,
> No wedded man so hardy be t'assaille
> His wyves pacience in trust to fynde
> Grisildis, for in certein he shal faille.
>
> O noble wyves, ful of heigh prudence,
> Lat noon humylitee youre tonge naille,
> Ne lat no clerk have cause or diligence
> To write of yow a storie of swich mervaille
> As of Grisildis pacient and kynde. . . .

The Merchant follows with the story of January and May—of an old husband and a young wife, who hoodwinks him with her young lover. A curious but effective mixture of antifeminist satire and magic, the story, told in decasyllabic couplets, makes skillful use of a great variety of literary sources. The Merchant's Tale ends this fragment, and another fragment begins with the Squire's Tale, an unfinished story of wonder and romance, set in "Sarray, in the land of Tartarye." It has the naïve enjoyment of wonders appropriate to the young squire, and its *Arabian Nights* atmosphere still has a certain appeal. Milton referred to it in his "L'Allegro" as the

> half told
> Story of Cambuscan bold.

The Franklin's Tale, which follows in this fragment, continues the marriage debate. It is a gentle and charming tale of a loving wife who, through no fault of her own, becomes involved in a promise to yield herself to another lover. Her husband, recognizing that promises must be kept, advises his wife, in tears, that she must fulfill her promise. The young man, when the lady presents herself to him and tells him in bitter grief that she is prepared to go through with it, releases her from her promise, and he in turn, who is indebted to a learned man for the means of having the lady put in his power, is released from payment of the large sum which he was to be charged for the service. Courtesy and "franchise" prevail, and "maistrye" gives way to "gentilesse." This is the final answer to the problem of who is to have the "maistrye" in marriage:

> Love wol nat been constreyned by maistrye.
> Whan maistrie comth, the God of Love anon
> Beteth his wynges, and farewel, he is gon!

The husband, the lover, and the "clerk" in the end all vie with each other in courteous and "free" behavior, and the Franklin concludes by asking his audience: "Which was the mooste fre, as thynketh yow?"

Another fragment begins with the Physician's Tale, the doleful story of Appius and Virginia, in which the daughter is killed by her father rather than be yielded to the lust of a corrupt judge. It is probably an earlier story of Chaucer and does not read like his maturer work. The Host is upset by the story and—thinking he knows his man—turns to the Pardoner for a merry tale:

> ". . . Thou beel amy, thou Pardoner," he sayde,
> "Telle us some myrthe or japes right anon."

The Pardoner demands a drink first, and then—somewhat the worse for liquor, for he has had more than one drink of "corny ale" that day—he begins. What he says constitutes perhaps the most brilliant single passage in all of Chaucer's work. Somewhat affronted by the Host's assumption that he is capable only of "a myrie tale," he begins by telling his audience of his skill and virtuosity as a Pardoner. But he is so anxious to display his cleverness (and his natural caution has been dissipated by drink) that he reveals himself as an unscrupulous trickster who uses false relics and every kind of dishonest cunning to wring money out of even the poorest people. He tells how he preaches, how he blackmails the congregation into giving him money, how he impresses, bullies, frightens, and overwhelms his hearers. It is a picture of extraordinary virtuosity, whose motive is wholly evil. Having thus vindicated his cleverness at the expense of his character he proceeds to his story—which is not a merry tale, but another example of his professional skill, an *exemplum*, a story with a moral to move and impress his hearers. His tale of the three rioters who set out to find Death and find him unknowingly in a heap of treasure—for sole possession of which each treacherously kills the others—is perfectly done. Beginning with overt moralizing, which rises to an eloquent attack on drunkenness, he proceeds to paint a vivid picture of the riotous, blasphemous, and avaricious young men at the tavern. The story then moves with somber speed to its violent conclusion. It is a professional performance of the very highest quality. Having completed the story, the Pardoner, either led by the momentum of his own eloquence or deceiving himself into believing that his eloquence and narrative skill have effaced the effect of his earlier self-revelation, offers to sell the company pardons:

> Paraventure ther may fallen oon or two
> Doun of his hors, and breke his nekke atwo.
> Looke which a seuretee is it to you alle
> That I am in youre fellaweshipe yfalle,
> That I may assoille yow, bothe moore and lasse,
> Whan that the soule shal fro the body passe.
> I rede that oure Hoost heere shal bigynne,
> For he is moost envoluped in synne.
> Com forth, sire Hoost, and offre first anon,
> And thou shalt kisse the relikes everychon,
> Ye, for a grote! Unbokele anon thy purs.

This invitation to kiss (for a fee) relics which he has already confessed are pigs' bones naturally outrages the Host, who replies with eloquent coarseness. The professional virtuosity of his tale clearly was not enough to pull the wool over the eyes of a tough-minded character like Harry Bailly. The Pardoner is enraged by his reply to his suggestion, and the Knight has to intervene to restore order.

Another fragment begins with the Shipman's Tale, an amusing *fabliau* with a folk source: there is some evidence that it was originally intended for the Wife of Bath and was transferred to the Shipman after Chaucer had decided to give the Wife another story instead. It is another tale of the wife and her lover fooling the husband. The Prioress' Tale, which follows, is a "miracle of our Lady," the story of little Saint Hugh of Lincoln murdered by "cursed Jewes" for singing a hymn to the Virgin as he walked through the Jews' quarter. It would of course be unrealistic and anachronistic to imagine that Chaucer or any of his contemporaries would have seen the fantastic and cruel libel perpetrated by such a story: there were no Jews in England in Chaucer's day, and they were known to Englishmen of the time solely in terms of anti-Semitic folklore. If we forget the implications, the story has a naïve charm which reflects something of the character of its teller. It is told in rhyme royal, and represents one of Chaucer's most assured handlings of this stanza.

The Host then turns to Chaucer himself,

> And sayde thus, "What man artow?" quod he;
> "Thou lookest as thou woldest fynde an hare,
> For evere upon the ground I see thee stare. . . ."

"Cheer up," says the Host to the timid and humble Chaucer of "elvyssh contenaunce,"

> "Tells us a tale of myrthe and that anon."
> "Hooste," quod I, "ne beth nat yvele apayd,
> For oother tale certes kan I noon,
> But of a rym I lerned longe agoon."

So the author of *The Canterbury Tales,* representing himself as the least skilled of all the narrators (this kind of humor was characteristic of him: we remember his respectful monosyllables before the eagle in *The House of Fame*), embarks on "Sir Thopas," that brilliant parody of the metrical romance. In the steady plod of the meter, in the mechanical piling up of detail, in the long catalogues of objects, in the language, situation, and tone, "Sir Thopas" burlesques all the main characteristics of run-of-the-mill popular romance in English verse. We have quoted from it in Chapter 2, but two more stanzas, illustrating the catalogue of the knight's physical attributes, will give some idea of the burlesque element:

> Sire Thopas wax a doghty swayn;
> Whit was his face as a payndemayn,
>   His lippes red as rose;
> His rode is lyk scarlet in grayn,
> And I yow telle in good certayn,
>   He hadde a semely nose.
>
> His heer, his berd was lyk saffroun,
> That to his girdel raughte adoun;
>   His shoon of cordewane.
> Of Brugges were his hosen broun,
> His robe was of syklatoun,
>   That coste many a jane.

The Host shuts him up after some thirty stanzas:

> "Namoore of this, for Goddes dignitee,"
> Quod oure Hooste, "for thou makest me
> So wery of thy verray lewednesse
> That, also wisly God my soule blesse,
> Myne eres aken of thy drasty speche.
> Now swich a rym the devel I biteche!
> This may wel be rym dogerel," quod he.

Chaucer then offers to tell "a litel thyng in prose," which turns out to be the long, tedious moralizing tale of *Melibee,* translated from the French. Whether Chaucer meant this to sound as it does to modern ears is not quite clear: he may not have been aware of how lacking in artistry his prose was compared to his verse. At any rate, the Host approved of the tale, and expressed the wish that his wife had the patience advocated and practiced by Melibeus' wife Prudence. The Host then calls on the Monk to tell a tale, assuming—as he had done with the Pardoner—that this secular-minded cleric will tell something lively. He addresses the Monk in a tone of cheerful agreement with his assumed opinion that clerical celibacy was a bad thing. But the Monk's professional dignity is offended, and he tells a series of tragedies—"De Casibus Virorum Illustrium." "Tragedy" to the medieval mind was a story of reversal of fortune from high to low. As the Monk says:

> Tragedie is to seyn a certeyn storie,
> As olde bookes maken us memorie,
> Of hym that stood in greet prosperitee,
> And is yfallen out of heigh degree
> Into myserie, and endeth wrecchedly.

This is presumably an earlier work of Chaucer's. It tells, in eight-lined stanzas rhyming *ababbcbc,* of the falls of Lucifer, Adam, Samson, Hercules, "Nabugodonosor," Balthasar, Cenobia, Pedro, king of Castille, Peter, king of Cyprus, Bernabo Visconti, Ugolino (see Dante's *Inferno,* Canto XXIII, which was presumably Chaucer's source), Nero, Holofernes, Antiochus, Alexander, Julius Caesar, and Croesus, before he is interrupted by the Knight, who can stand no more of these dreary stories:

> "Hoo!" quod the Knyght, "good sire, namoore of this!
> That ye han seyd is right ynough, ywis,
> And muchel moore; for litel hevynesse
> Is right ynough to muche folk, I gesse.

And the Host agrees fervently:

> "Sire Monk, namoore of this, so God yow blesse!
> Youre tale anoyeth al this compaignye."

He asks the Monk for a story of hunting, but the Monk replies sullenly that he doesn't want to play. The Nun's Priest is now called upon.

The Nun's Priest's Tale of Chauntecleer and Pertelote is perhaps the best known of all Chaucer's works, and justly so, for it represents Chaucer at absolutely the top of his form. The quiet, realistic opening describing the poor widow and her way of life, the account of the cock and the hen with its superb satire on human marital relationships, the use of learning in the discussion of the causes and meaning of dreams with the deftly drawn differences of approach between Chauntecleer and Pertelote, the ironic effect achieved by the application of human psychology to the behavior of the birds—all this has been discussed and praised often enough. Drawing on material from the medieval beast epic and on medieval notions of medicine, astrology, and psychology, Chaucer has produced a story so aerated with wit, so cunningly wrought at all points, so artfully blended of mockery and sympathy, of irony and understanding, that the traditional nature of the materials is lost sight of in the brilliant finish of the performance. But there is much of medieval thought and attitude in the tale, which in fact makes one of the handiest windows onto the Middle Ages for anybody who wishes to enter directly into that world. Yet the story is permanently modern, kept alive by artistry, wit, and insight into human (presented as animal) weakness.

Another fragment begins with the Second Nun's Prologue and Tale. These are conventional religious performances, probably written by Chaucer considerably earlier. The Prologue contains an invocation to the Virgin Mary, drawing on a variety of sources including the *Paradiso* and several Latin hymns, and the tale itself is an account in rhyme royal of the life and martyrdom of Saint Cecilia. The company are then enlivened by the appearance of a Canon and his Yeoman, who join them after hard riding. The Canon is an alchemist, and the Yeoman tells the company something of his master's methods for tricking people out of their money, which so enrages and shames the Canon that he rides off again. The Yeoman then tells his tale, which differs from all the others in that it is represented as something in which he was recently involved. It is the story of an elaborate plot on his master's part to obtain money fraudulently from credulous people who imagined that his alchemy could obtain riches for them. The theme was common enough in Chaucer's time, but it is told here with an immediacy and a freshness that correspond perfectly to the situation out of which it is made to arise.

Another fragment contains the Manciple's Prologue and Tale. The Prologue contains a lively quarrel between the Manciple and the Cook, the latter of whom is drunk. The Manciple's brief tale is of the telltale crow who tells the husband of his wife's infidelity: it was a story common in one form or another throughout Europe and the Orient. Finally, there is in another fragment the Parson's Pro-

logue and Tale, which follows directly after the Manciple's Tale,
for it begins with a reference to its having just ended. The Host
asks the Parson for a story, and the Parson replies that he will tell
no story but a sermon.

> Why sholde I sowen draf out of my fest,
> Whan I may sowen whete, if that me lest? . . .
> But trysteth wel, I am a Southren man,
> I kan nat geeste 'rum, ram, ruf,' by lettre,
> Ne, God woot, rym holde I but litel bettre; . . .

He does not hold with the alliterative poetry of the North, or with
rhyme. He will tell his tale in prose, "to knytte up al this feeste,
and make an ende." He then delivers a long sermon on penitence,
which includes a treatise on the seven deadly sins. The prose is
somewhat featureless, and the work is more interesting to students
of medieval preaching than to the literary critic. After it, in all the
manuscripts which contain the complete tale, is Chaucer's "Retraction," a conventionally pious renunciation of his works "of worldly
vanitees," including the *Troilus, The House of Fame, The Legend
of Good Women, The Parliament of Fowls,* and those of *The Canterbury Tales* "that sownen into synne." Neo-orthodoxy hails this
as a commendable turning from this world to eternity, but it is
difficult to be satisfied with a point of view which so blithely renounces what has made a man immortal.

The conclusion is self-evident. With Chaucer, the English language and English literature grew at a bound to full maturity. No
other Middle English writer has his skill, his range, his complexity,
his large humane outlook. Unfortunately, the English language (as
Chaucer foresaw in a stanza at the end of *Troilus and Criseyde*)
was still in the process of rapid change, and major shifts in pronunciation and accentuation were to occur in the following century
and a half. This meant that Chaucer's achievement in establishing
English as a fully developed literary language could not be adequately exploited by his immediate successors. It was not long before
readers were unable to scan him properly. This fact helps to emphasize Chaucer's loneliness. His followers lack both his technical brilliance and his breadth of vision, leaving him the one undisputed master in medieval English literature. Not until Shakespeare is there
an English writer with Chaucer's combination of technique and insight and his ability to put each at the service of the other, and
Shakespeare's genius, which was the greater, ran in different channels. But no other English narrative poet is his equal.

The large canvas on which *The Canterbury Tales* are painted, the
varied view of humanity in action which Chaucer gives us, were

later to become characteristic qualities of English literature, represented in both the drama and, later, the novel. The often quoted phrase of Dryden's, "Here is God's plenty," referring to *The Canterbury Tales*, can be applied to much in Shakespeare, Fielding, and Dickens, to name only a few. However much attention is paid to the principal character or characters in the foreground, English dramatists and novelists have had a fondness for filling in the background with a large range of characters diminishing in subtlety, but not in life, the further in the background they are. Men tend to be seen against the colorful pattern of a stratified society rather than only in intimate relation with the select few in contact with whom their destiny is determined. This is not, of course, always true, and less true of tragedies than of other kinds of work (compare *Othello* with *Henry IV*, for example or Jonson's *Bartholomew Fair* with his *Sejanus*), but on the whole the crowded canvas, with the characters shading off from fully realized individuals to types and oddities, seems to be a preference of the English literary genius. Chaucer, however, does not go in for Jonsonian "humours" (though he knows and uses the psychological theory behind them) or Dickensian eccentrics. His vision, if ironic, is central; his tone, if often comic, is never merely funny; and each of his characters represents some essential truth about men.

If Chaucer's work helped to make the East Midland dialect of Middle English into the English literary language, we are reminded by the work of his contemporary, John Gower (died 1408), who wrote in French and in Latin as well as in English, that the claims of the other two languages were still strong. French, however, was rapidly giving way to English, and it is significant that of his three major works—*Miroir de l'Homme, Vox Clamantis*, and *Confessio Amantis*—the first is in French (in its Anglo-Norman variety) and the last, written toward the end of his career with Chaucer's example before him, is in English. Gower's reputation has been eclipsed by Chaucer's, but he was popular in his own day and was still read by the Elizabethans. He is a more typical representative of his age and class than Chaucer could claim to be: conservative, moralistic, drawing with considerable technical skill but without any great originality of perception or liveliness of imagination on the traditional materials that were available to him. His long French poem is a manual of sins and sinners, a detailed and gloomy account of the prevalence of vice springing from man's corrupt nature. Repentance is, of course, the remedy. The *Vox Clamantis*, a dream allegory in Latin, deals with the Peasants' Revolt of 1381, giving a savagely gloomy picture of violence and disorder and of the general corruption of the age. The *Confessio Amantis* is a collection of tales in English octosyllabic couplets linked by a not very helpful framework. The poet announces, with a certain reluctance, that he will leave morality for love, for readers prefer the latter. He then describes the conventional May morning, with himself going out into a wood and meeting Venus, the Queen of Love, who advises him to make his confession to Genius, her priest. Genius considers it necessary to discuss the seven deadly sins, with the numerous sub-sins in each category, and he proceeds to illustrate each one by a story; it is these stories which make up the main material of the poem. The relation between the story and the sin it is meant to illustrate is often forced and sometimes preposterous, and it would have been better if Gower had rid himself altogether of this cumbrous machinery. But the tales themselves are told with a quiet skill. Gower lacks altogether Chaucer's vivacity and humor: he tends to be merely fluent. Here, for example, is part of his description of the cave of sleep from his tale of Ceyx and Alcione (which Chaucer told in *The Book of the Duchess*):

> Under an hell there is a cave,   [hill]
> Which of the sonne mai noght have,
> So that noman mai knowe ariht
> The point between the dai and nyht:
> Ther is no fyr, there is no sparke,
> Ther is no dore, which mai charke,   [creak]
> Whereof an yhe scholde unschette, [an eye should open]
> So that inward there is no lette. . . .

The stories are interspersed with digressions on a great variety of subjects. His views are always the conventional views of his age. There is no originality in his imagination or in his ideas. The constant moralizing wearies, and though many of the tales hold the interest, the smooth flow of over thirty thousand lines becomes infinitely tiresome. "Moral Gower," as Chaucer called him in the dedication of the *Troilus*, is one of the most interesting examples in medieval English literature of verse craftsmanship without genius; he is an excellent mirror of his age; he is more disturbed by the upheavals in contemporary society than Chaucer ever shows himself to be; but he is a dull fellow, lacking the true spark, and we cannot read him for any length of time without making historical allowances.

Moral in a more passionate and personal way and more deeply concerned with the religious, social, and economic problems of his time is the author of *Piers Plowman*, an impressive allegorical poem (or series of related poems) written in the old alliterative meter in the latter part of the fourteenth century. The author is traditionally taken to be William Langland, and he certainly refers to himself as Will in the poem; but the attribution is uncertain, and in any case it is possible that the later two of the three main versions of the poem which exist represent revisions and alterations by one or more other writers. The Prologue describes how the author fell asleep on a May morning on the Malvern Hills and saw in a dream "a faire felde ful of folke," with ploughmen, wasters, hermits, merchants, jesters, beggars, pilgrims, and friars, each going about his business; the list closes with a pardoner with his papal bulls offering to "assoil" the people, and neglectful priests deserting their flocks for an easy life in London. A king appears, and an angelic voice admonishes him in Latin to follow justice and mercy; then—with that dream logic where one scene suddenly transforms itself into another—we find a group of rats and mice deciding to put a bell on the cat so that they can have warning of his approach, then finding none of them willing to tie the bell on to the cat, and finally being warned that that is not how to handle the problem of a dangerous ruler. The Prologue ends with another crowded picture of the social scene, with barons, burgesses, tradesmen, and artisans of different kinds, laborers, and innkeepers crying "Hot pies!" at the doors of their taverns.

We can see at once that this is a new use of the dream allegory. The gentle movement of the traditional variety of love vision, generally told in rhymed couplets, has here given way to the more vigorous rhythms of the older alliterative line, obviously handled by someone who had long been familiar with it. There is a rapidity and a bustling quality about the verse, a sense of men at work, that is not easily paralleled in medieval English literature:

> A faire felde ful of folks   fonde I there bytwene,
> Of alle maner of men   the mene and the riche,
> Worchying and wandryng   as the worlde asketh.
> Some putten hem to the plow   pleyed ful selde,
> In settyng and in sowyng   swonken ful harde,
> And wonnen that wastours   with glotonys destruyeth.
>   And some putten hem to pruyde   aparailed hem thereafter,
> In contenaunce of clothyng   comen disgised.
>   In prayers and in penance   putten hem manye,
> Al for loue of ower lorde   lyueden ful streyte,
> In hope forto haue   heueneriche blisse. . . .
>   There preched a Pardonere   as he a prest were,
> Broughte forth a bulle   with bishopes seles,
> And seid that hym-self myghte   assoilen hem alle
> Of falshed of fastyng   of vowes ybroken.

The vision then develops into an allegorical interpretation of life. The first "passus" (the name given to the divisions of the poem) introduced Holy Church, a fair lady who expounds the way of salvation to the dreamer. In the second, Lady Mede (reward, bribery) appears, richly dressed, and is to be married to Falsehood; but Theology objects and the various characters proceed to London to have the matter decided by the King. The King threatens punishment to Falsehood and the other figures surrounding Lady Mede (Flattery, Guile), who run off and leave Mede alone to face the court. In the third passus, Mede tries her tricks on the justices. She confesses to a friar and is shriven, and makes a good impression by promising to pay for new windows in a church (which leads the author to utter a warning against those who hope to attain heaven by having their names engraved as benefactors on church windows: that is not the way to salvation). She recommends the acceptance of bribes to mayors and justices. The King is fooled, and proposes a marriage between Mede and Conscience, but Conscience objects and delivers a formidable indictment of the lady. Some lively argument follows, in the course of which Conscience gives an eloquent account of a time coming when

> Shal na more Mede   be maistre, as she is nouthe,   [now]
> Ac love and lowenesse   and lewte togederes,   [loyalty]
> Thise shal be maistres on molde   treuthe to save.   [earth]

Passus IV develops the argument, with Wit, Wisdom, Peace, Reason, and Wrong taking part: the King is convinced by Reason in the end, and asks him to stay with him always.

In Passus V the poet awakes briefly, then falls asleep again "and thanne saw I moche more." He sees the same field full of folk, and describes first Reason preaching to the people that recent plagues and tempests were punishment for sin. The Seven Deadly Sins hear Reason's call to repentance, and are moved to repent. This introduces one of the liveliest and most interesting sections of the poem. Pride, Luxury, Envy, Wrath, Avarice, Gluttony, and Sloth, each personified, give accounts of themselves before their repentance, and some of these accounts, taken together with the author's description, amount to brilliantly drawn portraits. There is of course no more individualization than is necessary to make the particular vice clear and to illuminate the behavior which it implies, but within these limits the character drawing is vivid and skillful. The most appealing is the picture of Gluttony in the tavern, where he stops on his way to church. The interior of a medieval tavern is described with Hogarthian realism: Gluttony's fellow drinkers are not personifications, but real people:

> Cesse the souteresse   sat on the benche,   [female shoemaker]
> Watte the warner   and hys wyf bothe,
> Tymme the tynkere   and tweyne of his prentis,
> Hikke the hakeneyman   and hughe the nedeler,
> Clarice of cokkeslane   and the clerke of the cherche,
> Dawe the dykere   and a dozeine other. . . .   [ditcher]

The level of the allegory is not consistent. Gluttony is a gluttonous person, who does not repent until he has made himself drunk and awakes two days later with a hangover. Sloth appears to be a self-indulgent and lazy priest who prefers to read "rymes of Robyn hood" to performing his priestly duties.

The repentant company then determine to journey in search of Truth, but they do not know the way. It is at this point that Piers Plowman first appears on the scene. The company have vainly inquired of a returned pilgrim if he knows where a saint called Truth is to be found. Then

> "Peter!" quod a plowman   and put forth his hed,
> "I knowe hym as kyndely   as clerke doth his bokes;
> Conscience and kynde witte   kenned me to his place."
>
> [kynde = natural]

Piers takes over the moral leadership of the company and tells them the way to Truth in Bunyanesque allegorical geography. This passus ends with a pardoner deciding that he cannot go without his papal bulls and letters of indulgence, and a common woman telling Piers simply that she will follow him.

Passus VI continues the story. Piers says he will act as guide to the company after he has ploughed his half-acre. He gives further moral advice to the company, in particular to a knight, who recognizes his duty to protect the church and the common people. Piers directs everybody to hard work, and those who shirk are disciplined by Hunger. A discussion of labor, wages, and similar economic factors, which illustrates the author's conservative view of such matters (he is looking back to an ideal stability before the present discontents) concludes this passus. In Passus VII, Truth sends Piers a pardon intended for all (though lawyers and merchants are eligible only with reservations), and a priest argues against its validity. The priest says that he can find no pardon there, but only a statement that those who do well shall find salvation and those who do evil shall not. The ensuing argument awakens the dreamer, and the passus concludes with the poet's passionate remarks on the superiority of good works to indulgences and papal bulls as means of pardon.

The remainder of *Piers Plowman*—most of it existing only in the two later versions—contains the vision of Dowel (Do Well), Dobet (Do Better), and Dobest. It is difficult to follow the somewhat rambling course of the prologues and ten passus of this extension of the poem; the author seems to be allowing his moral views and his religious emotion to deflect the poem at any point, and lively contemporary references, grand moments of religious passion, and flat didactic passages jostle each other. The author does not seem to have been able to subdue his material to an adequate literary form. But the main design is nevertheless visible. Underlying all the digressions, outbursts, symbolic incidents, moral indignation, prophecies, preaching, and visions is the notion of the quest, the search for the good life, for salvation, for truth, and for God. This search can be conducted on different levels and described from different points of view, and almost anything that men can do or think or feel or imagine is relevant to it. As the poem proceeds and the lives of Dowel, Dobet, and Dobest unfold with all the digressions and excursions, we get a picture of the fight against evil carried on simultaneously on different planes: the fight for the spirit against the dead letter, the fight against corruption in the Church, the fight against false religion. Faith, hope, and charity constitute the way; they follow from one another, culminating in charity, as Dobet follows Dowel to culminate in Dobest. The account of Dowel concludes with a triumphant description of the victory of Life over Death, of Light over Darkness, the meeting of Truth and Mercy, of Peace and Righteousness, with Christ's descent into Hell and his victory over Satan. The poet wakes to hear the joyous pealing of Easter bells. But in the ensuing account of Dobest we see Antichrist taking control after Christ's departure, and a sad picture of corruption and decay on the earth succeeds. Piers Plowman now reappears, as a symbol of Christ himself, of God *quasi homo* and of God's grace vouchsafed to all men. With a picture of a hard fought *psychomachia*, the vices pressing the virtues hard, and with Conscience finally rousing himself to seek in pilgrimage for Piers Plowman in his new symbolic meaning, the dream concludes, and the poet awakes in tears.

Though it lacks artistic unity and the author shows only sporadic control over his material, *Piers Plowman* is a remarkable work, with its alternation of bitter satire and tenderness, of vivid description of contemporary life and the stringing together of Latin tags, of social realism and religious vision. And the handling of the alliterative line is always easy and confident. There is none of Chaucer's relish of

the human scene as a human scene, nor of his joy in his verbal artistry; *Piers Plowman* is the work of a religious idealist who is genuinely distressed by the social and moral condition of England and
who is endeavoring to create a large and cumulative vision of what
is wrong and where we must look for improvement. If the two later
versions represent the work of other writers, then it seems clear that
the original author succeeded in creating a tradition, a vehicle for
carrying both a satirical and a religious content, which was exploited
by those similarly troubled. There is something of the popular imagination as well as of the individual vision in *Piers Plowman;* even in
its most visionary moments it is never private; the author is always
thinking of the people, and in Piers himself he creates a symbol who
eventually united the ideal of the common man with the ideal of
God made man. Like Chaucer, the author of *Piers Plowman* made
use of traditional material, and they both draw on the facts of contemporary society: but what different pictures they present! The
difference is one of attitude, both personal and social, and it is a
salutary check to hasty generalizations about the spirit of an age to
consider that the same age produced *Piers Plowman* and *The Canterbury Tales.*

CHAPTER FIVE

The End of the Middle Ages

THE ENGLISH LITERARY SCENE after the death of Chaucer is not inspiring. The fifteenth century, though it saw a significant increase in lay literacy and marked an important stage in the rise of the middle class, suffered from the confusions and demoralization of the long reign of Henry VI and of the Wars of the Roses which followed it. Significant new forces were indeed working in the national culture; the victory of English over French was now clear and complete, a new class of readers was slowly developing, the new movement of Humanism was beginning to awaken English interest, and social and economic changes were bringing about the transformation of the feudal system into a freer society based on a money economy; but it was some time before these changes were reflected in any important new movement of the mind or the spirit. At the beginning of the fifteenth century it was clear that none of Chaucer's followers had his technical brilliance, his imagination, or his understanding of men, and there was none who could combine the courtly and the bourgeois tradition as Chaucer had done. Fifteenth-century courtly poetry sometimes uses the old modes with a certain freshness: *The Flower and the Leaf*, long wrongly attributed to Chaucer, uses traditional material with charm, giving a new twist to the handling of tapestry figures of allegorical significance by having the narrator a woman and by having the two opposing sets of characters (worshipers of the flower and of the leaf, the idle and the faithful) treat each other with gentle friendliness; and other works of the "Chaucer Apocrypha" have their own appeal, though none is as fresh as *The Flower and the Leaf*. *The Cuckoo and the Nightingale* is a *débat* using familiar properties; *La Belle Dame sans Merci* (which gave Keats a title) has a lover pleading in vain with a lady whose matter-of-fact indifference to his love almost breaks out of the whole courtly love tradition; *The Assembly of Ladies* tells in heavy allegorical detail of pleadings before the Lady Loyalty. We see here a tradition working itself out.

128

Thomas Hoccleve and John Lydgate are the best known of Chaucer's followers in England; their lives overlapped Chaucer's, and Hoccleve apparently knew the master personally, yet they seem to belong to a different age. Hoccleve wrote less than Lydgate, but he is the more interesting, for, though there is little to choose between the two on grounds of poetic merit (or lack of it), there are realistic and autobiographical touches in Hoccleve's work that help to enliven it for us. He was a minor civil servant, a connoisseur of London night life and a tavern hunter, perpetually in need of money, seeking noble patrons and writing them begging verse letters. His *Mâle Règle* tells the story of his misspent life and ends with an appeal to the Lord Treasurer to pay him his overdue pension. There are some fairly vivid touches:

> Wher was a gretter maister eek than y
> Or bet aqueyntid at Westmynstre yate
> Among the taverneres namely   [especially]
> And cookes? Whan I cam, eerly or late,
> I pynchid nat at hem in myn acate,   [purchasing]
> Wherfore I was the welcomer algate
> And for a verray gentil man yholde.

And there is the well-known line

> Excesse at borde hath leyd his knyf with me.

His longer works are mechanical and tedious. They include many translations, among them the *Regement of Princes*, compiled from a variety of sources. His religious and didactic works have little value as literature, though they seem to reflect a genuine piety, for all his love of taverns. Technically, his verse is extraordinarily unaccomplished: he is content if he produces the requisite number of syllables in the line, paying no attention to how they are stressed (while Lydgate, on the other hand, is happy if he has the requisite number of stresses and does not seem to care how many or what kind of unstressed syllables he has). He had a genuine admiration for Chaucer, and introduced into the *Regement of Princes* stanzas in praise of him:

> O mayster deer and fadir reverent,
> My mayster Chaucer flour of eloquence,
> Mirrour of fructuous endendement,
> O universel fader in science . . .

Elsewhere he hails him as

> The firste foundere of oure faire langage.

Chaucer, it is clear, became a legend soon after his death; but this does not mean that any of his English admirers had the ability to follow in his footsteps.

Lydgate is almost universally written off as a bore, and though he has occasional felicitous touches there is little reason to disagree with this verdict. Unlike Hoccleve, Lydgate led a cloistered life as a monk, mostly at Bury St. Edmunds, and though this did not prevent him from managing to see a good deal of men and affairs—and certainly did not prevent him from reading widely, for the library at the Benedictine Abbey at Bury was one of the best-stocked in England—he had nothing of Chaucer's gift of turning both his reading and his experience to lively account in his own writing. Over one hundred forty-five thousand lines of his verse survive, including the mammoth *Fall of Princes* (from a French prose version of Boccaccio's *De Casibus Illustrium Virorum*), the almost equally lengthy *Troy-Book* (from Giudo delle Colonne's *Historia Troiana*), several lives of saints (done for different patrons), several translations from the French, and many miscellaneous shorter poems, both secular and religious in subject. There is a deadening lameness in his versification, together with a syntactical looseness, which makes the reading of his longer didactic works a severe penance. Lydgate's were the routine didactic interests of the unadventurous spirits of his time, and we can at least console ourselves with the thought that his work illustrates the early fifteenth-century English mind. He contributed something, too, both to the themes of English literature and to the vocabulary of English. His *Fall of Princes* is the first full-dress collection of "tragedies" (in the medieval sense of stories of falls from high to low estate) of the many that were to influence English thought and literature up to Shakespeare's *Richard III*. His *Dance Macabre* introduced to England (from the French) a theme of great significance in medieval thought and art of the period: Death the leveller, who addresses in turn all classes of men, Pope, Emperor, cardinal, king, and so on down the scale to laborer, friar, child, clerk, and hermit, points the grim moral of a common mortality which is found so often stressed in the fifteenth century. Lydgate added many new words to the English vocabulary, though he rarely employed them with much sensitivity or poetic force; they are mostly polysyllabic words from Latin or French, such as "inexcusable," "credulity," "tolerance," and "adolescence." But what the reader is most conscious of is his frequent use of tag phrases— "sothly to telle," "ther nis namor to say," "as to myn intent," "yiff I shal not lye," et cetera.

Lydgate is at his best in his shorter poems, and in those where the demands of the narrative compel him to some liveliness of detail (and it might be added that his feeling for small children has been noted in his favor). A good example is his tale, "The Churl and the Bird," rendered from the French. The churl has caught the bird and put it in "a praty litel cage"; the bird speaks:

> . . . And though my cage forged were of gold
> And the penacles of byral and cristal,
> I remember a proverbe said of olde
> Who lesith his fredome in faith he lesith al,
> For I had lever upon a branche smal
> Merely to sing amonge the wodes grene
> Thenne in a cage of silver bright and shene.
>
> Songe and prison han noon accordaunce;
> Trowest thou I wol synge in prisoun?
> Songe procedith of ioye and of pleasaunce
> And prison causith deth and distructioun . . .

But even emotion seeks, in Lydgate, to express itself in didactic or proverbial form.

The professions of literary incompetence made by so many of these fifteenth-century poets represent doubtless a mere fashion; but they spoke more truly than they knew. Among the little surviving verse of Benedict Burgh is a short poem of compliment to Lydgate which begins in this common self-deprecatory vein:

> Nat dremyd I in the mownt of Pernaso,
> ne dranke I nevar at Pegases welle,
> the pale Pirus saw I never also
> ne wist I never where the muses dwelle . . .

John Walton, whose translation of Boethius into English verse shows better metrical control than most of his fifteenth-century contemporaries, begins his prologue in similar strain:

> Insuffishaunce of cunnyng & of wyt,
> Defaut of langage & of eloquence,
> This work fro me schuld have withholden yit . . .

The anonymous author of *The Court of Sapience* (he may have been Stephen Hawes), a long allegorical, didactic poem in two parts, the first dealing with the dispute between Mercy, Peace, Righteousness, and Truth concerning the fate of man and the second a conducted tour of medieval learning, varies the formula somewhat and speaks in livelier accents. He asks Clio to "forge my tonge to glad myn audytours," professing his own deficiencies:

I knowe my self moost naked in al artes,
My comune vulgare eke moost interupte,
And I conversaunte & borne in the partes
Wher my natyf langage is moost corrupt,
And wyth most sondry tonges myxt & rupte . .

The Court of Sapience dates from about 1470: it is more vigorous in expression and competent in metrics than anything by Lydgate, but in theme it represents the uninspired development of the allegorical didactic tradition.

It seems as though the simple story romance, so popular with an earlier generation of Englishmen, had been pushed out by allegory and didacticism. And, with the decay of feudalism and the slow but steady rise of a realistic and iconoclastic bourgeoisie, there was no new source of idealism to revivify the increasingly uninspired and conventional didactic allegory. But by a fruitful coincidence, the last flare-up of chivalry in the courts of Europe, a last Indian summer of knightly ideals in the earlier manner, occurred at the same time that printing came in. Caxton, who had been in Burgundy witnessing this revival at the French-speaking court of the Duke of Burgundy, brought with him (from the Low Countries) the art of printing on his return to England. The revival of interest in the chivalric story romance which accompanied chivalry's final fling was just in time to take advantage of Caxton's imported art; which accounts for the fact that some of the first works printed in England were chivalric stories of the older kind. This revival of interest in romance, though influential, was brief; it was killed in the sixteenth century partly by the new movement of Humanism, which in England in its early phase took a narrow view of romantic tales and, with Roger Ascham, protested against idle stories of chivalry, and partly by the growing bourgeois taste for a more realistic, picaresque kind of story.

The attenuated courtly tradition; satirical, topical, and political verse of little literary merit but of considerable historical interest; didactic, moralistic, and religious writing: these were the three main categories of fifteenth-century English literature, and the third is the largest. The religious lyric, following the types discussed in Chapter 3, flourished during the period: indeed, most of what has been said of the fourteenth-century lyric applies to the fifteenth century also, though new themes and attitudes begin to make their appearance as the century advanced, and will be discussed later.

That the fifteenth century was a period of transition in England is obvious enough to the political and economic historian. The Wars of the Roses, where the nobility destroyed each other and the middle class rose steadily; William Caxton's introduction of printing into

England (Caxton's translation of Raoul de Fevre's *Le Receuil des Histoires de Troye*, printed by him as *Recuyel of the Histories of Troye* at Bruges in 1474, was the first printed book published in English, and his return to London in 1475 was followed by his printing in 1477 of *Dictes and Sayings of the Philosophers*, the first book printed in England); the gradual impact on English thought of the Humanism of the Renaissance; the establishment of the Tudor monarchy in 1485—these are obvious and significant marks of change. In the literature of the period, however, we see for the most part simply the progressive exhaustion of earlier medieval modes. Yet much that appears at first sight merely to exhibit this exhaustion can be seen on a closer view to be influenced in some degree by new ways of thinking. Stephen Hawes' allegorical romance, *The Pastime of Pleasure*, dedicated to Henry VII in 1506, continues the lame versification and the mechanical allegorizing of Lydgate, with even less notion of the true nature of allegory than his immediate predecessors:

> The light of truoth, I lacke cunnyng to cloke,
> To drawe a curtayne, I dare not to presume
> Nor hyde my matter, with a misty smoke
> My rudenes cunnyng, dothe so sore consume
> Yet as I may, I shall blowe out a fume
> To hyde my mynde, underneth a fable
> By covert coloure, well and probable.

It is a curious view indeed that the function of allegory is to obscure truth. Yet this "smokey," didactic, allegorical romance, telling (in first person narrative) of the pursuit and eventual attainment by the hero, Graunde Amour, of La Bell Pucell shows some interesting new features. The hero, encouraged by Fame (a lady) and accompanied by Governaunce and Grace (two greyhounds), receives an elaborate education in the Tower of Doctrine before engaging on the knightly adventures which culminate in his marriage to La Bell Pucell. Here we have the union of the active life and the contemplative life, which had hitherto been sharply distinguished in medieval thought, following St. Augustine's influential statement in *The City of God* that "the study of wisdom is either concerning action or contemplation, and thence assumes two several names, active and contemplative, the active consisting in the practice of morality in one's life, and the contemplative in penetrating into the abstruse causes of nature, and the nature of divinity." The knight and the clerk are united in Graunde Amour, representing a new ideal of lay education; further, the hero's love for La Bell Pucell is chaste and Christian and leads to marriage—something quite impossible in the earlier courtly love tradition. The interest—one might say the obsession—with education is characteristic of the age; the combination of the didactic romance with the romance of knightly adventure in a context of education looks forward to Spenser's *Faerie Queene*. And at the end, after the hero has married and lived happily ever after, he addresses the reader from the grave in the one memorable stanza of the poem:

> O mortall folk, you may beholde and se
> How I lye here, somtyme a myghty knyght.
> The ende of Joye and all prosperite
> Is dethe at last through his course and myght;
> After the day there cometh the derke nyght,
> For though the day be never so longe
> At last the belles ryngeth to evensonge.

The Seven Deadly Sins, and Fame, Time, and Eternity, all play their part in the final pageant, which shows a certain grandeur of conception in spite of the technical inadequacy of the verse.

How dismal—to the point of being positively comic—the verse can become is illustrated by the following passage, describing the hero's education in grammar at the hands of Dame Doctrine:

> . . . To whom she answered, right gently agayne,
> Saiyng alwaye, that a nowne substantyve
> Might stande without helpe of an adjectyve.
>
> The latyne worde, whiche that is referred
> Unto a thing, whiche is substantiall
> For a nowne substantive is well averred,
> And with a gender is declinall.
> So all the eyght partes in generall
> Are latyn wordes, annexed proprelye
> To every speache, for to speake formally.

This intolerable doggerel is representative of a whole area of late medieval English didactic verse. Yet not only does *The Pastime of Pleasure* have its moments of perception and even of eloquence; it is also a work of considerable historical importance in that it illustrates an attitude toward love, education, and the relation of the active to the contemplative life which foreshadows both the courtesy books of the Renaissance and the use of romance made by Spenser. Hawes saw himself, however, as a follower rather than as a pioneer, and he mentions Gower, Chaucer, and Lydgate (in that order) as his masters, listing the major works of the latter two. He seems utterly unaware of Chaucer's superiority to the other two, and Lydgate is especially praised for his eloquence:

> O master Lydgate, the most dulcet spryng
> Of famous rethoryke, wyth ballade royall,
> The chefe originall of my learnyng,
> What vayleth it, on you for to call
> Me for to ayde, nowe in especiall,
> Sythen your bodye is now wrapte in chest.
> I pray God to give your soule good rest.

Hawes' other allegorical-didactic romance, *The Example of Virtue,* is shorter and less interesting, and few other late medieval exercises in this mode have any special appeal. William Nevill's *Castell of Pleasure* (1518) is worth mentioning only because its printer, Robert Copland, himself (like Caxton) a translator and dabbler in letters, introduces a dialogue between the printer and the author at the beginning of the poem, and because, in its mechanical use of the allegorical formulas, it sinks to probably record depths of dullness. Nowhere is the popular medieval *ubi sunt* theme handled so flatly:

> Where is Tully, whiche had pryncypalyte
> Over all oratours in parfyte rethoryke?
> Where be all the foure doctours of dyvynyte?
> Where is Arystotyll for all his phylosophy & logyke?

Alexander Barclay (*ca.* 1475–1552) is a transitional figure of some importance. His *Ship of Fools* (1509) provided a new metaphor for English satire. It is a rendering of the *Narrenschiff* of the German Sebastian Brant through the Latin translation of Locher, a Swiss, but Barclay's own comments expand the poem to many times the length of his original. Satire, of course, was not unknown in the earlier Middle Ages; the *fabliau* tradition, as we have seen, is largely satirical, and Jean de Meun, Chaucer, and Langland have each his own satirical vein. The conception of the important people of the world as a collection of fools—courtiers, ecclesiastics, scholars, and merchants alike—seems to have become popular in the later Middle Ages, and Brant's idea of putting them all in a boat sailing off to Narragonia gave a new liveliness to the whole conception. It is a development of the older handling of the seven deadly sins, and the shift of attention from moral evil to intellectual folly is significant of a new temper in European civilization. *The Ship of Fools* looks forward to Erasmus' *Praise of Folly* as much as it looks backward to the theme of the seven deadly sins. Its interest is more in the contemporary social scene than with moral types, and this again marks an important development. Barclay's rhyme royal stanzas are pedestrian enough in movement, but the self-characterization of the representatives of different kinds of folly provides some vivid glimpses of the society of the time. Satire, so long directed against ecclesiastical abuses, is beginning to turn to wider themes, including life at Court (increasingly important with the establishment of the new national state with its centralized monarchy) and intellectual fashions. The satiric stream widens and deepens after Barclay, with Skelton's *Bowge of Court* and *Speak, Parrot* concentrating on the contemporary scene. The changes which Renaissance Court life and the first effects of Renaissance Humanism brought with them stimulated conservative minds to angry satire, and while the attack on folly is itself a Humanist theme, attacks on Humanism as well as on other novelties are made by angry conservatives. Indeed, angry conservatives have always produced the greatest satire, from Aristophanes to Swift, and while neither Barclay nor Skelton can be regarded as a great satirist they do share the great satirist's sense of outrage at what contemporary man is making of himself.

The pastoral also becomes at this time a vehicle for satire in English; it comes to replace the dream as the commonest kind of machinery for satirical as well as many other purposes. Barclay produced five eclogues, three translated (with many expansions) from the *Miserae Curialium* of Pope Pius II (Aeneas Sylvius Piccolomini) and two from the late fifteenth- and early sixteenth-century Italian poet, Baptista Mantuanus, known as Mantuan in England where he was much admired for his Latin pastorals in the sixteenth and seventeenth centuries. Thus a new breath from classical literature comes, though indirectly, into English literature, the first of very many such. The use of the pastoral for satire of Court life, urban life, ecclesiastical corruption, and other abuses of the time, as well as to discuss literary questions, established itself early in the Renaissance; Barclay is the first English writer to use a device, already common in Italy, which was to be developed significantly by succeeding generations of English poets, notably by Spenser in his *Shepherd's Calendar*. And as *The Shepherd's Calendar*, as we shall see, is in some sense both the manifesto and the first-fruits of the "new" English poetry, the pastoral tradition is clearly of prime importance in English literature; we shall have to look at it more closely later.

John Skelton (ca. 1460–1529) is the most interesting and original of all the transitional poets who, while considering themselves in the tradition of Chaucer, Gower, and Lydgate, are in fact Janus-faced, looking both toward the medieval past and to the Renaissance future. As a satirist, Skelton attacks the abuses of courtly life, new fashions in thought, religion and behavior, personal enemies, Scots, and aspects of the contemporary scene which he found annoying. *The Bowge of Court* is a satire of Court life in the traditional rhyme royal stanza, combining traditional medieval allegorical figures with the ship of fools device, the characters being sometimes allegorical personages and sometimes lively representatives of the contemporary scene. Less traditional in form and content is *Speak, Parrot*, a bubbling satirical piece mostly in rhyme royal but with some parts in other meters; the poet speaks through the bird in a characteristic mixture of bitterness and clowning. But *Colin Clout* and *Why come ye not to Court* represent his most characteristic and original satirical vein. The verse here is that short two-beat line which has become known as "Skeltonics"; the poems move with breathless abandon from point to point, highly personal in tone, deliberately discursive in progression, mingling fierce abuse, clowning humor, and bitter irony. Latin tags and even whole passages in rhymed Latin couplets, echoes or parodies of the Church liturgy or of the arguments of the schoolmen, are sprinkled freely among the wild and whirling verses. The life, the abandon, the high spirits, the reckless vitality of these pieces make them utterly unlike anything that English literature had yet produced. In *The Book of Philip Sparrow* he uses a similar technique to lament the loss of a young girl's pet sparrow: the lament is put into the mouth of the girl, and ends with Skelton's own tribute to the girl's charm and beauty. Its parody of the Office for the Dead and other aspects of the Latin liturgy of the Church is done with a cheerful recklessness reminiscent of the goliardic literature of the Middle Ages. The verse itself is crudely accentual—whether it derives from the breakup of a longer line or from medieval Latin poetry or from another source cannot be precisely determined—but it moves with extraordinary speed and vigor:

> Sometyme he wolde gaspe
> Whan he sawe a waspe;
> A fly or a gnat,
> He wolde flye at that
> And prytely he wold pant
> Whan he saw an ant;
> Lorde, how he wolde pry
> After the butterfly!
> Lorde, how he wolde hop
> After the gressop!
> And whan I sayd, Phyp, Phyp,
> Than he wold lepe and skyp,
> And take me by the lyp.
> Alas, it wyll me slo,
> That Phillyp is gone me fro!
>   *Si in-i-qui-ta-tes,*
> Alas, I was evyll at ease!
>   *De pro-fun-dis cla-ma-vi,*
> Whan I sawe my sparrowe dye!

The color and life of Skelton's most characteristic verse is perhaps best seen in *The Tunning*[1] *of Elinor Rumming*, a remarkable description of an alewife and the goings-on in her alehouse:

> Come who so wyll
> To Elynour on the hyll,
> Wyth, Fyll the cup, fyll,
> And syt there by styll,
> Erly and late:
> Thyther cometh Kate,
> Cysly, and Sare,
> With theyr legges bare,
> And also theyr fete
> Hardely full unswete;
> Wyth theyr heles dagged,
> Theyr kyrtelles all to-iagged,
> Theyr smockes all to-ragged,
> Wyth tytters and tatters,
> Brynge dysshes and platters,
> Wyth all theyr myght runnynge
> To Elynour Rummynge,
> To have of her tunnynge:
> She leneth them of the same,
> And thus begynneth the game.

His *Garland of Laurel* is an elaborate set piece in praise of himself: Fame and Pallas discuss his qualifications; Gower, Chaucer, and Lydgate hail him; a group of noble ladies make a laurel wreath with which to crown him. The incidental lyrics addressed to these ladies are in a new vein of lyrical tenderness, notably that addressed to Margery Wentworth:

> With margerain jentyll,
>   The flowre of goodlyhede,
> Enbrowdred the mantill
>   Is of your maydenhede . . .

Magnificence is a morality play with allegorical characters, showing how Magnificence is deceived and undone by vices, conquered by Adversity, and finally redeemed by Goodhope and Perseverance. It is aimed at Wolsey, but also has its general application.

Skelton moved in a Humanist atmosphere without fully realizing it; his attire was conservative in intention but in fact revolutionary in unconscious implication. His fiercely individual temperament, the

---

[1] Tunning: putting of beer into casks.

vigor which he infused into his rough accentual verse, his ambiguous relation with the courts of Henry VII and Henry VIII, his attacks both on Church abuses and on radical reformers like Wyclif and Luther, his bitter feuds with so many of his contemporaries, his strange mixtures of anger and tenderness, of self-conceit and moral indignation, of prophetic elevation and low abuse, show a highly individual temperament coping in a strongly individual way with some of the bewildering crosscurrents in the civilization of his day. His lively and unpolished verse and his violently personal manner attracted English poets in the 1920's and 1930's who were looking for a style in which to express similar reactions, and Pope's verdict of "beastly Skelton" has in recent times been enthusiastically reversed.

Meanwhile, the revival of interest in feudal ideals which, paradoxically but understandably, accompanied the final decay of feudalism in England, produced in the prose Arthurian tales of Sir Thomas Malory the greatest of all its monuments. Malory, who appears to have been a mid-fifteenth-century knight of lawless behavior who wrote his stories in prison, turned, first the English alliterative romance known as *Morte Arthure*, and then a variety of French romances about Arthur's knights, into a series of tales of Arthur and his knights in which the ideals of practical chivalry replaced the sentimental and doctrinal elements which figure so prominently in his French sources. He cut his way through the tangle of complexly interwoven tales, fitted together in pieces like a Chinese puzzle, with which his originals so often presented him, and, to use Caxton's term, "reduced" his material to a coherent group of related stories in which incidents followed each other with less interruption and the emphasis was on action and motive rather than on sentiment or doctrine. Caxton published the work in 1485, giving it a false unity by applying the title of the last group of stories—"The Morte Arthure Saunz Gwerdon"—to the whole collection. The discovery in 1934 of the Winchester MS of Malory's stories makes it clear that "Le Morte Darthur" is Caxton's title for the whole, not Malory's. Malory's work is in eight tales or groups of tales, each group originally written separately as an independent work, except for the sixth and seventh, which are explicitly linked in Malory's colophon to the sixth. The first (though apparently the second in order of writing) is the comprehensive "Tale of King Arthur"; it begins with the death of Uther Pendragon and Arthur's accession, and tells of Arthur's victorious wars against rebels and hostile neighbors, the stories of Balin, Gawain, Torre and Pellynor, much about Merlin, the plottings of

Morgan le Fay, Arthur's half sister, and a group of adventures engaged in by Gawain, Ywain, and Marhalt. The second group, "The Tale of the Noble King Arthur that was Emperour Himself through the Dignity of his Hands," was apparently the first to be written and derives from the alliterative *Morte Arthure:* it tells of Arthur's struggle against the claims of Rome, the battle between Arthur and Lucius, Arthur's triumph and coronation as Emperor in Rome. The third, "The Noble Tale of Sir Launcelot du Lake," turns for its hero from Arthur to Sir Lancelot, who appears here, not as the lover of Guinevere, but as an active and gallant knight who proceeds from adventure to adventure before returning to King Arthur's court, where the knights whom he has overcome testify to his prowess. "The Tale of Sir Gareth of Orkney" follows; it is a characteristic story, from an unknown French source, of a questing knight who champions a scornful lady, Lynet, who later comes to admire him, but too late to prevent his marrying her sister Lyonesse. "The Book of Sir Tristram de Lyones" is the fifth; it is a simplified and "reduced" version of the French prose *Romance of Tristan*, with the Grail material omitted, the love of Tristram (Tristan) and Isode (Isolde) treated with emotional gusts and with no sense of doom, Tristram's adventures and achievements as a Knight of the Round Table emphasized, and the lovers left at the end happily in Joyous Gard. Even so, Malory's "Book of Sir Tristram" is far from being a single tale; it is made up of many separate adventures, and is divided into seventeen parts—easily the longest of Malory's seven books. "The Tale of the Sankgreal" is Malory's fifth book; it is translated from the French *Queste del Saint Graal*, but emphasizes what might be called chivalric humanism as the underlying ethical pattern, at the expense of the religious. Lancelot is less the repentant sinner of the French original than the former hero of the Round Table whose chivalric ideals are never made to appear as basically inimical to the truly religious life. Malory plays down the basic dichotomy between Carbonec and Camelot, so important in the *Queste,* though of course something of it does come through from his original. "The Book of Sir Launcelot and Queen Guinevere" is partly based on the French *Mort Artu*, the final branch of the prose Arthurian Cycle. This goes together with the final book, "The Most Piteous Tale of the Morte Arthur Saunz Gwerdon" (based partly on the *Mort Artu* and partly on the English stanzaic *Morte Arthur*), and the two books again show Malory's characteristic minimizing of the religious in favor of the chivalric moral. Lancelot loves both his mistress and his king; these two chivalric loyalties are incompatible, and in the end they destroy him. It is not the clash between courtly love and heavenly love so much as the clash between courtly love and feudal loyalty that interests Malory. Here, indeed, the sense of doom rises; Lancelot becomes involved in battle against those he loves; and in the end, with the Round Table destroyed, Arthur "hurt to the death" in the final battle in which the treacherous Mordred is slain, and Guinevere retired to a nunnery, Lancelot decides to forsake the world too, out of love and despair rather than from a religious impulse. Guinevere dies repentant; Lancelot follows soon after, and Sir Ector speaks his obituary:

"A, Launcelot!" he sayd, "thou were hede of al Crysten knyghtes! And now I dare say," sayd syr Ector, "thou sir Launcelot, there thou lyest, that thou were never matched of erthely knyghtes hande. And thou were the curtest knyght that ever bare shelde! And thou were the truest frende to thy lover that ever bestrade hors, and thou were the trewest lover of a synful man that ever loved woman, and thou were the kyndest man that ever strake wyth swerde. And thou were the godelyest persone that ever cam amonge prees of knyghtes, and thou was the mekest man and the jentyllest that ever ete in halle amonge ladyes, and thou were the sternest knyght to thy mortal foo that ever put spere in the reeste."

It ends in desolation, with no comfort but memory of knightly deeds once done.

Malory's prose style, which moves with a simple cogency always perfectly adapted to the narrative line which he is developing, is not easily placed in the history of English prose. He is outside the tradition of English devotional prose which continues from Anglo-Saxon times to the Tudor and Elizabethan translations of the Bible. He begins by capturing something of the rhythms, and using some of the alliterative devices, of Middle English alliterative verse as represented by the verse romance *Morte Arthure;* he simplifies, tightens up, adds weight and precision and, at the same time, a conversational flow. He learns as he writes, and the later books show a fine ease in dialogue together with a dignity and eloquence which derive at least in part from the heroic element in the *Morte Arthure.* The flow is simple enough, marked by such conjunctions as "and," "for," "but," "then," and "therefore." The underlying rhythms provide a quiet emotional ground swell to the narrative; the dialogue is lively and often captures the individual quality of a character; the accounts of action rise and fall with a restrained epic movement which has quiet gravity without magniloquence. The result of it all is an impressive summing up of the "Matter of Britain" as seen through the perspective of the Indian summer of the Age of Chivalry; excessive sentiment, the pure devotional note, and over-abundant narrative complication are equally pruned away, and Malory gives us the

Arthurian stories set to an uncomplicated chivalric morality. But the epic note does not really belong to these nostalgic stories of a lost way of life; the defects of the code are manifest in the actions which are based on it, and in the end the heroic key is modulated into elegy.

It is paradoxical that William Caxton, who brought the art of printing to England, should have been so interested in chivalry and old romance. But the late fifteenth and early sixteenth century was a transitional period in which all sorts of paradoxical things were likely to happen. The work of Barclay and Hawes showed both old medieval modes and new Humanist influences. Humanism itself was one element in that complex movement we call the Renaissance, a movement whose reality has recently been questioned but which certainly was real, though its manifestations were not as sudden nor its causes as simple as was once thought. The world of medieval Christendom, set against the militant Moslem world, which bounded it on the south and east, had a significant religious and cultural uniformity; its intellectual and imaginative boundaries were limited, the scholar moving within the limits of "Latinitas," the philosopher and the scientist working deductively on truths taken from authority, the poet rendering his vision of past and present through notions of order and significance common to the whole of medieval Europe. The Holy Roman Empire, we know, was never more than an ideal, but the ideal represented a view of history and of society that lay behind most of the superficially differing attitudes which intelligent men in the Middle Ages expressed. The shift from the view of the Roman Empire as divinely ordained machinery for the Christianizing of the Western world to a view of the pagan culture of Greece and Rome as something more civilized, more splendid, more fully illustrative of what man can make of himself by cultivation of the arts and sciences than any subsequent phase of history, represented a real revolution in thought. And while it would be wrong to see this shift as simply the rapid result of the fall of Constantinople to the Turks in 1453, with the consequent emigration of Greek-speaking Christians from the Eastern Empire to Italy—for it was a slow process that had been going on since long before 1453—it would be ridiculous to assert that because the movement was gradual it did not take place. The writing of history is impossible without making generalizations, and it is impossible to make generalizations unless one deliberately cultivates the proper perspective. A cause is known as a cause by its effect; if looked at by itself it is simply an isolated phenomenon, and if looked at with reference to preceding events it becomes itself an effect. History is continuous; "movements" are arbitrary categories of the historian; but significant changes do occur, attitudes do alter radically, the old order does give place to the new. And the Renaissance is not a fiction of the historian's imagination.

Medieval Christendom established itself in the chaos that followed the collapse of the Roman Empire; it took over what it could from the Roman world, compromised where it had to with both old pagan and new barbarian, and achieved a synthesis in which the thought and institutions of the classical world played a certain limited part. Humanism, that movement which represented the desire to recover the purest ideals of Greek and Latin expression and to assimilate the most civilized aspects of classical thought, was essentially an attempt to get behind the medieval synthesis, to approach the original sources of classical culture directly, not through the medium of clerical "Latinitas." Italy had known this movement since the fourteenth century, and long before it reached England it had exerted its influence on Italian literature. North of the Alps the Humanist movement became more directly involved in religious and moral questions. The ambitious and ubiquitous machinery of the medieval Church was ceasing to function effectively; satire of clerical abuses, amusedly ironical in Chaucer, soon swelled to an angry and bitter chorus, and this in turn encouraged the *avant garde* to turn to the secular thought of the classical world for guidance and enlightenment. That secular thought, touched with the moral earnestness of Christian protest against abuses of Christian institutions, produced a school of Christian Humanists which was to include reformers who remained within the Roman Catholic fold as well as Protestants. It must be remembered, too, that the "New Learning," as it was often called in the sixteenth century, encouraged the study of Hebrew as well as of Latin and Greek, and that the great German Humanist Reuchlin was even more important for the development of Hebrew studies in Europe than the great Dutch Humanist Erasmus was for the study of Greek. Hebrew and Greek, the languages of the Old and New Testaments respectively, were essential tools in any new approach to the Bible. If pre-Protestant reforming thought demanded vernacular Bible translation, it was the new scholarship of the Humanists that eventually made that translation possible from the original sources. Thus Humanism in spite of itself was drawn into new religious movements.

We have already noted the changes in the economic bases of society that were bringing about the end of feudalism. In the towns, a new upper class of merchants and professional men joined hands with the landowners in the country, where a prospering "gentry" were enclosing common land in the interests of sheep farming, to the distress of the peasants who were thus deprived of the opportunity of tilling the soil and forced to roam the countryside in search of work. Individualism asserted itself in economic as in other areas. The political genius of Henry VII, whose accession to the throne in 1485 after his victory over Richard III brought to an end the Wars of the Roses and ushered in the new Tudor despotism, enabled him to win the loyalty of merchant, professional man, gentry, and nobility alike and so to maintain a political stability in the country of which it was in desperate need, and at his death to leave a secure throne to his son. Henry VII thought of himself as a medieval monarch, re-establishing a medieval monarchy, and did not see the implications of his own reign. He was no friend to Humanists. But with the accession of Henry VIII in 1509, the Humanists in England had their chance, and the early years of his reign were years of promise and excitement for English culture. The scene changed in the latter part of Henry's reign, when Henry's insistence on divorce from Catherine of Aragon, his break with Rome, his suppression of the monasteries and the consequent destruction of so many English art treasures, and his assumption of the supreme headship of the English Church lost him the approval of such a moderate Catholic Humanist as Sir Thomas More, whose execution for high treason in 1535 marks the end of Henry's alliance with the most attractive elements of contemporary Humanism and arrested the Humanist movement in England for a generation. More, scholar, statesman, diplomat, political theorist (the ideal commonwealth described in his Latin work *Utopia* represents a Humanist rather than a Christian conception of the state), and patron of the arts, represented all that was best in the new ideal of culture. His piety led him to seek to purify, rather than radically to reorganize, the Church, and he remained devoted to papal supremacy; like Erasmus, he wished to remove corruption without changing theological doctrine or ecclesiastical structure, but unlike the Dutch Humanist he became involved in practical affairs to his own undoing. He remains the glory and the tragedy of Henry VIII's reign.

The "New Learning" had made itself felt in England as early as the fifteenth century, but these early manifestations left no permanent mark. John Tiptoft, Earl of Worcester, William Grey (later Bishop of Ely), John Free of Balliol College, Oxford, and John Gunthorpe (later Dean of Wells) all visited Italy in the latter part of the fifteenth century and returned with Latin manuscripts which they left to Oxford college libraries. But it was not until the introduction of Greek learning into England that a more permanent enthusiasm for classical scholarship was aroused. Thomas Linacre, William

Grocyn (who returned from Italy in 1490 to teach Greek at Oxford), and William Latimer, put Greek studies on a firm footing at Oxford, while at Cambridge the teaching of Greek by Erasmus from 1510 to 1513 gave a great impetus to Greek studies. John Colet, who had studied in Paris and Italy and was a friend of Erasmus, lectured on the New Testament at Oxford at the turn of the century and in 1510, then Dean of St. Paul's, endowed the Cathedral school of St. Paul's to bring the "New Learning" into secondary education. Richard Croke, who had studied Greek at Oxford with Grocyn and then studied at Paris and lectured at several continental universities, returned to Cambridge in 1518, where, the following year, he was appointed reader in Greek. He was succeeded by Sir Thomas Smith, and in 1540, when five new regius chairs were founded by Henry, Smith got that of civil law, while Sir John Cheke became professor of Greek. Cheke (hailed by Milton in one of his sonnets as having "taught Cambridge and King Edward Greek") later became tutor to the young King Edward VI: he did more than any other single person to make Greek studies popular in England.

The history of scholarship becomes important for the history of literature at this time because the new classical scholarship meant the establishment of direct contact with the achievements of classical culture and this in turn meant not only new ideals in literary style but new concepts of civilization and a sense that the Middle Ages had represented a vast deflection of progress of the arts and sciences off their true course. Further, the recovery of Greek science—which was one of the great achievements of Humanism, far too little realized—meant that Renaissance science could begin where Greek science had left off. Astronomy, physics, and medicine profited by this renewed contact with Greek thought: the scientific discoveries of the sixteenth and seventeenth centuries were made possible by the work of the fifteenth-century Humanists. In the Middle Ages, Greek science (and, indeed, much Greek philosophy) was only available in fragmentary and often distorted form through Latin translations from the Arabic, for the Moslem world were earlier heirs of Greek thought; now it became freely and directly available. No wonder that Renaissance thinkers came to regard the Middle Ages simply as an obstacle standing between them and the pure knowledge of the classical world. The ages of "Gothic superstition," which was all the seventeenth and, still more, the early and middle eighteenth century could see in the Middle Ages, were so regarded because they blocked the light of classical culture.

But this survey has taken us well beyond the transitional period. In the next chapter we shall examine, in some detail, the new movement and its consequences for literature.

CHAPTER SIX

The Early Tudor Scene

THE HISTORIAN of sixteenth-century English culture is liable to find himself devoting all his space to charting the different ways in which that vast complex of movements which we call the Renaissance affected men's minds and imaginations. But in a history of literature one must resist the temptation to dwell at too great length on the intellectual background, important and fascinating though it is, and let the works of literature tell their own story. We have already said something of the new interest displayed by the Humanists in the cultural monuments of Greece and Rome. Humanism had many aspects: the scholarly, concerned with the recovery or reconstitution of accurate texts of the classics; the stylistic, concerned with classical rhetoric and literary criticism and their application to an improved vernacular literature; the ethical, concerned with the highest ideals of Greek and Roman thought (which could be combined with or modified by Christian teaching); and what might be called the positively secular, the replacement of a theocentric universe by one based on man and his potentialities, the acceptance of human life and human values as of permanent significance if ordered and controlled by a sense of proportion, interpreted in the light of the best thought of antiquity, and enriched and illuminated by the arts. It would be difficult to find a writer who was influenced by all these aspects of Humanism simultaneously; many of the most active Humanists were pedantic and narrow in their view of classical "purity" and in their exaltation of Ciceronian Latin; but the sixteenth-century French essayist Montaigne—secular-minded, but not anti-religious; curious about and tolerant of human foibles and attitudes; continually fascinated by the problems posed both by his own psychological and physical self and by the external world—could perhaps be taken as a typical representative of the humanist attitude in the broadest sense of that term. It was an attitude which found no such single typical representative in England, yet the attitude was influential in England; it was in the air, and people were touched by it and had to reckon with it.

The influence of the new geographical discoveries on men's imaginations (though it developed later than one might have expected) is one of the more obvious points to be noted. Spenser can speak for that when, justifying in the prologue to the second book of *The Faerie Queene* his setting the scene in "that happy land of Faery," he observes:

> But let that man with better sense advise,
> That of the world least part to us is read:
> And daily how through hardy enterprise,
> Many great regions are discoveréd,
> Which to late age were never mentionéd.
> Who ever heard of th' Indian Peru?
> Or who in venturous vessel measuréd
> The Amazon's huge river now found true?
> Or fruitfulest Virginia who did ever view?
>
> Yet all these were, when no man did them know;
> Yet have from wisest ages hidden been:
> And later times things more unknown shall show. . . .

And John Donne addresses his mistress with

> O my America! my new-found-land, . . .
> How blest am I in thus discovering thee!

It was Donne, too, who, in often-quoted lines, expressed the effect on many men's minds of the new astronomy:

> And new philosophy calls all in doubt,
> The element of fire is quite put out;
> The sun is lost, and th' earth, and no man's wit
> Can well direct him where to look for it.

The new astronomy was made necessary by the navigational needs of the voyagers; and the voyagers themselves began by seeking for a new route to the spices of the East after the land route had been blocked by the fall of Constantinople; and spices were necessary in order to preserve the cattle killed in the winter; and the cattle were killed in the winter because no winter cattle-feed was yet known. So the complex chain of cause and effect keeps on expanding. Further, the new astronomy depended on the work of the Humanists. The notion that the earth is a planet revolving round the sun had been put forward by the Greek astronomer Aristarchus of Samos in the third century B.C., and Copernicus was first led to consider such a view by reading in a work attributed to Plutarch that the Pythagoreans had taught it. The editing and translating (into Latin) of Greek scientific works provides the bridge between Humanism and science in the Renaissance.

New geographical, astronomical, philosophical, and religious notions boil up and mingle in the most diverse ways throughout the sixteenth and seventeenth centuries. The new concept of the national state was helping to alter the medieval view of Christendom. On the accession of Henry VIII in 1509, the Court became the center of fashion and culture, and after the suppression of the monasteries the great country houses, which were so often built with their wealth and even from their ruins, took over the patronage of the arts. With the art of printing flourishing, books proliferated and reached an ever wider public. Religious and political questions were debated in multitudes of polemical pamphlets, so that it might be said that printing made the new ideas socially important at a speed unprecedented in earlier history. The religious controversies that raged throughout Europe were hastened and exacerbated by the printing press. Other new ideas reached less far down the social scale. The new ideal of the gentleman, combining the alternative medieval choices of the life of action and the life of contemplation, was reflected in the Italian "courtesy books" (of which the most influential, Castiglione's *Il Cortegiano*, was translated by Sir Thomas Hoby in 1561) and other works of education that appeared all over Europe to teach—in the words of Milton's pamphlet on education—"all the arts, both public and private, of peace and war." The Baconian view of the function of knowledge as "the relief of man's estate," as control over nature rather than abstract metaphysical insight, was even more limited in its influence, but it was nevertheless part of the intellectual climate. And with the establishment of Queen Elizabeth's court, with its *mystique* of the Virgin Queen, its patriotic self-confidence culminating in 1588 with the defeat of the Spanish Armada, and the growing sense of pride in the vernacular and its potentialities, the scene was set for a remarkable efflorescence of national culture.

All this, of course, is to simplify. The literary pattern to be set against this background can be traced more adequately if we go back and inquire about the state of poetry in the reign of Henry VIII. George Puttenham, the Elizabethan critic whose *Art of English Poesie* appeared in 1589, tells us in that work that in the latter part of Henry VIII's reign (1509–47) "sprang up a new company of courtly makers [poets], of whom Sir Thomas Wyatt the elder and Henry Earl of Surrey were the two chieftains, who having travelled into Italy and there tasted the sweet and stately measures and style of the Italian poesie as novices newly crept out of the schools of Dante, Ariosto and Petrarch, they greatly polished our rude and homely manner of vulgar poesie from that it had been before, and for that cause may justly be said the first reformers of our English metre and style." Wyatt (also spelled Wyat and Wiat) was the older of the two, living from 1503 to 1542, and in one sense it can be said that with him modern English poetry begins. He and the "courtly makers" who followed him exercised the language by translating from foreign models and experimenting with a great variety of lyric measures, to restore to English metrics the combination of flexibility and regularity which they had lost in the century following Chaucer, a century during which the rapid shift from that stage of the language we call Middle English to the stage we call Modern English had wrought havoc with the polished and controlled Chaucerian line. They were thus essentially craftsmen, treating a conventional subject matter over and over again in their attempts to hammer out a disciplined yet flexible poetic style. They borrowed, imitated, and translated from Italian and French poets as well as from one another, and had they not done so their ultimate achievement would have been less. They circulated their work in manuscript (publication during the poet's lifetime was not at this time common) and engaged in mutual encouragement and criticism. In 1557 (after the death of both Wyatt and Surrey) the printer Richard Tottel put out a collection of poetry by the "courtly makers" with the title *Songes and Sonnettes, written by the ryght honorable Lorde Henry Haward late Earle of Surrey, and other*, generally known as *Tottel's Miscellany*, which was a somewhat belated manifesto of the new poetry. Many more collections of songs and poems followed in Queen Elizabeth's reign (1558–1603), bearing such attractive titles as *The Paradise of Dainty Devices, A Gorgeous Gallery of Gallant Inventions, A Handful of Pleasant Delights, A Banquet of Dainty Conceits, The Arbor of Amorous Devices, England's Helicon*, and *England's Parnassus*. Many of the poems in these collections are little more than exercises; some are over-ingenious, some crude and mechanical; but by and large they demonstrate the immense success with which the earlier poets of the century had flexed the muscles of the English language to make it suitable for graceful poetic expression.

Some of Wyatt's most interesting—though not his most successful —poems are his sonnets. Like Chaucer, he had been sent on diplomatic missions abroad, and had visited Italy among other countries, to come (as so many poets in Italy and France had already done) under the spell of the fourteenth-century Italian poet, Francesco Petrarca (Petrarch), the great master of the sonnet of idealized love. The sonnet, one of the most popular verse forms not only of Elizabethan literature in England but of Renaissance European literature as a whole, developed first in Italy in the twelfth century before passing into France and then into England. Wyatt, facing the problem of restoring gravity and cogency of utterance to English verse after a period of linguistic change during which pronunciation had altered and metrical patterns had gone to pieces, turned to the Italian sonnet for help. Here was a highly conventional verse form, a form which demanded discipline and craftsmanship on the poet's part, a form which challenged the poet to mold his thought with wit and aptness to the precise shape of those fourteen balanced lines.

The sonnet was not simply a stanza of fourteen lines with a certain rhyme scheme: the lines were deftly balanced, the links and pauses between them creating a movement which, in most Italian sonnets, was in four parts—two of four lines each (*quatrains*) and two of three lines each (*tercets*). There were other ways of balancing the sonnet—such as Shakespeare's; he balanced it on a final couplet of rhyming lines—but the pattern most common in Italy employed two quatrains with a single pair of rhymes, *a b b a, a b b a,* the first and fourth rhyming and the two middle lines rhyming (as in Tennyson's *In Memoriam*), followed by two tercets in any one of a variety of arrangements—*c d c, c d c;* or *c d c, d c d; c d e, c d e;* or other groupings. In such a scheme the four parts of the sonnet really resolve themselves into two, the first consisting of two pairs of four lines (the *octave*) and the second of two pairs of three lines (the *sestet*). There were many other ways of patterning the fourteen lines, but the pattern just described was that most frequently used by Petrarch, whose sonnets celebrating his ideal love of Laura were immensely influential and represent the most important single influence on later love sonnets throughout Europe.

There are periods in the history of any literature when what poets need most is a formal convention which will enable them to study the demands of the medium quite objectively, with a craftsman's eye, and prevent them from merely splashing about in language that has not been tempered to meet the precise curve of the meaning. The sonnet form met this need for English poets in the sixteenth century, and Wyatt's sonnets represent one of the most interesting movements toward metrical discipline to be found in English literary history. Wyatt's problem was to handle the ten-syllabled iambic line with gravity in the individual line and at the same time to achieve a significant unity in the poem as a whole. The metrical tradition established by Chaucer had lost its usefulness because of changes in the language. While these changes (which brought with them a certain flexibility in accentuation during a transitional period) made it possible for Wyatt to experiment freely and effectively in numerous short-line stanzas where the sustained gravity of regular metrical utterance throughout a series of long lines was not required, they seriously handicapped him in writing the heavier kind of line demanded by the sonnet. As a result, his sonnets are less good than his lighter lyrics: he is not always quite sure where the accent falls in a given word, nor is he always able to keep before the reader's ear the basic swell of the metrical design, so necessary in this kind of formal utterance. In the lighter lyrical measures he was also helped by the rhythm of lute music.

It was not only the sonnet form that later poets got from Petrarch; the whole nature of the relation between the poet and his beloved became conventionalized in terms of an idealized courtly-love attitude which Petrarch manifested toward Laura in his love sonnets. This notion of the lover as the humble servant of the often cruel fair, wounded by a glance of her eye, tempest-tossed in seas of despair when his love is rejected, changing in mood according to the presence or absence of his beloved, is derived from the medieval view of courtly love which we have discussed in an earlier chapter. Petrarch moved this courtly love to a high, ideal plane of his own, and subsequent sonneteers for the most part kept it there. The Petrarchan sonnet thus provided the English poet with both a conventional form and conventional sentiments. (It should be added that innumerable Italian and French sonneteers after Petrarch had helped to conventionalize both form and content by the time the English sonneteers began writing.)

The difficulties Wyatt found in handling the iambic pentameter line in the sonnet can be illustrated by the opening line of the following sonnet (from Petrarch):

> Ever myn happe is slack and slo in commyng,
>> Desir encresing, myn hope uncertain,
>> That leve it or wayt it doeth me like pain,
> And Tigre-like, as swift it is in parting.

Wyatt's own spelling has been retained, because to modernize it is often to prejudge the question of pronunciation. The third line here has ten syllables but in no other way resembles an iambic pentameter line. "Uncertain" in the second line is accented on the final syllable; the verbal "-ing" ending is apparently accented at the end of the first and fourth lines. Wyatt's rhyming of verbal endings such as "-ing" and "-eth" and noun endings such as "-ness" and "-aunce" is a common habit, and shows much awkwardness. In a line such as

> Which holdeth the divine parte of nature

it is uncertain whether "nature" is accented on the first syllable, as it certainly was by Shakespeare's time, or on the second syllable, as Chaucer pronounced it. The rhyming of "nature" with "master" hardly helps us to decide. Or the opening of another sonnet from Petrarch—

> The longe love, that in my thought doeth harbar—

shows how far from the iambic beat Wyatt could get. Or is this line meant to be scanned as an iambic pentameter? One is tempted to scan it

> The lónge lóve, that in my thóught dœth hárbar

with perhaps the "e" of "longe" pronounced. But did Wyatt mean

> The lóng love, thát in mý thought dóth harbár?

Or something between these two? Either way, "doeth" is a mono-syllable, though it is apparently disyllabic in other poems. The rhyming of "harbar" with "baner" (banner) leaves the accentuation of both words still in doubt. And what are we to make of such a quatrain as this (from the same sonnet)?

> She that me lerneth to love and suffre,
> And willes that my trust and lustes negligence
> Be rayned by reson, shame and reverence,
> With his hardines taketh displeasur.

"Reason" is apparently pronounced like the modern "reason," not like the Chaucerian "resóun," though no doubt Wyatt could pro-nounce it in the Chaucerian way if it suited the line. "Displeasur" is accented on the second syllable, one assumes, rhyming (if it can be called a rhyme) with "suffre," yet it might just as easily be pro-nounced with the accent on the final syllable. The pronunciation of English was changing even as Wyatt wrote. At the end of the remarkable poem beginning "They fle from me that sometyme did me seke" occur the lines:

> But syns that I so kyndely ame served,
> I would fain knowe what she hath deserved.

This scans regularly if we pronounce the "e" in "kyndely" and (which Wyatt surely did not do) in "knowe." But Tottel, printing the poem in 1557, emended these lines to

> But, since that I unkindly so am served:
> How like you this, what hath she now deserved?

This is neat and regular. But more than metrical changes have taken place. In the twenty or thirty years since Wyatt wrote, not only had it become impossible to pronounce "kyndely" as three syllables, it had also become impossible to construe "so kyndely" in the sense that Wyatt had intended, meaning "in such a fashion," and Tottel had to change it to "*un*kindly," thus giving a quite different force to the line. Sometimes we find in Wyatt remarkable effects of metrical subtlety achieved through cunning irregularity: but we can never be sure whether the irregularity really is the product of cunning or whether the effect was not intended—or whether, indeed, Wyatt scanned the passage as we do.

These difficulties, which are so apparent when Wyatt wrote the iambic pentameter line, seem to have largely disappeared when he wrote in lighter lyric meters, with (presumably) the help of musical accompaniment. There is nothing tentative or awkward about this (one can safely modernize the spelling now):

> Forget not yet the tried intent
> Of such a truth as I have meant,
> My great travail, so gladly spent,
>   Forget not yet.
>
> Forget not yet when first began
> The weary life ye know, since whan
> The suit, the service none tell can,
>   Forget not yet. . . .
>
> Forget not yet, forget not this,
> How long ago hath been, and is,
> The mind that never meant amiss,
>   Forget not yet.
>
> Forget not, then, thine own approved,
> The which so long hath thee so loved,
> Whose steadfast faith yet never moved,
>   Forget not this.

The same serene control can be seen in such lyrics as "Marvel no more" and "My lute, awake!"

> My lute, awake! perform the last
> Labour that thou and I shall waste,

> And end that I have now begun;
> For when this song is sung and past,
> My lute be still, for I have done. . . .

The refrain seems to help Wyatt, and his best songs are those balanced on the concluding short-line refrain, "forget not yet," "Blame not my lute," "Say nay, say nay!" Yet these poems do not represent any startling new development in the English lyric: their verse-forms and rhyme-schemes are often to be found in medieval Latin poetry and in Middle English lyrical poetry too. The Middle English lyrical tradition flows directly into the Tudor song tradition, and the reader who comes from fourteenth- and fifteenth-century lyrics to the songs of Wyatt is conscious of no break. A fifteenth-century manuscript, for example, has the following poem:

> Wimmen beth bothe goud and schene,   [schene: beautiful]
>   On handës, fete, and facë clene;
> Wimmen may no beter bene.
>   Witnesse on Marie.
>
> Wimmen beth gentel on her tour;
>   A wimman bare oure Saviour;
> Of all this world wimman is flour.
>   Witnesse on Marie. . . .

This is the exact stanza form of "Forget not yet." The lively movement and metrical assurance of "The Nutbrown Maid" (first printed about 1502) shows all the virtuosity of later Tudor poetry; its internal rhyming is handled with great artfulness:

> Be it right, or wrong, these men among
>   On women do complaine,
> Afferming this, how that it is
>   A labour spent in vaine,
> To love them wele, for never a dele
>   They lofe a man againe;
> For let a man do what he can,
>   Ther favour to attaine,
> Yet if a newe to them pursue,
>   Ther furst trew lover than
> Laboureth for nought, and from her thought
>   He is a banisshed man. . . .

This spirited dialogue between "Squire" and "Puella" runs on for thirty lively stanzas, each concluding with the phrase "banisshed man." It seems clear that the sung lyric was not affected by the changes in the language that seems to have caused the iambic decasyllabic line to disintegrate. "Skeltonics" may represent a deliberate abandonment of metrical polish in favor of a rough, if effective, accentual measure, but while Skelton wrote, anonymous singers were keeping a smoother kind of verse alive so that it could be transmitted to later generations.

Wyatt's most perfect poems are not, then, his most original in form. In subject matter, he is as a rule even less original, content to appear in the conventional guise as the hopeless lover of a cruel mistress. Yet every now and again he handles the heavier line with a force and splendor that mark him as a pioneering original poet of extraordinary strength. Only a complete poem can illustrate this:

> They flee from me that sometime did me seek,
> With naked foot stalking in my chamber.
> I have seen them gentle, tame and meek,
> That now are wild, and do not remember
> That sometime they have put themselves in danger
> To take bread at my hand; and now they range,
> Busily seeking with a continual change.
>
> Thanked be fortune it hath been otherwise,
> Twenty times better; but once in special,
> In thin array, after a pleasant guise,
> When her loose gown from her shoulders did fall,
> And she me caught in her arms long and small,
> Therewith all sweetely did me kiss,
> And softly said, "Dear heart, how like you this?"
>
> It was no dream; I lay broad waking:
> But all is turned, thorough my gentleness,
> Into a strange fashion of forsaking;
> And I have leave to go, of her goodness,
> And she also to use newfangleness.
> But since that I so kindely am served,
> I would fain know what she hath deserved.[1]

The variations from the regular iambic line here are strangely moving, and the whole poem has the air of having caught, and rendered into impressive art, the very essence of an emotional situation. Wyatt occasionally does this even in those sonnets where the handling of the meter seems to be a hit-or-miss affair. Surrey never achieves the strength and subtlety of Wyatt at his best. Wyatt's three "satires," though derived from Horace (two) and the Italian poet Alamanni (one), have a freshness and a conversational tone which please in a different way. The first begins

---

[1] From this point on, now that we are in the period of "modern" English, the spelling of quotations is modernized except when the original spelling is necessary for reasons of meter or of poetic suggestiveness.

Mine own John Poins, since ye delight to know
The cause why that homeward I me draw,
And flee the press or courts where so they go,
Rather than to live thrall, under the awe
Of lordly looks, wrappid within my cloak, . . .

and the second

My mother's maids, when they did sew and spin
They sang sometimes a song of the field mouse, . . .

His version of the seven penitential Psalms (deriving from Aretino's prose paraphrase) has its impressive moments; the prologues are in *ottava rima* and the psalms themselves in *terza rima,* both of which forms Wyatt handles with some skill, though unevenly. But on the whole Wyatt's Psalms can be classed among the Tudor exercisings of the vernacular. His most consistently good poems are his song lyrics; his few really remarkable pioneering poems in heavier meters flash out from a mass of uncertainly handled traditional material. And even where his sonnets are not successful, they do represent the first English attempt of the age at this verse form.

Henry Howard, Earl of Surrey, the only one of the "courtly makers" whose name appeared on Tottel's title page, was some fourteen years younger than Wyatt, whose poetic disciple he was. His execution in 1547, when he was barely thirty, on a trumped up charge of treason, put an end to one of the most spirited and promising careers of the time: Surrey was born into one of the noblest families of England and educated, at both the English and French courts, in a consciously aristocratic tradition. Like Wyatt, he was sensitive to the literary fashions that had invaded much of Europe from Italy, and like him he endeavored to exercise and enlarge the English poetic tongue in translations and adaptations from Italian and Latin and in variations on conventional themes. The first thirty-six poems in *Tottel's Miscellany* are by Surrey, and four more are included later in the book. The difference between Wyatt and Surrey can be summed up in a phrase: Surrey has less strength and more polish. He is more consistently successful than Wyatt in fitting the metrical accent to the normal accentuation of the word and stress of the spoken language, but he lacks Wyatt's moving and surprising touches. Wyatt is a greater poet, wielding a less perfect instrument, Surrey is the competent and graceful craftsman; his sonnets run with greater metrical smoothness than Wyatt's. The metrical control is clear in the following:

The soote season that bud and bloom forth brings
With green hath clad the hill and eke the vale,
The nightingale with feathers new she sings,
The turtle to her make hath told her tale: [make : mate]
Summer is come, for every spray now springs,
The hart hath hung his old head on the pale,
The buck in brake his winter coat he flings,
The fishes float with new repairéd scale,
The adder all her slough away she slings,
The swift swallow pursueth the flies smale,   [smale : small]
The busy bee her honey now she mings,   [mings : mingles]
Winter is worn that was the flowers' bale.
And thus I see among these pleasant things
Each care decays, and yet my sorrow springs.

This is a rendering of a sonnet of Petrarch's:

Zefiro torna, e 'l bel tempo rimena, . . .

but Surrey's nature imagery is livelier and more English than Petrarch's finely stylized picture, and, unlike Petrarch, he prolongs the description of spring for twelve lines, to turn suddenly on a final couplet. This handling of the sonnet form with the lines rhyming *abab abab abab aa* is unusual in having only two rhymes, but its grouping of three quatrains and a final couplet is characteristic of Surrey and was to become a mark of the English form of the sonnet. Surrey also uses the forms *abab abab abab cc, abba cddc effe gg*, and *abab cdcd efef gg*. This last is the "Shakespearean" form, and Surrey seems to have settled on it as the most convenient. It relieves the poet from the necessity of running the same rhymes right through (which is easier in Italian than in English) and so gives him more freedom. Wyatt, like Petrarch, preferred five rhymes to the "Shakespearean" seven; he, too, ended his sonnets with a couplet, the majority of them being in the form *abba abba cddc ee*.

Much of Surrey's verse handles the traditional Petrarchan theme of love. More interesting are his autobiographical pieces, such as the poem, in alternately rhyming iambic pentameter lines, which he wrote on his temporary imprisonment in Windsor in 1545. The poet is remembering his happy boyhood at Windsor with the king's illegitimate son, the Duke of Richmond:

So cruel prison how could betide, alas,
As proud Windsor? Where I in lust and joy
With a king's son my childish years did pass
In greater feast than Priam's sons of Troy;

Where each sweet place returns a taste full sour:
The large green courts where we were wont to hove
With eyes cast up into the maidens' tower,
And easy sighs, such as folk draw in love;
The stately seats, the ladies bright of hue,
The dances short, long tales of great delight;
With words and looks that tigers could but rue,
Where each of us did plead the other's right; . . .

Among the verse forms with which Surrey experimented was the so-called "Poulter's Measure," a curious jog-trot which became very popular in the sixteenth century: it consists of lines of twelve and fourteen syllables alternating:

Such wayward ways hath love, that most part in discord,
Our wills do stand, whereby our hearts but seldom doth accord.
Deceit is his delight, and to beguile and mock
The simple hearts which he doth strike with froward, divers stroke.
He causeth hearts to rage with golden burning dart,
And doth allay with leaden cold again the tother's heart. . . .

Surrey was partial to this measure, and rendered passages from Ecclesiastes and some of the Psalms in it. These renderings—which are adaptations, infused often with personal feeling—have their own kind of eloquence. He used *terza rima*, sometimes in pentameter lines and once in octosyllables, and a variety of short stanzas. He could be didactic, moralistic, reminiscent, satirical, and epigrammatic as well as conventionally amorous. All in all, Surrey was an accomplished versifier whose responsiveness to the cultural movements of his time, together with his aristocratic idealism of mind, his quickness of wit, and his technical curiosity about his craft enabled him on occasion to write poetry of grace and eloquence. And to write English poetry of grace and eloquence in the first half of the sixteenth century was a historically important achievement, and one which had great influence on the subsequent course of English poetry.

Perhaps the most obvious pioneering achievement of Surrey was his use of blank verse in his translation of the second and fourth books of Virgil's *Aeneid*. This translation was apparently suggested to him by an Italian version of book four which appeared in 1534, and by the Italian version of the first six books which appeared in 1540: he presumably thought of blank verse as his medium because that was the English equivalent of his Italian models. Surrey was also influenced by the important translation of the *Aeneid* (in rhymed couplets) by Gavin Douglas, the late fifteenth- and early sixteenth-century Scottish poet. Surrey's translation, published by Tottel as a separate book in 1557, has been praised for its speed and vigor, but the end-stopped lines soon prove wearisome and the verse on the whole has a wooden quality. Here is clearly a case where the historical importance outweighs the intrinsic worth.

The only other author named in Tottel is Nicholas Grimald: after thirty-six poems by Surrey and ninety-one by Wyatt, Tottel prints forty by Grimald, in a variety of styles and on a variety of subjects. The first is a love poem in Poulter's Measure:

> What sweet relief the showers to thirsty plants we see,
> What dear delight the blooms to bees, my true love is to me. . . .

There are other love poems in iambic pentameter couplets, poems of compliments in seven-foot iambic couplets, poems translated from the Latin of the sixteenth-century French Calvinist theologian Theodore Beza, as well as from other sources, some of which are in blank verse and some brief epigrams. Grimald's poems are followed by ninety-four attributed to "uncertain authors," among whom Thomas, Lord Vaux, has been identified, though most of Vaux' identifiable work appeared in a larger miscellany, *The Paradise of Dainty Devices*, 1576. Other authors who have been probably or certainly identified are: J. Canand, Sir John Cheke, William Gray, John Harington, John Heywood, Thomas Norton, Sir Anthony St. Leger, and an unknown D. Sand. Oddly enough, among the poems by uncertain authors is included a short lyric by Chaucer (beginning, as Tottel prints it, "Flee from the prese and dwell with sothfastnes") probably taken from one of the sixteenth-century editions printed by William Thynne. Sir Thomas Bryan and Thomas Churchyard are among the poets whose names have been associated with *Tottel's Miscellany* but whose poems have not been identified. These uncertain authors play variations on the themes set by Wyatt and Surrey. There are love poems, elegies, moralizing poems, poems of compliment, and poems of proverbial philosophy. The verse forms include couplets, both octosyllabic and decasyllabic, iambic hexameters, *ottava rima*, a variety of stanza forms, and nine sonnets. There are no outstanding poems in this section, which is interesting only as an exercising ground for Tudor poetry.

Tottel's aim is indicated in his introductory note to the reader which begins: "That to have well written, yea and in small parcels, deserveth great praise, the works of divers Latins, Italians, and other, do prove sufficiently. That our tongue is able in that kind to do as praiseworthy as the rest, the honorable style of the noble Earl of Surrey, and the weightiness of the deepwitted Sir Thomas

Wyatt the Elder's verse, with several graces in sundry good English writers, do show abundantly . . ." The work was published, as Tottel goes on to say, "to the honor of the English tongue and for profit of the studious of English eloquence." National pride in the vernacular, and the desire to improve it to the point where it could compete with or surpass Italian or even approach the classical tongues of ancient Greece and Rome, were important motives in sixteenth-century English poetry, which helped to form the ambitions of Spenser and, later still, of Milton. Indeed, the words with which in 1627 the young Milton broke off from a Latin vacation exercise to dedicate himself to writing poetry in English could fittingly speak for these Tudor experimenters:

> Hail native Language, that by sinews weak
> Didst move my first endeavouring tongue to speak,
> And mad'st imperfect words with childish trips,
> Half unpronounc't, slide through my infant lips,
> Driving dumb silence from the portal door,
> Where he had mutely sat two years before:
> Here I salute thee. . . .

Tottel's Miscellany went into nine editions between 1557 and 1587, later editions introducing new poems. This is sufficient evidence of the popularity of the "courtly makers," while the miscellanies that followed Tottel's (of which *The Paradise of Dainty Devices*, 1576, was the most popular) testified equally to the interest in the handling of the various lyric and other measures with which the poets of the time experimented. There was no real progress in the latter part of Henry VIII's reign and in the short reigns of his successors, Edward VI and Mary, but the versifying went on, with a great deal of mechanical jingling and much use of the jog-trot Poulter's Measure. Metrical regularity, once achieved, was apt to fall into the wearisome cadence of repetitious and inflexible arithmetical correctness. Of individual poets who were writing in the mid-sixteenth century, Thomas Churchyard (ca. 1520–1604) and George Gascoigne (ca. 1525–77), deserve mention. Churchyard, who began writing in the reign of Edward VI (1547–53) if not of Henry VIII, produced a great many poems in the styles of the day, most of them little more than mechanical exercises, but there is an occasional happy lyric in his collection called *Churchyard's Chips* (1575). Churchyard's longevity and versatility won him some reputation by the end of the century: Spenser referred to him in 1591 as "old Palemon . . . that sung so long until quite hoarse he grew." Gascoigne is a more interesting poet. His play *The Supposes*, acted at Gray's Inn in 1566, was a prose translation of a comedy by

Ariosto and is the earliest extant comedy in English prose, and his blank verse tragedy *Jocasta*, translated from the Italian of Ludovico Dolce's *Giocasta*, with the collaboration of Francis Kinwelmersh, was also presented in 1566. (Dolce's play was an adaptation of the *Phoenissae* of Euripides.) His blank verse satire *The Steel Glass* (1576) presents a picture of the failures of the different orders of society with that medieval sense of hierarchy and function in society which was carried undimmed into the Renaissance: the versification is dogged rather than effective, but it provided further exercise for the developing English form of blank verse, which Gascoigne at least uses rather more flexibly than Surrey. Among his varied other work are *Certain Notes of Instruction Concerning the Making of Verse or Rhyme in English* (1575), a pioneer critical essay on English prosody, primitive enough but showing remarkable good sense; moralistic prose pamphlets; a collection of meditative poems, or elegies; and a number of attractive lyrics of which the best known (either because or in spite of most readers' lack of awareness of its sexual theme) is "Gascoigne's Lullaby":

> Sing lullaby, as women do,
> Wherewith they bring their babes to rest,
> And lullaby can I sing too
> As womanly as can the best.
> With lullaby they still the child,
> And if I be not much beguiled,
> Full many wanton babes have I
> Which must be stilled with lullaby. . . .

The *Epitaphs, Epigrams, Songs and Sonnets* (1567) of George Turberville contains some pieces of genuine lyrical grace, and if his translations from Ovid and Mantuan are of less interest as poetry they at least show him helping to exercise the language by translation. George Whetstone (ca. 1544–87), a friend of Gascoigne's and usually coupled with Churchyard, wrote a considerable amount of miscellaneous verse in the styles of the time, but is remembered chiefly for his unacted play in two parts, *Promos and Cassandra*, in crude enough verse which, together with a prose version of the same story, provided the plot for Shakespeare's *Measure for Measure*. Finally, we must mention Edward de Vere, Earl of Oxford (1550–1604), whose poems in *The Paradise of Dainty Devices* and in other Elizabethan collections show the earlier Tudor lyrical tradition carried successfully into Elizabethan court poetry: contemporaries placed him at the head of the courtly poets of his day, but to the retrospective eye of the historian he seems rather to constitute a bridge between Tottel's courtly makers and such Elizabethan poet-courtiers as Sidney, Ralegh, and Fulke Greville, who are discussed in a later chapter.

The most ambitious single poetic achievement of the mid-sixteenth century was not, however, the work of those who "wrote well in small parcels." It was *A Mirror for Magistrates*, a composite didactic work intended originally as a continuation of Lydgate's *Falls of Princes* (itself derived from Boccaccio's *De Casibus Virorum Illustrium*). The printer J. Wayland suggested such a sequel to William Baldwin, who had already turned the biblical Song of Songs into English verse and written a prose *Treatise of Moral Philosophy*. Baldwin sought collaborators, and between them they produced seven new stories from English history, in the form of imaginary monologues spoken by the ghosts of eminent men who had suffered drastic reversals of fortune. These seven stories, originally published as a supplement to an edition of *The Falls of Princes*, were expanded to nineteen and published separately in 1559. Later editions included new stories and other changes, the most notable addition to the edition of 1563 being Thomas Sackville's "Complaint of Henry Duke of Buckingham" preceded by an "Induction" which remains the best known part of the *Mirror*. Thomas Churchyard's "Shore's Wife" also appeared in the 1563 edition. Other editions appeared in 1578 and 1587. Besides Baldwin, Sackville and Churchyard, the authors (who have not all been identified) included George Ferrers, Thomas Chaloner, Thomas Phaer (who translated the *Aeneid*), John Dolman, and Francis Seager.

A Mirror for Magistrates contains monologues written in rhyme with varying degrees of metrical facility and different kinds of rhythmic movement, from the impressive elegiac cadences of Sackville's "Induction" to reminiscences of the old alliterative measure and various kinds of jog-trot. The poetic quality of much of the work is low indeed, but Sackville possesses a Virgilian gravity and handles imagery with a fine original power, and Churchyard effectively introduces the note of passion in his account of Jane Shore. The stories are linked by prose discussions among the authors, in which they exchange views about the significance of the stories they tell, the ethical and political ideas underlying them, and the most effective ways of presenting them, thus showing themselves concerned both with the technical problems of their craft and with the intellectual currents of their time. For *A Mirror for Magistrates* is not merely a series of medieval "tragedies" after Lydgate, even though it was begun as a sequel to Lydgate, who remained popular in the sixteenth century. It embodies the Renaissance interest in the didactic aspect of history, in a study of the past as the proper education of a prince, teaching him by example what to follow and what to avoid. The authors are concerned with the nature of order and of justice, with the reasons for human suffering, with the ways in which divine retribution overtakes human crimes, and with cause and effect in human affairs. They are concerned with the proper behavior of a prince and the proper relation between ruler and ruled. In taking characters from English history from the time of Richard II to that of Henry VIII and making them speak of their fortunes, the authors were seeking to project the moral and educational meaning of history. The notion of history as the great teacher was common in the Renaissance and is to be found again and again in sixteenth-century European literature. And the idea of selected episodes of history constituting a mirror in which the consequences of good and bad government can be seen, for the proper instruction of those who govern, was a commonplace in Elizabethan England. The title *A Mirror for Magistrates* emphasizes the political didacticism of the work; and this concern with political didacticism arose from the concern of the age with the whole question of the education of the prince as well as from the specifically English interest in the moral of the Wars of the Roses and the possibilities of maintaining a unified and stable government without reverting to the bad old days, still vividly in men's minds, of civil war. Queen Elizabeth's being unmarried and thus having no direct heir increased English preoccupation with the problem of government, succession, and order. Writers of the age looked to history and biography to help them show, as in a mirror, the truth about human affairs with special reference to the relationship between power and virtue and between crime and suffering. *A Mirror for Magistrates* thus reinterpreted the medieval concept of the wheel of fortune and unpredictable fate to show the political and ethical background of those spectacular falls from high estate which the Middle Ages saw as "tragedy." The Tudor historians from whom Shakespeare drew the material for his history plays shared, in differing degrees (Edward Hall had it much more than Raphael Holinshed), this Renaissance view of the educational function of history: the most eloquent expression of this view in English is to be found in Sir Walter Ralegh's preface to his *History of the World* (1614).

In moralizing history, the Renaissance made it more amenable not only to treatment by philosophers but also to handling by poets and dramatists. An understanding of the true relation of history

Spenser and His Time

Looking back on the poetry of the sixteenth century with the historian's perspective, we can see clearly enough that the endeavor to establish English as a poetic language at least the equal of Italian and French prompted much of the experimentation and exercising that went on in Tudor verse. It is true that among the production of poets between Wyatt and Spenser we do find some accomplished lyrics and an occasional success in longer and graver kinds of verse; but an air of uncertainty still hung over everything, and the poet who could turn out a deft song at one moment might very well fall, on another occasion, into the crudest jog-trot or the most wooden kind of labored regularity. England awaited the poet who could pull together the diverse elements that had been operating in Tudor verse; who could profit by Renaissance Latinists, by Italian and French developments in the vernacular, by new ideas about the function and prestige of the poet, by classical example, by new currents in religious and philosophical thought, as well as by the exercising of the English language that had been going on; who could at the same time look back to Chaucer and, while absorbing and benefiting from all the new currents, re-establish contact with the great medieval master of English verse; and who would be simultaneously Elizabethan and European, drawing inspiration both from the national excitement of his own time and country and from the larger movements of the mind and the imagination which were agitating the whole of Western civilization Classical, medieval, and Humanist; inspired equally by the new Puritan idealism and by the reawakened interest in Platonic thought; moved both by the new Protestant gravity and by the Catholic sense of the unity of Western culture; supreme craftsman with a great synthesizing imagination—such was the poet the times now required if the full riches of Elizabethan England were to find adequate expression in poetry. The greatest genius that England produced at this—and at any—time did not turn directly to this synthesizing task but used all this material with careless brilliance in the dramatic exploration of the relation between the moral and emotional aspects of man: Shakespeare was not the New Poet the Elizabethans were looking for; his genius was too large and too unself-conscious for him to see himself as contributing to any specific historical end. It was Edmund Spenser (1552–99) who saw himself, as he was seen by his contemporaries, in the role of the New Poet who was to draw the threads together and mark both a culmination and a new beginning in English poetry. Spenser was the great synthesizer for whom English nondramatic poetry was waiting.

The publication of *The Shepherd's Calendar* in 1579 marked Spenser's formal entry as the New Poet. An unpretentious and uneven work to modern eyes, not much read today except by specialists and students, *The Shepherd's Calendar* is the perfect example of a work of greater historical importance than of permanent and intrinsic poetic interest. The title, in Spenser's (or his printer's) spelling is worth recording: "The Shepheardes Calendar, Conteyning twelve Aeglogues proportionable to the Twelve monethes. Entitled to the Noble and Vertuous Gentleman most worthy of all titles both of learning and chevalrie M. Philip Sidney." The eclogue, or pastoral dialogue (spelled "aeglogue" by Spenser and many of his contemporaries because of a false derivation from the Greek word for goatherd) has its origin in Sicilian folk song and comes first into literature in the work of Theocritus, Bion, and Moschus, Greek Sicilian poets of the third century B.C. It was a form widely used in the Renaissance, deriving more often from the eclogues of Virgil than directly from the Greek pastoralists. By the time Spenser was writing there were eclogues in Italian and French as well as in Renaissance Latin, and pastoral poetry (i.e., poetry dealing with shepherds, or ideal shepherds) was established as an accepted poetic form, ranking below epic or heroic poetry, which was at the top of the poetic ladder in Renaissance criticism, and below tragedy, but laudable nevertheless and especially appropriate for a poet beginning his poetic career. Virgil had started with eclogues and moved on at last to his great epic: the proper course for an ambitious new poet was clear. Not only was the pastoral well established in Renaissance poetry by Spenser's time; it had also been frequently used in an allegorical manner for moral and satirical purposes. Pastoral allegory was thus an established note. Almost any aspect of human life could be presented through the elemental activities of shepherds. Rural work has always been an obvious prototype of all human endeavor, being, as it were, the primal human activity. And the work of the shepherd is not only an obvious example of rustic labor; it also includes the element of guardianship, which makes it easy to discuss either political rulers or spiritual leaders in pastoral terms. The elemental background of pastoral activity also makes pastoral poetry an appropriate vehicle for the presentation of the more elemental human emotions, such as love or grief. The Renaissance poets, excited at the potentialities of the literary use of the pastoral, exploited it to the point of exhaustion, with the result that it is now regarded as one of the most faded of literary forms. But for Spenser it was a richly promising medium, and an obvious one for a manifesto of the new poetry.

Linking his eclogues together in a calendar, Spenser found a happy way of combining unity with diversity, as well as of combining the simple and rustic with the elaborate and sophisticated. By varying the degree to which his shepherds were allegorical, he could vary the tone from the naïvely pastoral to the elaborately formal. And by making his shepherds compete in singing matches, in a formula that goes back to the Greek pastoralists, he was enabled to introduce into his pastoral framework a diversity of lyrical poems in different styles. The poet who influenced him most in his allegorical use of the pastoral was the fifteenth-century Italian, Baptista Spanuoli, known in literature as Mantuanus or Mantuan, whose ten Latin eclogues on moral and religious themes were used as a schoolbook throughout Europe. But Spenser also knew Theocritus and Bion (and there were Latin and French versions, if he needed help with the original), the Latin eclogues of Petrarch, Boccaccio, and Iacopo Sannazaro, and the two French eclogues of Clement Marot, which he imitated in his November and December poems. In short, Spenser was working confidently in a European tradition, both classical and Humanist.

Spenser sent *The Shepherd's Calendar* into the world with an introduction and commentary by "E. K.," who was probably Edward Kirke, who had been a fellow student of Spenser's at Cambridge, and who certainly had been briefed carefully by Spenser about his intentions in producing the poem. One is reminded of Stuart Gilbert's commentary on James Joyce's *Ulysses*, which was also an explanation of a new kind of work by someone who had had the benefit of talks with the author about its meaning and purpose. E. K. could make claims for Spenser that the poet was too modest to make himself but which nevertheless must have fairly represented Spenser's own view of his function and ambitions. E. K.'s

introduction, addressed to Spenser's friend, the scholar and man of
letters Gabriel Harvey, makes all the points necessary to emphasize
the importance of the work. He begins with a quotation (or rather,
misquotation) from Chaucer, and links Spenser both with Chaucer
and with Virgil. He goes on to refer to Spenser's "wittiness in devis-
ing, his pithiness in uttering, his complaints of love so lovely, his
discourses of pleasure so pleasantly, his pastoral rudeness, his moral
wiseness, his due observing of decorum everywhere, in personages,
in seasons, in matter, in speech, and generally in all seemly simplicity of handling his matter and framing his words: the which of
many things which in him be strange, I know will seem the
strangest, the words themselves being so ancient, the knitting of
them so short and intricate, and the whole period and compass of
speech so delightsome for the roundness and so grave for the
strangeness." The emphasis on decorum is significant: decorum
meant propriety and fitness of tone and diction and verse form, the
suiting of the style to the matter, the deliberate avoidance of anything disproportionate or incongruous. It was an important Renaissance esthetic ideal, and in showing himself concerned with it
Spenser is not only exhibiting a debt to the critical thought of his
age but also showing his awareness of a prime need of English
poetry at this time. Decorum was conspicuously lacking in the
majority of the earlier Tudor poets. Biblical paraphrase in Poulter's
Measure, for example, such as we find more than once in *Tottel's
Miscellany*, is a clear violation of decorum:

> Knock and it shall be heard, but ask and given it is,
> And all that like to keep this course of mercy shall not miss.
>   For when I call to mind how the one wandering sheep
> Did bring more joy with his return than all the flock did keep,
>   It yields full hope and trust my strayed and wandering ghost
> Shall be received and held more dear than those were never lost.

Spenser put an end to this sort of thing. E. K. refers with contempt
to the Tudor versifiers as "the rakehelly rout of our ragged rhymers
(for so themselves use to hunt the letter [i.e., practice alliteration])
which without learning boast, without judgment jangle, without
reason, rage and foam, as if some instinct of poetical spirit had
newly ravished them above the meanness of common capacity."
That is poetry without decorum, which Milton was later to call "the
chief masterpiece to be observed."

E. K. praises Spenser for preserving the continuity of English
poetry by using a certain number of older words, and using them
appropriately. Spenser, he says, "hath laboured to restore, as to

their rightful heritage, such good and natural English words as have been long time out of use and almost clean disherited." Pride in the vernacular comes out strongly in E. K.'s remarks on the English language and its potentialities. He praises Spenser both for his choice of words and for his "knitting of sentences, . . . and for all the compass of the speech," which he calls "round without roughness and learned without hardness." He classes him with the great classical and Renaissance poets, suggesting that *The Shepherd's Calendar* is the pioneer work of a new English poet worthy to be ranked with them: "So [i.e., in eclogues] flew Theocritus, as you may perceive he was all ready full fledged. So flew Virgil, as not yet well feeling his wings. So flew Mantuan, as being not full somd.[1] So Petrarch. So Boccaccio. So Marot, Sanazarus, and also divers other excellent both Italian and French poets, whose footing this author everywhere followeth, yet so as few, but they be well scented, can trace him out. So finally flieth this our new Poet, as a bird, whose principals be scarce grown out, but yet as that in time shall be able to keep wing with the best."

Though the modern reader may feel a certain anticlimax in coming from this enthusiastic preface to the poems themselves, he cannot fail, if he comes to *The Shepherd's Calendar* from earlier Tudor poetry, to be struck by the control and the assurance of Spenser's verse. In the January eclogue, the shepherd Colin Clout, who is Spenser himself (the name comes from an anticlerical satire of Skelton's), is complaining of his unrequited love for Rosalind. Spenser thus adapts a Petrarchan mood to a pastoral setting. The stanza has six lines, rhymed *ababcc:*

> A shepherd's boy (no better do him call)
> When winter's wasteful spite was almost spent
> All in a sunshine day, as did befall,
> Led forth his flock, that had been long ypent.
> So faint they woxe, and feeble in the fold,
> That now unnethes their feet could them uphold.
>
> All as the sheep, such was the shepherd's look,
> For pale and wan he was (alas the while);
> May seem he loved, or else some care he took;
> Well couth he tune his pipe and frame his style.
> Then to a hill his fainting flock he led,
> And thus him plained, the while his sheep there fed.
>
> "Ye gods of love, that pity lovers' pain
> (If any gods the pain of lovers pity),

[1] Full somd: a falconer's term, meaning full fledged.

> Look from above, where you in joys remain,
> And bow your ears unto my doleful ditty.
> And Pan, thou shepherds' God, that once didst love,
> Pity the pains that thou thyself didst prove. . . ."

We see here the deliberate archaisms that Spenser was to experiment with much more before he settled on the diction for *The Faerie Queene.* Spenser is trying to combine rusticity with formality. The February eclogue, which tells the story of the oak and the briar, is written in a rougher accentual measure, which Spenser seems to have considered a genuine English verse-form and one suitable for the handling of more deliberately rustic themes. Whether this looser meter represents how Spenser and his contemporaries read Chaucer, not understanding the pronunciation of the final *e,* or whether Spenser was trying to do something resembling what Coleridge did in *Christabel,* is not clear; but it *is* clear that Spenser used this accentual verse deliberately, as a style appropriate to the subject of this eclogue. He used it again in the May and September eclogues. The March eclogue gives the dialogue of two shepherds in the old romance stanza that Chaucer had used so mockingly in *Sir Thopas:* Thomalin tells Willy how he saw Cupid in a bush, and they exchanged shots, but the naturalistic pastoral setting makes the incident sound rather incongruous: we expect a grouse or a partridge rather than "the little god." The April eclogue, after an introductory dialogue between Thenot and Hobbinol in flexible decasyllabic quatrains, introduces a formal song in praise of Elizabeth. The verse form, though perhaps suggested by Ronsard and his group, la Pléiade, is an interesting original experiment:

> Ye dainty nymphs, that in this blessed brook
>   do bathe your breast,
> Forsake your watery bowers and hither look,
>   at my request;
> And eke you virgins that on Parnasse dwell,
> Whence floweth Helicon, the learned well,
>   Help me to blaze
>   Her worthy praise
> Which in her sex doth all excell.

There is a careful chiming of vowels through the song (which has thirteen stanzas) and cunning variations of *tempo,* foreshadowing Spenser's later achievements in sound and movement.

The May eclogue is a dialogue between two shepherds in which, through the obvious pastoral disguise, Spenser attacks idle, deceitful, and worldly High Church clergy, whose fondness for elaborate ritual offended Spenser's Protestant idealism. June brings another complaint, in an eight-line stanza rhyming *ababbaba*. Colin complains not only of his lack of success in love, but of his lack of success in his poetry and his generally unsettled condition. The slow-moving verse rises and falls in a fine plangent cadence. The July eclogue is another Protestant satire, made, as E. K.'s "argument" tells us, "in the honour and commendation of good shepherds, and to the shame and dispraise of proud and ambitious pastors." The proud shepherd, Morrell (probably denoting John Elmer, the High Church bishop of London), argues with the humble and conscientious Thomalin, who concludes by praising Algrin (i.e., Edmund Grindal, Archbishop of Canterbury and Puritan sympathizer) as the type of the good shepherd. The verse form is alternately rhyming eight-syllabled and six-syllabled lines, handled with ease and assurance.

August gives a singing match, with a charming roundelay by Perigot and Willy followed by a much more formal *sestina* by Cuddie. The roundelay is fresh and artfully artless:

Perigot:	It fell upon a holy eve,
Willy:	hey ho holiday,
Per.	When holy fathers wont to shrieve,
Wil.	now ginneth this roundelay.
Per.	Sitting upon a hill so high,
Wil.	hey ho the high hill,
Per.	The while my flock did feed thereby,
Wil.	the while the shepherd self did spill,
Per.	I saw the bouncing Bellibone,
Wil.	hey ho bonibell,
Per.	Tripping over the dale alone,
Wil.	she can trip it very well. . . .

This draws on the popular tradition, but embodies more skill than may be at first apparent. The chiming repetitions and modifications of Willy's lines are handled with effective variety. The *sestina*, an elaborate verse-form from Petrarch, is a slow moving six-line stanza, with each stanza using the same words to end the lines, but in a different order. It opens:

Ye wasteful woods, bear witness of my woe
Wherein my plaints did oftentimes resound;
Ye careless birds are privy to my cries,
Which in your songs were wont to make a part.

> Thou pleasant spring hast lulled me oft asleep
> Whose streams my trickling tears did oft augment.

The lines of the second stanza end, respectively, with "augment," "woes," "resound," "cries," "part," "sleep." Those of the third stanza end "sleep," "augment," "woe," "resound," "cries," "part." Those of the fourth, with "apart," "sleep," "augment," "woe," "sound," "cries." And so on. Elaborate though this is, it is less elaborate than the Petrarchan *sestina*. Spenser is here performing a deliberate *tour de force*: it is Colin's (i.e., Spenser's) poem that Cuddie recites, and Perigot provides the applause afterward:

> O Colin, Colin, the shepherds' joy,
> How I admire each turning of thy verse. . . .

The September eclogue is a dialogue between Hobbinol and Diggon Davie. The latter is "a shepherd, that in hope of more gain drove his sheep into a far country. The abuses whereof, and loose living of Popish prelates, by occasion of Hobbinol's demand, he discourseth at large." Spenser takes many suggestions here from Mantuan, but the Protestant content is his own.

The October eclogue is in many ways the most important of all, for it voices, for the first time in English, the high Renaissance ideal of poetry. "In Cuddie is set out the perfect pattern of a poet," runs the argument, and though the presentation of this perfect pattern is accompanied by Cuddie's complaints that the age of great poetry is dead, the exhortations of his friend Piers sound the louder note. The argument reads like a summary of Sidney's "Defence of Poetry." Cuddie

> . . . complaineth of the contempt of poetry, and the causes thereof; specially having been in all ages, and even amongst the most barbarous, always of singular account and honour, and being indeed so worthy and commendable an art; or rather no art, but a divine gift and heavenly instinct not to be gotten by labour and learning, but adorned with both; and poured into the wit by a certain ἐνθουσιασμὸς and celestial inspiration, as the author hereof else where at large discourseth . . .

The verse has a gravity suited to the subject:

> Abandon then the base and viler clown,
> Lift up thyself out of the lowly dust,
> And sing of bloody Mars, of wars, of jousts.
> Turn thee to those that wield the awful crown,
> To doubted knights whose woundless armour rusts,   [doubted:
> And helms unbruiséd waxen daily brown.   redoubted]

> There may thy Muse display her fluttering wing,
> And stretch herself at large from East to West; . . .

And again, Piers breaks out on hearing Cuddie lament the present decline of poetry:

> O peerless poesie, where is then thy place?
> If nor in Princes palace thou do sit
> (And yet is Prince's palace the most fit)
> Ne breast of baser birth doth thee embrace.
> Then make thee wings of thine aspiring wit,
> And, whence thou camest, fly back to heaven apace.

The strain of lament here is conventional; the note of faith in poetry's high destiny rings out clearly above it.

The November eclogue is a lament for "the death of some maiden of great blood, whom he calleth Dido." It is based on a similar poem by Marot. The lament is introduced as a song sung for pleasure rather than an expression of personal grief: the eclogue opens with Thenot asking Colin:

> Colin my dear, when shall it please thee sing,
> As thou were wont, songs of some jovisance?

And Colin replies that a joyful song is not seasonable in "sad Winter," when the "mournful Muse" is more appropriate. Like the poem in praise of Elizabeth in the April eclogue, the lament which Colin proceeds to sing is an exercise in the handling of vowel music and variations in *tempo:*

> Why do we longer live (ah, why live we so long?)
> Whose better days death hath shut up in woe?
> The fairest flower our girlond all among
> Is faded quite and into dust ygoe.
> Sing now, ye shepherds' daughters, sing no moe
>   The songs that Colin made you in her praise,
>   But into weeping turn your wanton lays,
>   O heavy hearse.
> Now is time to die.   Nay, time was long ygoe,
>   O careful verse.   [careful: sorrowful]

The short lines "O heavy hearse" and "O careful verse" are repeated as a refrain at the end of each stanza.

The December eclogue is an imitation of Marot's *Eclogue au*

Roy, in which the poet looks back over his poetic career. It is suited to the time of the year, the poet reviewing the change from the springtime of his days to the present time:

> So now my year draws to his latter term,
> My spring is spent, my summer burnt up quite.
> My harvest hastes to stir up winter stern,
> And bids him claim with rigorous rage his right.
> So now he storms with many a sturdy stour,
> So now his blustring blast each coast doth scour.

So ends this varied collection of eclogues in which Spenser tried out his genius and presented himself to the public as England's New Poet. Technically, they are of the very greatest interest: the thirteen different verse forms which Spenser includes in the twelve eclogues (two of them new to English verse and five Spenser's own invention) show what English verse craftsmanship was capable of in 1579, and they also point forward to later developments. But besides their importance for the craft of English verse, they are important for drawing together traditions from the golden age of medieval English poetry, from the Latin and Greek classics, and from the Renaissance literature of Italy and France, and domiciling them happily in English poetry, where they were to remain for three centuries. We see here, too, Spenser's Protestant idealism, something of his neo-Platonic philosophy, and his high claims for poetry. All of these elements were to combine later more richly and subtly in *The Faerie Queene.*

It is appropriate, and not merely a matter of historical convenience, to see all Spenser's earlier work in the perspective provided by *The Faerie Queene,* which is the culmination toward which Spenser was always moving and the great synthesis of themes and influences which the Elizabethan age had been awaiting. Spenser was well fitted, both by temperament and education, to absorb and to handle creatively the moral and intellectual currents of his time. At the Merchant Taylors' school, then presided over by Richard Mulcaster, a scholar with all the Renaissance enthusiasm for education and for the new ideal of the perfect gentleman, and at Cambridge, where he formed a lasting friendship with the scholar and critic Gabriel Harvey, who was both Puritan and Humanist, he came into contact with the kind of scholarship and enthusiasms to which his own high idealism responded immediately. Spenser's combination of Italian neo-Platonism with English Protestantism, his imaginative handling of his own very considerable scholarship, his responsiveness to the challenge and excitement of his age, reflect

the interaction of his education and environment with his temperament. He was never the complete courtier, for place-seeking at
Elizabeth's court was hardly in accordance with his own concept
of the perfect Christian gentleman, and besides, his Puritanism led
him to oppose aspects of Elizabeth's compromise between the
extremes of Protestantism and Catholicism; his failure to secure a
higher government position than that of a civil servant in Ireland,
where he spent most of his life from 1580 until his death in 1599,
or a more substantial governmental recognition of his claims than a
pension of fifty pounds a year, is not surprising. But he became a
friend and admirer of Sir Philip Sidney, whom, together with so
many of his contemporaries, he regarded as the beau ideal of knighthood and courtesy, and was an active participant in the most significant literary discussions of his time. And much of his "occasional"
writing deals, either directly or indirectly, with the contemporary
scene. Indeed, he never withdrew from contemporary religious and
political controversies into an unreal world of the imagination: he
was always concerned with the problems of his day, as well as with
broader issues, and *The Faerie Queene* itself is an allegorical commentary on the religious, political, and social scene as well as a
more general poetic exploration of the nature of virtue.

Spenser's confident entry as the New Poet with *The Shepherd's
Calendar* was not immediately followed up by anything spectacular.
The first three books of *The Faerie Queene* were not published until
1590, and books four to six appeared in 1596, but in the interval he
had written a variety of other verse of varying degrees of high
seriousness. A volume of minor poems appeared in 1591, entitled
Complaints: Containing sundry small Poems of the World's Vanity.
This contains "The Ruins of Time," an elegiac poem written in slow-
moving rhyme royal: its structure is borrowed from du Bellay's
"Antiquités de Rome," and its theme combines the general medieval
ubi sunt motif with reflections on the deaths of the Earl of Leicester,
Sir Philip Sidney, and Sir Francis Walsingham: there is also the
notion that poetry can confer immortality. "The Ruins of Time" is
an uneven poem, which shows signs of having been put together in
haste; but the verse is never out of control, and there are passages
of richly musical elegy. "The Tears of the Muses" is the second of
the *Complaints:* written in a stanza rhyming *ababcc*, it is more
satirical than elegiac in tone and laments the decay of the arts and
other abuses of the time in a rather mechanical manner. Each of the
nine Muses speaks her complaint, and the whole apparatus is somewhat old-fashioned for a New Poet: it probably represents fairly
early work. More interesting is the third poem in the collection,

"Virgil's Gnat," a lively rendering in *ottava rima* of the Latin *"Culex,"* an epyllion or little epic attributed to Virgil. But by far the most interesting poem in the book is "Mother Hubbard's Tale," a skillful and spirited satire on contemporary affairs in the form of a beast fable. Chaucerian in tone, with the rhymed couplets moving in a deliberately conversational cadence, this vigorous attack on abuses in economic, ecclesiastical, court, and government affairs, shows what Spenser could do when he kept his eye sharply on the contemporary English scene. Here is a very different poet from the author of *The Faerie Queene:*

> But if thee list unto the Court to throng,
> And there to hunt after the hopéd prey,
> Then must thou thee dispose another way.
> For there thou needs must learn to laugh, to lie,
> To face, to forge, to scoff, to company,
> To crouch, to please, to be a beetle stock
> Of thy great master's will, to scorn or mock;
> So may'st thou chance mock out a Benefice,
> Unless thou canst one conjure by device,
> Or cast a figure for a bishopric,
> And if one could, it were but a school-trick.

This links the accents of Chaucer with those found in the satires of Dryden and Pope.

The *Complaints* volume also contains some translations from Marot and du Bellay of no great interest in themselves, and the charming and sprightly "Muiopotomos, or The Fate of the Butterfly," a mock-heroic account in *ottava rima* of the capture and destruction of a beautiful butterfly by a baleful spider: it may or not have an allegorical meaning. The same year, Spenser published *Daphnaida: An Elegy upon the Death of the Noble and Virtuous Douglas Howard, Daughter and Heir of Henry Lord Howard, Viscount Byndon, and Wife of Arthur Gorges, Esquire*, a formal piece in a stanza which chimes interestingly in a rhyme scheme *ababcbc*. The model appears to have been Chaucer's *Book of the Duchess*, but Spenser's style is more rhetorical and his verse more highly wrought. *Colin Clout's Come Home Again*, published in 1595, is one of the freshest, most personal, and most attractive of Spenser's occasional poems. It tells, through a simple and easily penetrated pastoral allegory, of Sir Walter Ralegh's visit to Spenser in Ireland and Spenser's subsequent visit to London with Ralegh; there he was graciously received by Queen Elizabeth, but realized that court life was not for him, and he returned to Ireland. The poem is decasyllabic quatrains with alternating rhymes; occasionally the rhymes are repeated or otherwise linked in successive quatrains, with a highly musical effect. The ease and flow of the style, the combination of the autobiographical and the formal, the wholly successful mixture of the pastoral with the courtly, the rustic with the artificial, constitute one of Spenser's happiest attempts at synthesis.

The premature death of Sir Philip Sidney at the battle of Zutphen in 1586 called forth the usual spate of elegies, and Spenser's contribution was a pastoral elegy entitled "Astrophel," an uninspired performance in stanzas rhyming *ababcc*, modeled on Bion's lament for Adonis. That the death of so cherished a friend should have inspired such a highly conventional piece of work is an interesting commentary on the place of convention in Elizabethan art, while the fact that the poem is dedicated to Sidney's widow while referring in some detail to Sidney's love for "Stella," traditionally identified with Penelope Devereux, Lady Rich, who did not return Sidney's love, poses a problem in the relation between art and life that the modern mind finds hard to solve. The problem reminds us of how purely formal the notion as well as the handling of courtly love could be in Elizabethan times (and presumably earlier) and warns us against interpreting Spenser's allegorizing habit too naïvely.

A more interesting example of Spenser's handling of a convention of his time is provided by his *Amoretti*, love sonnets in the Petrarchan mode so dear to the Elizabethans. To what extent these sonnets celebrate his love for Elizabeth Boyle, his marriage to whom he celebrated in his "Epithalamion," is an unprofitable question: they tell the story of the poet's wooing of a mistress who at first rebuffed him, then relented and returned his love, and finally, as a result of some unhappy incident, turned against him again. If the "Epithalamion" represents the true end of this story, then we must suppose that the lady changed her mind yet again, and permanently this time. But again we must remember the place of the sonnet sequence in Elizabethan poetry and the place of convention in Elizabethan art. Spenser's sonnets may well have been a graceful Petrarchan exercise with a constantly shifting relationship to his personal experience. Just as in *The Faerie Queene* the allegory keeps shifting in perspective, as it were, at one point logically worked out in every detail and in another yielding to the psychological realism of the characters who are given emotions and actions beyond their allegorical role, so in other phases of his work Spenser was in the habit of varying the relation of his art to his life. A sonnet sequence was a formal handling of language which tested the skill and craftsmanship of the poet, and it was to be appreciated for the poetic life kindled within it, not for its autobiographical revelations. "Sincerity" in art does not mean autobiographical accuracy, but a full

and subtle exploitation of the artist's medium so that the poem
creates as it moves its own world of experience. That world, of course,
does have reference to and does illuminate the real world of human
experience, but not necessarily through a direct projection of the
poet's autobiography. We should bear these obvious points in mind
when we read the Elizabethan sonnet sequences, whether Spenser's,
Sidney's, Daniel's, Drayton's, or Shakespeare's.

The eighty-nine sonnets that make up the *Amoretti* move with a
limpid flow and show a remarkably consistent level of craftsmanship,
though they never rise to some overwhelming moment like Drayton's
famous "Since there's no help, come let us kiss and part," Sidney's
"Leave me, O love which reachest but to dust," or some of Shakespeare's. There are, naturally, many echoes of Petrarch, and some of
Tasso, Ronsard, Desportes, and others. The usual, though not in-
variable, rhyme-scheme is *ababbcbccdcdee*, with the first twelve
lines deftly linked by rhyme and movement and separated from
the final couplet. The best known of the sonnets of the *Amoretti*
is a fair sample of the controlled flow Spenser achieves in these
poems:

> One day I wrote her name upon the strand,
>   But came the waves and washéd it away:
>   Again I wrote it with a second hand,
>   But came the tide and made my pains his prey.
> Vain man, said she, that dost in vain assay
>   A mortal thing so to immortalize,
>   For I myself shall liké to this decay,
>   And eke my name be wipéd out likewise.
> Not so, (quoth I) let baser things devise
>   To die in dust, but you shall live by fame;
>   My verse your virtues rare shall eternize,
>   And in the heavens write your glorious name.
> Where, whenas death shall all the world subdue,
>   Our love shall live, and later life renew.

The "Epithalamion" is an altogether more remarkable piece of
work, and one of Spenser's highest achievements. This celebration
of his own wedding (which took place in Ireland, probably in 1594)
roused all Spenser's genius for enriching and transfiguring bare
fact by poetic imagination and by the appropriate use of imagery
and of rhythms. Convention and personal feeling here find their
perfect meeting, and it is testimony to the way in which the whole
tradition of European poetry had become part of Spenser's very
personality that he should exploit that tradition most fully, most

happily, and most originally when he came to express one of the supreme moments of his own life. The elaborate verse paragraph derives from the Italian *canzone*, but the handling of the melody, the use of the refrain, the adaptation of a lyrical poem to a narrative structure, the blending of descriptive details with the celebratory mood, the mingling of elements from Catullus, from Chaucer's *Parliament of Fowls*, from Irish setting, English folklore, and from classical tradition, shows original poetic genius in control of its richly diversified materials to a degree that English poetry had not yet seen. The architectonic quality both of the individual stanza and of the poem as a whole is remarkable, and the chiming refrain subtly varied yet sufficiently the same to bind the poem together with its incantatory repetition is something to marvel at. Here is the New Poetry reaching to heights of complex lyrical expression that were not before possible in English.

The narrative basis is simply the story of the wedding day: first the poet's announcement of his subject, then an account of the preparation for the wedding and the bidding of the guests, then a summons to the nymphs of the local woods, streams, and mountains to bring garlands for the bride and sing her praise, then dawn and the awakening of the bride. With the bride's appearance the verse takes on a new richness and a new excitement: her progress is described in language that echoes the Psalms:

> Lo where she comes along with portly pace,
> Like Phoebe from her chamber of the East,
> Arising forth to run her mighty race,
> Clad all in white, that 'seems a virgin best.
> So well it her beseems that ye would ween
> Some angel she had been.
> Her long loose yellow locks like golden wire,
> Sprinkled with pearl, and pearling flowers atween,
> Do like a golden mantle her attire,
> And, being crownéd with a girland green,
> Seem like some maiden Queen.
> Her modest eyes, abashéd to behold
> So many gazers as on her do stare,
> Upon the lowly ground affixéd are.
> Ne dare lift up her countenance too bold,
> But blush to hear her praises sung so loud,
> So far from being proud.
> Nathless do ye still loud her praises sing,
> That all the woods may answer and your echo ring.

The bride's beauty, both physical and spiritual, is now praised, and by this time the wedding procession has reached the church, and the bride enters to the sound of the organ:

> Open the temple gates unto my love,
> Open them wide that she may enter in, . . .

There follow the ceremony, the homecoming, the poet longing for the end of day—

> Ah! when will this long weary day have end,
> And lend me leave to come unto my love?
> How slowly do the hours their numbers spend!
> How slowly does sad Time his feathers move!
> Haste thee, O fairest planet, to thy home,
> Within the Western foam. . . .

The bride's attendants are dismissed, night descends, and the poet invokes peace and blessing on his bride. The moon rises and looks in at the window, and she too is invoked to bless the marriage; Juno and Genius are asked to grant the blessing of fruitfulness, and the poem ends on a note of calm yet eloquent benediction, with a seven-line coda in which the poet commends his song to his love.

This is poetic celebration carried as far as it can go: it is Spenser at the very height of its genius. Only quotation of the whole poem could demonstrate to those who are not familiar with it its extraordinary artistry, for each part gains immensely by contributing to the total movement. Not quite so rich, but equally brilliant in imagery and movement, is the "Prothalamion," a wedding poem written for the double wedding of Lady Elizabeth and Lady Catherine Somerset, daughters of the Earl of Worcester, to Henry Guilford and William Petre in 1596. Here again we have the massive and musical stanza with its concluding refrain ("Sweet Thames, run softly, till I end my song"), the adroitly varied line lengths, the movement from a hushed picture of early morning by the Thames to the ceremonious entry of the two swans who symbolize the two bridegrooms. The "Prothalamion" is more deliberately stylized than the "Epithalamion"; it has a tapestry quality, an almost heraldic tone; yet the personal note is effectively blended with this, and the poet himself is the vividly presented observer of the ceremonious scene. The benediction pronounced on the swans by one of the nymphs has a grave stateliness unsurpassed in English poetry:

> Ye gentle birds, the world's fair ornament,
> And heaven's glory, whom this happy hour

Doth lead unto your lovers' blissful bower,
Joy may you have and gentle heart's content
Of your love's couplement;
And let fair Venus, that is queen of love,
With her heart-quelling son upon you smile,
Whose smile, they say, hath virtue to remove
All love's dislike, and friendship's faulty guile
For ever to assoil.
Let endless peace your steadfast hearts accord,
And blesséd plenty wait upon your board,
And let your bed with pleasures chaste abound,
That fruitful issue may to you afford,
Which may your foes confound,
And make your joys redound,
Upon your bridal day, which is not long:
   Sweet Thames, run softly, till I end my song.

In 1596 Spenser published his *Four Hymns,* the first two, in honor of Love and of Beauty, being early works, and the latter two, in honor of Heavenly Love and of Heavenly Beauty, being written much later. These hymns have been a favorite study of those interested in the influence of Platonism on Spenser, for they reflect that influence more explicitly and consistently than any other of his shorter poems; they are not otherwise of any great interest, for, while displaying Spenser's usual control over his medium and rising occasionally to a fine rhetorical eloquence, they do not exhibit any new powers or outstanding poetic qualities. The renewed interest in Plato during the Renaissance is a commonplace of intellectual history; Spenser had met it at Cambridge and he had met it, too, in the works of the Italian neo-Platonists, in Giordano Bruno's treatise on love, *Degli Heroici Furori,* in Marsilio Ficino's Latin translation of Plato, his treatise on Plato's doctrine of immortality, and his commentary on Plato's *Symposium,* in Castiglione's essay on the perfect courtier, *Il Cortegiano,* translated into English by Sir Thomas Hoby in 1561, and in many other works. The Platonic doctrine that one ascends from a specific embodiment of beauty to a contemplation of the idea of beauty as an end in itself, this idea being divine and its contemplation being a religious activity, was elaborated by the Italian Platonists in a variety of ways. It was also often grafted on to the medieval notion of courtly love to which at first sight it appears so antithetical (for no medieval courtly lover would have considered it proper to move from contemplation of his mistress's beauty to contemplation of beauty in others and then of beauty in the abstract). Medieval courtly love, Platonism, and Christianity were blended in many interesting ways by Renaissance writers, and Spenser's combination of Protestant idealism, Platonism, and native amorousness represented his own version of a synthesis common enough in his day.

In the "Hymn in Honour of Love" Spenser takes numerous ideas from the *Symposium*, the *Phaedrus*, and from the Italian neo-Platonists to present an account of the importance and significance of love, its loftiness and exalting capacity, the difference between true love and mere lust, and the necessarily long and arduous road to the enjoyment of true love. Similarly, in the "Hymn in Honour of Beauty" he celebrates true beauty, which is more than surface appearance, but the physical reflection of something much more profound and universal. In the former poem he declares:

> For Love is lord of truth and loyalty,
> Lifting himself out of the lowly dust
> On golden plumes up to the purest sky
> Above the reach of loathly, sinful lust
> Whose base affect through cowardly distrust
> Of his weak wings dare not to heaven fly,
> But like a moldwarp in the earth doth lie.

And in the latter:

> So every spirit, as it is most pure,
> And hath in it the more of heavenly light,
> So it the fairer body doth procure
> To habit in, and it more fairly dight
> With cheerful grace and amiable sight.
> For of the soul the body form doth take:
> For soul is form and doth the body make.

Beside this we might put the following passage from Hoby's translation of Castiglione:

I say that beauty cometh of God and is like a circle, the goodness whereof is the centre. And therefore, as there can be no circle without a centre, no more can beauty be without goodness. Whereupon doth very seldom an ill soul dwell in a beautiful body. And therefore is the outward beauty a true sign of the inward goodness, and in bodies this comeliness is imprinted more or less, as it were, for a mark of the soul, whereby she is outwardly known: as in trees, in which the beauty of the buds giveth a testimony of the goodness of the fruit.

In the hymns of Heavenly Love and Heavenly Beauty, Spenser implicitly repudiates the Platonic notion of the ladder, expresses regret for his earlier celebrations of earthly love and beauty, and speaks in a specifically Christian manner of divine love made manifest by the career on earth of Christ, and of the beauty and wisdom of God which infinitely transcends anything visible on earth. Calvin's *Institutes* and the Hebrew Wisdom literature are influences here alongside more obvious Christian sources and the Italian neo-Platonists, and the tone is far from Platonic in spite of Platonic echoes. These poems illustrate how literary and intellectual fashions affected Spenser's style and subject matter, but Spenser's genius was not for explicitly philosophical poetry, and the hymns are of more interest to the student of Renaissance thought than to the historian of English poetry.

Of Spenser's toying with the idea of writing English verse in classical quantitative measure instead of in traditional English metrical forms, all that need be said is that this interest in the possibilities of writing classical verse in English was an inevitable part of Humanist enthusiasm for the classics and for imitating the achievements of classical literature; Spenser's letters to Gabriel Harvey show the two writers exchanging views and experiments which had no effect on Spenser's poetic achievement. The suspicion of rhyme as a barbarous nonclassical invention was another phase of the same Humanist attitude, which had more fruitful results than the interest in classical measures for it led to blank verse and, in particular, led Milton to choose blank verse for his *Paradise Lost*. But Spenser needed rhyme, which he handled more richly and musically than any other English poet, and his classicizing was a brief and transient phase of his poetic career.

All Spenser's earlier poetry is in a sense but preparation and exercise for his unfinished epic, *The Faerie Queene*, one of the few great inclusive attempts made by an English poet to bring together in one rich pattern all the various strands of civilization with which he was acquainted. Drawing on the medieval allegorical tradition in both its secular and religious forms, on medieval romance, classical epic, Aristotelian ethics, Plato and Italian neo-Platonism, Renaissance Humanism, Protestant idealism, Malory, the Italian epic, English history, geography and folklore, Elizabethan patriotism and political thought, and almost every current of European thought and expression and convention which had reached the sixteenth century, he constructed his comprehensive poetic vision of *la condition humaine* as it was, in a context of ideal suggestion of what it should be. His immediate model was Ariosto's *Orlando Furioso,* which, as he told Gabriel Harvey, he hoped to "overgo," though his tone is quite different from Ariosto's and he lacks the Italian's comic exuberance and astonishing fertility of lively invention. The Italian epic provided the mold into which he could pour his serious and complex vision:

the vision itself was Spenser's own, for all his use of older traditions. Spenser wrote a letter to Sir Walter Ralegh (prefixed to the edition of 1590) "expounding his whole intention in the course of this work," in which he declared that "the general end . . . of all the book is to fashion a gentleman or noble person in virtuous and gentle discipline." He pointed out that he had learned from Homer, Virgil, Ariosto, and Tasso, "by example of which excellent Poets I labour to portray in Arthur, before he was King, the image of a brave knight, perfected in the twelve private moral virtues, as Aristotle hath devised, the which is the purpose of these first twelve books, which if I find to be well accepted, I may be perhaps encouraged to frame the other part of politic virtues in his person, after that he came to the king." The letter continued:

In that Faery Queen I mean glory in my general intention, but in my particular I conceive the most excellent and glorious person of our soveraine the Queen, and her kingdom in Faery land. And yet in some places else I do otherwise shadow her. For considering she beareth two persons, the one of a most royal Queen or Empress, the other of a most virtuous and beautiful Lady, this latter part in some places I do express in Belphoebe, . . . So in the person of Prince Arthur I set forth magnificence [the Aristotelian *megalopsychia, magnanimitas*, greatness of soul] in particular, which virtue for that (according to Aristotle and the rest) it is the perfection of all the rest, and containeth in it them all, therefore in the whole course I mention the deeds of Arthur applicable to that virtue which I write of in that book. But of the xii other virtues I make xii other knights the patrons, for the more variety of the history. Of which these three books [i.e., the first three books, published in 1590] contain three, the first of the knight of the Redcross, in whom I express Holiness; the second of Sir Guyon, in whom I set forth Temperance; the third of Britomartis, a lady knight, in whom I picture Chastity.

He goes on to explain that he begins *in medias res* in proper epic fashion, and since only three books are here presented he had better explain what has happened before the events there narrated (an explanation which he intended, again in proper epic fashion, to unfold in a suitable retrospect in a later book). "The beginning . . . of my history, if it were to be told by an Historiographer, should be the twelfth book, which is the last, where I devise that the Faery Queen kept her annual feast xii days, upon which xii several days the occasions of the xii several adventures happened, which being undertaken by xii several knights are in these xii books severally handled and discoursed." And he goes on to give a brief account of how the adventures of the Redcross Knight, of Sir Guyon, and of Britomart first started. And "many other adventures are intermeddled, but rather as accidents than intendments."

Of the total plan of twenty-four books, Spenser only completed

six. The first three were published in 1590, and books four, five, and
six in 1596. In 1609, ten years after Spenser's death, a folio edition
was published containing the first six books and a fragment of book
VII entitled "Two Cantos of Mutability." *The Faerie Queene* is thus
very far from complete, a mere fragment of an epic. And in a work
of such complex design incompleteness is bound to present difficulties of understanding and interpretation. Nevertheless, the work as
we have it is noble and impressive, more than long enough to enable
us to assess its quality and significance—long enough, indeed, to have
frightened off generations of readers who have been content to judge
the work by brief extracts or merely by reputation. It remains one of
the great poems of the English language; but its greatness is of a
rather special kind.

The notion that *The Faerie Queene* consists of an endless series of
pictorial stanzas, each slow moving and musical, with an optional
allegorical significance which all readers since Spenser's time have
preferred to ignore, is still common enough to require correcting.
The surface of the epic consists, as Professor C. S. Lewis has well
put it, of "interlocked stories of chivalrous adventure in a world of
marvels," and it is this surface which it shares with the Italian epic.
The background is an indeterminate world of plains, woods, castles,
dens, islands, and shores, a deliberate dream world through which
we watch the characters move—

> And forth they pass, with pleasure forward led, . . .

> So forth they passed, and all the way they spent
> Discoursing of her dreadful late distress, . . .

> So forth he fared, as now befell, on foot, . . .

> So forth they pass, a well consorted pair, . . .

> So forth they rowéd, and that Ferryman
> With his stiff oars did brush the sea so strong, . . .

> So as they travelled, lo they gan espy
> An arméd knight toward them gallop fast, . . .

> Thus as she her recomforted, she spied
> Where far away one all in armour bright
> With hasty gallop towards her did ride; . . .

We watch, as it were in a trance, as characters approach and recede
across this magic landscape. The very opening of the first canto of
Book I strikes the note of observed adventure:

> A Gentle Knight was pricking on the plain,
> Y-clad in mighty arms and silver shield,

Wherein old dints of deep wounds did remain,
The cruel marks of many a bloody field;
Yet arms till that time never did he wield.
His angry steed did chide his foaming bit,
As much disdaining to the curb to yield.
Full jolly knight he seemed, and fair did sit,
As one for knightly jousts and fierce encounters fit.

Yet the poem is not a sequence of pictorial scenes, each with its moral and religious and political allegorical significance. The shifts in tone and tempo, the range from homely realism to liturgical solemnity or spiritual exaltation, the deliberate alterations in perspective and in levels of probability, and above all the flexibility of the allegory which mutates from simple personification to oblique suggestion in accordance with the needs of the narrative, the interest of the characters and the degree to which the poet is approaching or moving away from a climactic moment in the unfolding of his complex ethico-religious meaning—all this gives the poem variety and liveliness and prevents that aimless drowsiness which somehow so many people have come to associate with Spenser. Thus in Book I the Redcross Knight, who is Holiness, accompanied by Una, who is Truth, becomes involved in a series of adventures which suggest (at a variety of levels) how man's pursuit of holiness can be hindered by error, hypocrisy, false devotion, and so on. At the same time the Redcross Knight is also Everyman, facing the ordinary temptations of this world, and needing the help of Grace (Prince Arthur) as well as Truth in order to lead the good life and attain holiness. The Redcross Knight both represents a quality (holiness) and represents man in search of that quality. (Spenser is also talking about religious conditions in England, putting the Protestant against the Catholic view of the good life, and bringing in many contemporary references. But this is unimportant.) The adventures, as well as having meaning on these levels, also have their own interest and their own ethical suggestiveness, just as the incidental characters may or may not have human qualities which enrich the story psychologically and ethically as well as their more formal allegorical significance, which again may vary in its degree of literalness. The monster Error, which the Redcross Knight slays, is described as "most loathsome, filthy, foul and full of vile disdain," prolific of her poisonous young, and, in the midst of the fight, vomiting forth books and papers together with lumps of foul flesh and "loathly frogs and toads." The description is vigorous, skillful, and thoroughly "Spenserian" in the popular sense; the allegory is simple to the point of childishness. Then Spenser goes on to describe how the knight was harassed by the monster's "cursed spawn":

The same so sore annoyéd has the knight,
That wellnigh chokéd with the deadly stink
His forces fail, he can no longer fight.
Whose courage when the fiend perceived to shrink
She pouréd forth out of her hellish sink
Her fruitful curséd spawn of serpents small,
Deforméd monsters, foul and black as ink,
Which swarming all about his legs did crawl,
And him encumbered sore, but could not hurt at all.

This is vigorous and effective; both the literal and the allegorical meanings are perfectly clear. But the next stanza changes the tone:

As gentle Shepherd in sweet eventide
When ruddy Phoebus gins to welk in west,   [welk: fade]
High on an hill, his flock to viewen wide,
Marks which do bite their hasty supper best,
A cloud of cumbrous gnats do him molest,
All striving to infix their feeble stings,
That from their noyance he nowhere can rest,
But with his clownish hands their tender wings
He brusheth oft, and oft doth mar their murmurings.

The background of pastoral life introduced here in the simile is reminiscent of some of Milton's similes in *Paradise Lost,* where he provides relief from the acrid atmosphere of hell by a simile which invokes one of the simpler and more elemental activities of men in the fields or on the sea. The sudden and brief metamorphosis of the Redcross Knight battling with a cursed spawn of serpents into a shepherd brushing off the innocent but annoying gnats brings in a more normal human world and establishes, as it were, a middle term between the world of chivalric action on the one hand and the world of ethical and religious ideals on the other. Because it is introduced as a simile it does not interrupt or spoil the force of the incident; but it humanizes it, and reminds us of the everyday world in which our ethical problems are to be encountered and solved.

This is a fairly obvious example of a shift in tone in *The Faerie Queene.* Spenser can shift through a much wider range of tones. Still confining ourselves to Book I, we can pick out in a short space a great variety of kinds of expression. There is the note of romantic adventure pure and simple:

At length they chanced to meet upon their way
An aged Sire, in long black weeds yclad.

There is the pastoral:

> A little lowly Hermitage it was,
> Down in a dale, hard by a forest's side.

There is the popular satirical:

> He told of Saints and Popes, and evermore
> He strewed an *Ave Mary* after and before.

There is the mythological-romantic:

> There Tethys his wet bed
> Doth ever wash, and Cynthia still doth steep
> In silver dew his ever-drooping head,
> While sad Night over him her mantle black doth spread.

There is the homely proverbial:

> A dram of sweet is worth a pound of sour.

There is the moralizing, religious note:

> Ay me, how many perils do enfold
> The righteous man, to make him daily fall!
> Were not, that heavenly grace doth him uphold,
> And steadfast truth acquit him out of all.

There is the poetic-proverbial (but it is worth remembering that these lines are spoken to entrap the Redcross Knight into despair and suicide):

> Sleep after toil, port after stormy seas,
> Ease after war, death after life does greatly please.

There is the lofty chivalric:

> O goodly golden chain, wherewith yfere
> The virtues linkéd are in lovely wise,
> And noble minds of yore alliéd were
> In brave pursuit of chivalrous emprise.

Perhaps the most effective display of Spenser's range is found toward the end of Book I, when he is describing the Redcross Knight's slaying of the dragon:

> So down he fell, and forth his life did breathe,
> That vanished into smoke and cloudës swift;
> So down he fell, that th'earth him underneath
> Did groan, as feeble so great load to lift;
> So down he fell, as an huge rocky clift,

> Whose false foundation waves have washed away,
> With dreadful poise is from the mainland rift
> And, rolling down, great Neptune doth dismay.
> So down he fell, and like an heaped mountain lay.

This is formal and stylized. But after this comes:

> And after, all the rascal many ran,
> Heapéd together in rude rabblement,
> To see the face of that victorious man,
> Whom all admiréd, as from heaven sent,
> And gazed upon with gaping wonderment.
> But when they came where that dead Dragon lay,
> Stretched on the ground in monstrous large extent,
> The sight with idle fear did them dismay,
> Ne durst approach him nigh, to touch, or once assay.

> Some feared and fled; some feared and well it feigned.
> One that would wiser seem than all the rest
> Warned him not touch, for yet perhaps remained
> Some longering life within his hollow breast,
> Or in his womb might lurk some hidden nest
> Of many Dragonets, his fruitful seed.
> Another said that in his eyes did rest
> Yet sparkling fire, and bad thereof take heed;
> Another said, he saw him move his eyes indeed.

> One mother, when as her foolhardy child
> Did come too near and with his talons play,
> Half dead through fear her little babe reviled
> And to her gossips gan in counsel say:
> "How can I tell but that his talons may
> Yet scratch my son or rend his tender hand?"
> So diversly themselves in vain they fray,
> While some, more bold, to measure him nigh stand
> To prove how many acres he did spread of land.

This is shrewd comic realism, very different indeed from Spenser's high romantic strain. One could multiply examples of Spenser's different styles indefinitely. The sudden questioning with which he opens the eighth canto of Book II, for example, startles by its difference from what has gone before:

> And is there care in heaven? And is there love
> In heavenly spirits to these creatures base,
> That may compassion of their evils move?
> There is: else much more wretched were the case
> Of men, than beasts.

In the same canto we also get the following:

> Horribly then he gan to rage and rail,
> Cursing his gods and himself damning deep:
> Als when his brother saw the red blood rail
> Adown so fast, and all his armour steep,
> For very felness loud he gan to weep,
> And said: "Catiff, curse on thy cruel hand
> That twice hath sped; yet shall it not thee keep
> From the third brunt of this my fatal brand:
> Lo, where the dreadful Death behind thy back doth stand."

Book II is concerned with the adventures of Sir Guyon, who represents Temperance, and at the same time represents Everyman tempted from health of soul and body by various kinds of excess and disease. The allegory weaves in and out of the story easily and effectively, with images of health in man and in nature opposing images of illness and perversion. The House of Temperance, "in which doth sober Alma dwell," represents the human body ruled by the soul, and its defense of the health of both against the besiegers has a clear enough allegorical meaning. The various kinds of smoldering passion which threaten bodily and spiritual health are magnificently embodied in such characters as Furor, Strife, Pyrocles, and Atin (some representing the forces that incite to rage and similar passions, others exhibiting the result of such incitement on human behavior and attitude—as always, the allegory works easily on several different levels). But bodily and spiritual health is more subtly threatened by false pleasures than by anger and grief—

> A harder lesson, to learn continence
> In joyous pleasure than in grievous pain,
> For sweetness doth allure the weaker sense
> So strongly, that uneathes it can refrain   [uneathes: scarcely]
> From that which feeble nature covets fain;
> But grief and wrath, that be her enemies,
> And foes of life she better can restrain—

and the latter part of the book deals with these subtler temptations. The temptation of Mammon is a magnificent set piece, and the final victory of temperance over her foes, followed by the destruction of the Bower of Bliss, which represents nature corrupted by the misuse of art, enables Spenser to pull out all the stops.

Book II illustrates clearly the way in which Spenser combines his Christian ideals with his neo-Platonism and his humanism. Nature itself is good, and even Phaedria, the laughing girl with the boat who represents frivolous mirth, is not evil but merely empty; growth, nurture, fertility, satisfying and fruitful sexual activity, temperance, health, and virtue are on one side, and opposed to them are every kind of distorting passion, excess, corruption, disease, perversion, and prurience. There is a Greek as well as a Christian ideal at work here, though how far Spenser is successful in combining them into a consistent Christian humanism is perhaps doubtful, as it is with Milton also. Book III, dealing with Britomart, who represents chastity, and Book IV, ostensibly dealing with Cambel and Telamond (representing male friendship) but in fact developing the general theme of love and its different varieties and continuing the stories of Britomart, Amoret, Scudamour, Florimel, and the other characters who embody or suggest the varieties of real love and their relation to false love, reach out into a complex suggestiveness. Spenser's chastity is not virginity but lawful wedded love, which is contrasted with adulterous courtly love represented by Malecasta and Busirane. The development of the story of the allegory in these two books is rich and fascinating: Spenser is combining views from Plato's *Symposium* with elements from the courtly-love tradition and from a variety of other sources to create an ideal of true love against which he sets the barren, demoralizing, perverse, enslaving love of the courtly romances. He splits the courtly-love ideal in half, dismissing its fruitless afflictions and self-pityings but retaining its high passion, and associates the half he retains with Christian marriage. The characters here operate at several different levels, and it is profitless to try to pin down the precise resemblances and differences of significance between, say, Britomart, Amoret, Belphoebe, and Florimel. What is required here is for the reader to surrender himself to the story; if he does this, he will find the picture of the varieties of true love in man and nature opposed to love's perversion building itself up cumulatively as the adventures and descriptions unfold. The two books are rich in set descriptive pieces which teem with moral and psychological suggestions.

Book V is more restricted in theme: it deals with Sir Artegal, who represents Justice, and the political allegory here more than once comes to the foreground, to the distress of the modern reader, who neither agrees with the Elizabethan concept of justice nor retains any interest in the political problems of Spenser's Europe. The sense of the importance of order, both in nature and in human society, and the necessity of everything and every one knowing his proper place and performing his proper function, is strong throughout the book. Spenser provides the clue to the Elizabethan view of the vice which

Marlowe made central in *Tamburlaine* and with which Shakespeare, too, was fascinated:

> O sacred hunger of ambitious minds
> And impotent desire of men to reign,
> Whom neither dread of God, that devils binds,
> Nor laws of men, that common weals contain,
> Nor bands of nature, that wild beasts restrain,
> Can keep from outrage and from doing wrong,
> Where they may hope a kingdom to obtain.
> No faith so firm, no trust can be so strong,
> No love so lasting then, that may enduren long.

The hero of Book VI is Sir Calidore, representing Courtesy, and in this charmingly varied section of *The Faerie Queene* Spenser explores the concept of "gentilesse" as developed in the Renaissance by such writers as Castiglione. Everything is here, from Christian humility to gentlemanly good manners, from pastoral simplicity to knightly honor, and the various threats to the ideal of true courtesy, from brutality to over-sophistication, are also presented. The meaning here emerges from the behavior of the characters rather than through formal allegory; the characters tend more to illustrate than to represent or suggest the qualities they stand for as they do in the other books. The pace is fairly slow, and the writing both assured and relaxed. The two Cantos of Mutability present, with an impressive combination of masquelike pageantry and rich philosophic reflection, a discussion of the relation between change and order, between the principle of alteration and decay and the principle of Nature, the ever renewing heart of things. A debate between Mutability and Nature concludes the cantos, and the poet's reflections on its meaning proceed for only two stanzas before the poem as we have it comes to an end. It is clear only that Spenser is concerned to find the relation between time (over which Mutability rules) and eternity, where "all things firmly stay."

At intervals throughout *The Faerie Queene*, related in a variety of ways to the action, Spenser strikes the patriotic note. English and Welsh history and geography, genealogies going back to Brut, the Trojan founder of the British race, and the mythology of the English countryside presented with a proper sense of what is appropriate to different regions, punctuate the adventures of the various knights and ladies. For all its setting in Faeryland, for all the romantic vagueness of its topography and the immense variety of European sources that lie behind it, *The Faerie Queene* is an essentially English poem, and Spenser exhibits his pride in his country and in his Queen through a host of devices and allusions. *The Faerie Queene* is an English Christian Humanist epic.

The stanza which Spenser invented for his epic, with its carefully chiming rhyme-scheme and concluding alexandrine, is capable of a great variety of effects, and the popular notion that it is less suited for narrative verse than for static pictorial description is not borne out by the way it actually operates in the poem. Spenser does indeed excel in certain kinds of set descriptive piece, but he can vary the speed and movement of the stanza to produce contemplative, discursive, dreamlike, exclamatory, formal, colloquial, satirical, and other styles and moods. His use of deliberately antique word forms, Chaucerian and pseudo-Chaucerian, is largely for purposes of stylization appropriate to a heroic poem, but he can also use older words to give a homely, proverbial effect. Altogether, *The Faerie Queene* is a poem of extraordinary richness and diversity, a remarkable synthesis of Elizabethan culture whose total effect cannot be properly judged because the work was left unfinished but whose quality and splendor can nevertheless be easily discerned. Yet the synthesis was a personal one: the union of chivalric, patriotic, Christian, and Platonic, of medieval and Protestant, of courtly love and Christian marriage, of Italian romance and medieval allegory, of pageantry and philosophy, of shrewd observation and high imagination, was not something that could be handed on unchanged to future poets. The English poets of the period who imitated Spenser imitated only one aspect of his multiple work—his allegory or his topographical patriotic poetry or his pastoralism—and there were more who turned away from him than who followed him. Ben Jonson was right in a sense when he told Drummond of Hawthornden that "Spenser writ no language." It was no imitable language; there was no further road along that way—the way of the allegorical heroic poem deriving its form from the Italian epic—in English literature. Yet Spenser's place in the English poetic tradition is indisputable: he was the first modern poet to exploit the full poetic resources of the English language; he had the highest ambitions for poetry while at the same time retaining a freshness of approach characteristic of the more casual and "occasional" singer. He inspired both Milton and Keats, in very different ways: to the former he was "sage and serious Spenser," England's first epic poet, while to the latter he stood for enchantment and high romance. And to Wordsworth (who considered Spenser— with Chaucer, Shakespeare, and Milton—as an example to be studied and, if possible, equaled) he was

> Sweet Spenser, moving through his clouded heaven
> With the moon's beauty and the moon's soft pace.

"The poets' poet" he has been called: but this does not mean (as is sometimes thought) that his work represents the quintessence of poetic lushness, but rather that, combining so many strands and occupying such a central position in the history of the English poetic tongue, he has continued to arouse the professional interest of other poets. *The Faerie Queene* may be a blind alley in English literary history: but its author remains a figure of the utmost importance to all interested in the poetic handling of the English language and the technique of English verse.

Spenser dedicated *The Shepherd's Calendar* to "the noble and virtuous gentleman most worthy of all titles both of learning and chivalry," Sir Philip Sidney, and addressed his explanatory letter about *The Faerie Queene* to Sir Walter Ralegh. Each of these figures was in his way representative of his time. Sidney (1554–86), whose brief life of thirty-two years ended in a scene of characteristic gallantry after he had been fatally wounded in a minor battle before the city of Zutphen, came as near to achieving the Renaissance ideal of the gentleman as any Englishman ever did; scholar, poet, critic, diplomat, and courtier, he was at once a man of affairs and a high idealist, regarded in his own lifetime as the epitome of knighthood. Ralegh (ca. 1552–1618), less simply attractive in character, shared with Sidney the varied gifts of the Renaissance courtier: his life was more tempestuous than Sidney's, with greater changes of fortune; he had a vigorous mind, in touch with the most advanced thought and thinkers of his day, a restless and active temperament, and real poetic skill.

None of Sidney's work was published during his lifetime, though much of it circulated in manuscript. In 1591, his sonnet-sequence *Astrophel and Stella* appeared. Nine years earlier, the publication of *Hekatompathia, or a Passionate Century of Love* by Thomas Watson, a friend of Sidney's and of other men of letters in the 1580's, attracted new attention to the Petrarchan sonnet and helped to set the fashion for sequences of love sonnets. But only one original sonnet of Watson's in this volume was a poem of fourteen lines of the kind to which we now restrict the term "sonnet": Watson called it a "quatorzain." Further, Sidney's sonnets may well have been written and circulated in manuscript before Watson's collection appeared. At any rate, Sidney had the wider influence and wrote the better poems, and can be said to be largely responsible for the spate of sonnet-sequences that followed the publication of *Astrophel and Stella*. Fulke Greville's *Caelica* (written about 1580 but not published until 1638), Samuel Daniel's *Delia* (1592), Michael Drayton's *Idea's Mirror* (1594), Spenser's *Amoretti* (1595), and Shakespeare's sonnets, which, though not published until 1609, were probably written in the 1590's, are among the more important sonnet-sequences which followed Sidney's, and there were many more by lesser writers, including Henry Constable (*Diana*, 1592), Thomas Lodge (*Phillis*, 1593), Barnaby Barnes (*Parthenophe and Parthenophil*, 1593), and Giles Fletcher (*Licia*, 1593).

Petrarch's sonnets to Laura were, of course, the ultimate inspiration of all these sonnet-sequences, but Ronsard, du Bellay, and other French and Italian poets were also drawn on, often freely. Many of these late Elizabethan and early Jacobean sonnet-sequences are of more interest to the student of literary fashion than to the critic or reader of poetry, and they raise some interesting questions concerning the place of convention in art. A series of sonnets addressed to a single lady, expressing and reflecting on the developing relationship between the poet and his love, can tell a complex and even a dramatic love story, which is what we sometimes get. The story does not have to be literal autobiography, and questions of "sincerity" in this simple sense of the word are hardly relevant. Nevertheless, the best of these sonnets can project a psychological situation with power and originality, in spite of the often routine "conceits" which had become so much a part of the Petrarchan tradition. Of the English Petrarchan sonneteers it can be said, as Johnson said of the "metaphysical" poets of the seventeenth century, that "to write on their plan it was at least necessary to read and think." Indeed, the "conceit" of the Petrarchan sonneteer is not basically different from that of the metaphysical poet—each developing analogies with ingenious logic and subtle wit and making such analogies emblems of an emotional state. But whereas the metaphysical poet combined colloquial vigor and a devastating emotional integrity with their ingenuities, the Petrarchan sonneteer remained on the whole more formal, more rhetorical, and more "sugared."

Sidney's Stella was Penelope Devereux, betrothed to Sidney in her youth; for some reason the engagement was later broken off, and she became the wife of Lord Rich, while Sidney himself married Frances Walsingham in 1583. The 108 sonnets and eleven songs which make up the *Astrophel and Stella* series provide a record of his hopeless love for Stella in terms which combine traditional Petrarchan "conceits" with considerable individuality of expression and feeling. Many of the sonnets read like mere exercises, distinguished only by ingenuity, but a handful stand out as among the finest examples of their kind which the age produced. Sidney himself claimed complete originality both of feeling and expression—

"Fool," said my Muse to me, "look in thy heart and write."

But even in repudiating the conventional language of the sonneteer
he is likely to use that language, exclaiming

> Let dainty wits cry on the sisters nine
> That, bravely masked, their fancies may be told,

or

> I never drank of Aganippe well,
> Nor ever did in shade of Tempe sit.

The best are also the best known. "With how sad steps, O moon, thou
climb'st the skies" is a beautifully modulated sonnet, opening softly
on a note of slow plaintiveness and changing with deliberate abrupt-
ness in the third line as the poet moves from melancholy to bitterness. In "Come sleep! O sleep, the certain knot of peace," an invocation to sleep is deftly turned at the end into a love poem to Stella.
In "Having this day my horse, my hand, my lance," he turns a Petrarchan compliment neatly in a context of chivalry. In "Stella oft
sees the very face of woe," the sonnet winds cunningly to its startling
last line:

> I am not I; pity the tale of me.

Some with admirable openings fall away into pallid ingenuities;
others are well sustained and artfully modulated. Sidney does not
always use the same sonnet form, rhyming sometimes *abba* and
sometimes (but less often) *abab*. His commonest rhyme-scheme is
abba, abba, cdcdee. He almost always ends on a couplet, on which
the poem is often balanced. Some of the songs have a splendid immediacy, notably the fourth song, "Only joy, now here you are,"
where Astrophel, alone with Stella in her house with every one else
in bed and all silent, pleads with her to

> Take me to thee, and thee to me,

and she replies, at the end of each plea,

> No, no, no, no, my dear, let be.

The hushed atmosphere, the passion of the speaker and the lady's
responding love subdued by virtue are admirably captured in a poem
that breaks through the Petrarchan love convention to give us a sudden glimpse of forbidden love in dramatic action.

Sidney's best known sonnet is probably the great repudiation of
human love in favor of divine, "Leave me, O love which reachest but
to dust." This forms no part of the *Astrophel and Stella* series, and is
found among a group of twenty-seven poems from Sidney's manu-

scripts which is included in the 1598 edition of *The Countess of Pembroke's Arcadia* under the title "Certain Sonnets." There are also sonnets and other verses sprinkled throughout the *Arcadia*.

Arcadia, written to amuse his sister, the Countess of Pembroke, is a prose romance interspersed with verses, an odd work to modern eyes, yet in its own way very typical of its age as well as of its author. The original version, known as the *Old Arcadia*, was written in the later 1570's and was not printed until 1926. Sidney revised his original version, adding much new material and altering his method of presentation, but he did not live to complete the revision. The fragmentary revised version was published in 1590, and in 1593 the Countess of Pembroke brought out a text consisting of the new version as far as it went, with the story completed according to the text of the original version. This composite version, though it has long been the accepted one, is obviously a makeshift and is less satisfactory as a literary work than either the *Old Arcadia* or the incomplete revision.

Old Arcadia is a pastoral love story, with a political background, based on Greek romance, that Alexandrian form of literature which dealt episodically with Mediterranean adventure, and regularly included disguises, capture by pirates, infants lost and recovered many years later, mistaken identity, and true love winning in the end. It tells the story of Basilius, king of Arcadia, who retires to rural irresponsibility with his wife and his two daughters, Pamela and Philoclea. Two visiting princes visit Arcadia, and each falls in love with one of the daughters, one disguising himself as a shepherd and the other as an Amazon in order to gain access to Basilius' family. The pursuit of the girls by the disguised lovers is complicated by a variety of circumstances (including the fact that Basilius and his wife both fall in love with the Amazon prince, the former thinking him to be female, the latter penetrating his disguise). The kingdom of Arcadia meanwhile gets into difficulties, and everything is finally disentangled and put in order by Euarchus, model king of Macedonia and father of one of the princes. This involves his condemning both princes for the supposed murder of Basilius, but this misunderstanding is finally cleared up and everything ends happily. The pastoral element in the story is real rather than symbolic: shepherds are introduced because Basilius and his family have retired into the country and are liable to come into contact with shepherds. The shepherds do not stand for ecclesiastical or political or other kinds of character, as they so often do in Renaissance pastoral. The political background of the work is straightforward: Basilius has fallen into culpable weakness,

while Euarchus represents the ideal ruler. Against the political background the themes of love (between the princes and the princesses)
and friendship (between the two princes and between the two
princesses) are worked out with typical Renaissance high idealism
and a good deal of equally typical Renaissance subtlety. Though
from one point of view a "vain amatorious poem" as Milton called it
in a fit of pique after having long known and profited from it, it is
also, as Milton conceded, "a book in that kind full of worth and wit"
with a serious moral both ethical and political. Ideal love, ideal
friendship, and the ideal ruler are, directly and indirectly, discussed,
suggested, and embodied.

The revised *Arcadia* introduces considerable complications into
the plot and provides Basilius with a wicked sister-in-law, Cecropia,
who corrupts her son Amphialus. Cecropia's activities in persecuting
Pamela, Philoclea, and one of the princes gives Sidney an excellent
opportunity to demonstrate virtue triumphantly resisting every kind
of temptation, religion overcoming atheism, true love conquering
the cruelest inducements to unfaithfulness, and constancy, fidelity,
fortitude, and patience prevailing over every kind of evil persuasion
and physical compulsion. The ethical and didactic element is thus
considerably heightened in the revised version, and the relatively
simple romance of the *Old Arcadia* is overlaid with so much new
and more serious matter that the whole character of the work is
altered, to become in scope and intention parallel to *The Faerie
Queene*. The revised *Arcadia* is a noble work in the fullest sense of
the term. Like Spenser's epic, it had as its "general end" the fashion-
ing of "a gentleman or noble person in virtuous and gentle discipline"; both are the work of Protestant Humanists, combining Christian, Platonic, and Renaissance ideals.

The style of the *Arcadia* is highly "conceited," full of elaborate
analogies, balanced parenthetical asides, pathetic fallacies, sym-
metrically answering clauses, and other devices of an immature prose
entering suddenly into the world of conscious literary artifice. It has
its moments of idyllic simplicity and stylized pastoral charm, and
even passages of ironical humor and amused parody, but, on the
whole, Sidney's prose in the *Arcadia* (in both versions, but especially
in the revised) is a variety of that elaborate rhetorical prose which
the Elizabethans often employed in an endeavor to bring the level
of their prose artfulness and sophistication up to that of their poetry.
John Lyly's *Euphues, The Anatomy of Wit* (1578) and its sequel,
Euphues and his England (1580), had similarly tried to embellish
English prose style. Lyly takes his hero Euphues through a series of

adventures and experiences which involve debates on such standard Renaissance themes as youth and age, love and friendship, and other matters of interest to young gentlemen in search of amusement, education, and the idea of the good life. "Euphuism," as Lyly's prose style has since been called, differs in many fundamental respects from the style of Sidney's *Arcadia*, but there is a similarity of intention. Lyly's almost fantastic skill in arranging his sentences in antithetically balanced clauses (with both words and phrases answering to each other); his constant and ingenious parallelisms; his endless plays on words; his mathematically worked out alliteration and cross-alliteration; his comparisons and similes involving mythology and, more often, natural history (parodied by Falstaff in his speech in his own defense, *Henry IV Pt. I*, II, iv: "for though the camomile, the more it is trodden on the faster it grows, so youth, the more it is wasted the sooner it wears"); his frequent introduction of proverbs; and numerous other devices drawn from Renaissance rhetoricians—in these excessive efforts he wearies the reader and demonstrates clearly that Elizabethan prose had not yet grown up. Sidney is less consistent, less extreme, and less mechanical in his use of artifice.

Sidney's other important work is his *Defence of Poesie*, written in the early 1580's and first published in 1595 (in two editions, the other being entitled *An Apologie for Poetrie*). Here, with an ease of manner and grace of style, he answers the Puritan objections to imaginative literature in a series of arguments drawn largely from the Italian Humanist critics. The tone of the essay is that of a gentleman's conversation, and he works easily into his subject, with deliberate *sprezzatura* or nonchalance, by way of a casual discussion of horsemanship. Elizabethan criticism at this time was concerned mostly with practical matters of rhetoric and versification or with attack on or defense of the social influence of the theater. Sidney's is the first attempt in English of any significance to draw together the arguments about the nature, function, possibilities, and future of poetry into a unified critical discussion. Echoes of Aristotle and Horace as filtered through the Italian Renaissance critics can be found throughout the essay, but the tone and the spirit of the discussion are Sidney's own. The antiquity of poetry and its early civilizing function are stressed; the poet is a maker, a creator, who makes "things either better than Nature bringeth forth, or quite anew forms such as never were in Nature." Nature's "world is brasen, the Poets only deliver a golden." By creating a better world than the real world, and by presenting that world in such a persuasive and delightful manner that the reader is "moved" by it to try to embody this ideal world in his own living, poetry proves itself a better moral teacher than either philosophy (which lays down the precepts but does not move the reader to carry them out) or history (which is tied to the fact and can only tell what happened, and what happened is often most unedifying and not likely to lead the reader to virtue). The liveliness of the images which the poets create is contrasted with the dullness of historians and philosophers, and by this insistence on the poet's ability to captivate and move, Sidney provides himself with a theory of form and style. It is not enough for the poet to create a golden world: he must present that golden world in such a way that the reader believes it as he reads and is pleased and moved by it. From this point on he is free to discuss matters of form and style as achieving different degrees of conviction and "moving" in the reader. He goes on to discuss the different species of poetry and their several "excellences," before proceeding to a general account of the objections to poetry, which are dealt with easily enough on the principles he has laid down, with some amusing ironic characterization of the objectors. The essay concludes with an inquiry into the present state of poetry which shows Sidney unexpectedly cautious and precedent-ridden in his practical criticism. But it must be remembered that the essay was written just before the great flowering of Elizabethan literature in Spenser and Shakespeare.

Sir Walter Ralegh was an even more versatile character than Sidney—explorer, navigator, and chemist as well as soldier, courtier, politician, and historian. His poetical work is unequal and fragmentary, much of it remaining in manuscript until centuries after his death. Some of his poems appeared in Elizabethan miscellanies, but it seems certain that more were by him than were ascribed to him there. He has a notable sonnet on Spenser's *Faerie Queene*, in which he tells how Petrarch and Homer were overcome by the arrival of the Fairy Queen; but for the most part his poems lack the fashionable "conceits" of the time and have a masculine vigor of their own. His long *Cynthia* survives only in part in a first draft. It represents the Ocean addressing Cynthia (Queen Elizabeth); it is in alternately rhyming quatrains which lack smoothness but which often possess a rugged forcefulness not easily matched in the period. Some of his moralizing lyrics have a studied simplicity which must be the product of deliberate control:

> Go, soul, the body's guest,
> Upon a thankless arrant.
> Fear not to touch the best;

> The truth shall be thy warrant.
> Go, since I needs must die,
> And give the world the lie. . . .

This is the first stanza of a thirteen-stanza poem, "The Lie," in which every stanza except the last ends with "Give the world the lie." A similar studied simplicity is seen in:

> Give me my scallop-shell of quiet,
> My staff of faith to walk upon,
> My scrip of joy, immortal diet,
> My bottle of salvation,
> My gown of glory, hope's true gage,
> And thus I'll take my pilgrimage. . . .

One has the feeling that Ralegh, like the seventeenth-century Scottish poet the Earl of Montrose (who, like Ralegh, was a soldier and courtier who met death by execution), achieved poetry by sheer strength of character.

Another of Sidney's friends, who had been at school with him and traveled abroad with him, was Fulke Greville, Lord Brooke (1554–1628), courtier, poet, dramatist, Calvinist, Stoic, man of action. If Spenser and Sidney were able to resolve some of the conflicting currents of Renaissance thought, Greville tended to hold them separately in his mind, living in several worlds at once. His poetry and his plays (which followed the stricter Senecan form in protest at what he considered the looseness and triviality of contemporary dramatic practice) reflect a divided mind:

> Oh wearisome condition of humanity!
> Born under one law, to another bound;
> Vainly begot, and yet forbidden vanity;
> Created sick, commanded to be sound.
> What meaneth Nature by these diverse laws,
> Passion and Reason, self-division's cause?

This outburst, from the Chorus of Priests which concludes his play *Mustapha*, is typical of Greville in its sense of conflict. He has not Spenser's confident Platonic idealism, which can surround Christian and Humanist thought with a halo of philosophic optimism and enable him to work out a practical ideal of virtue which combines gentlemanliness with assurance of salvation. Indeed, Spenser's ability to combine notions of gentlemanliness with those of Christian faith and practice, typical though it was of a certain phase of Renaissance thought, looks somewhat odd to modern eyes, and Greville's eyes were surprisingly modern. The unworldly Christian life may be the

way to ultimate salvation, and divine Grace the only means by
which man can be enabled to lead that life; but life on earth as we
know it has its own problems and standards, and if we are to live in
the world we must concern ourselves with them. This seems to
have been Greville's attitude, and he is thus one of the first figures
in English literature for whom the "new philosophy" not only "called
all in doubt" but suggested the kind of problem by which Aldous
Huxley was tormented in his early novels. (It is significant that
Huxley quotes Greville as the epigraph to *Point Counter Point*.)
"I know the world and believe in God," Greville once wrote; but he
did not know how to reconcile that knowledge with that belief. In
practical political affairs he was Machiavellian; in personal ethical
matters he was a Stoic; in religious thought he was a Calvinist.

Greville's poetry has thus a somber intellectual quality. His
sonnet-sequence *Caelica* contains some powerful and striking poems,
none more so than the opening one (which is not a strict sonnet, but
a poem of three six-line stanzas):

> Love, the delight of all well-thinking minds;
> Delight, the fruit of virtue dearly loved;
> Virtue, the highest good that reason finds;
> Reason, the fire wherein men's thoughts be proved;
>> Are from one world by Nature's power bereft,
>> And in one creature, for her glory, left.

Or the remarkable Sonnet XXII (again, not a true sonnet):

> I with whose colors Myra drest her head,
> I that wore posies of her own hand making,
> I that mine own name in the chimneys read
> By Myra finely wrought ere I was waking:
>> Must I look on, in hope time coming may
>> With change bring back my turn again to play?

> I that on Sunday at the Church-stile found
> A garland sweet, with true-love knots in flowers,
> Which I to wear about mine arm was bound,
> That each of us might know that all was ours:
>> Must I now lead an idle life in wishes?
>> And follow Cupid for his loaves and fishes? . . .

> Was it for this that I might Myra see
> Washing the water with her beauties, white?
> Yet would she never write her love to me;
> *Thinks wit of change while thoughts are in delight?*
>> Mad girls must safely love, as they may leave:
>> *No man may print a kiss: lines may deceive.*

The indignant "I's" with which this poem opens, the contrast between simple rustic love and sophisticated betrayal, and the mingling of anger with reflection, give it an impressive immediacy.

Greville's verse treatises (of humane learning, upon fame and honor, and of wars) deal in strenuous though sometimes pedestrian verse with human weakness and pride, while his Senecan verse plays, *Mustapha* and *Alaham*, present the political implications of the human dilemma, the former dealing with imperial power abused, the second with royal weakness exploited. The verse of these plays is often rough and crabbed, and the thought is not adequately put at the service of character in action: the plays are commentaries on human affairs rather than the vivid and lively presentation of stories symbolic of human destiny. They have their magnificent moments, a piece of sad and thoughtful rhetoric or set recital of cogently phrased *sententiae*.

Meanwhile, miscellanies in songbooks poured from the presses, and Elizabethan lyrics of all kinds, fresh and faded, light and heavy, formal and gay, were printed in numerous collections throughout the latter part of the sixteenth and the early seventeenth centuries. It is the contents of these collections that has given the term "Elizabethan lyric" the connotation which it has so long had, and led us—rightly—to think of the middle and latter Elizabethan period as a great age of lyric and song. The improvement in the maturity and confidence of Elizabethan poetry between the poets represented in *Tottel's Miscellany* and the last decade of the century can be seen in the collection entitled *The Phoenix Nest* (1593), compiled by a certain R. S. *The Passionate Pilgrim*, put out by the printer William Jaggard in 1599 as "by W. Shakespeare," is actually a miscellany, with poems by a variety of authors. *England's Parnassus, Belvedere*, and *England's Helicon* all appeared in 1600; the last of these is one of the finest anthologies of English poetry ever produced, and contains poems by most of the poets of the middle and latter sixteenth century, including Sidney, Spenser, Drayton, Lodge, Peele, and Shakespeare. It includes poems from older miscellanies (including two from *Tottel*), songs from the madrigal books (a new fashion) and songbooks, and work by poets otherwise little known. The last of the Elizabethan anthologies was *A Poetical Rhapsody* (1602), a large and interesting collection whose second edition (1608) adds hitherto unprinted poems by Sir John Davies, Ralegh, and others, which might well have been lost if they had not been here published from manuscript.

Of the other Elizabethan sonnet-sequences, it can only be said that many of them show considerable skill in the handling of the

convention, but only occasionally does one of these poets rise to
the level of a memorable poem. Compliment, lament, hope, despair,
expressed with every variety of Petrarchan conceit and later development of such conceit, are the commonest themes. We hear Giles
Fletcher addressing his Licia:

> When as her lute is tuned to her voice,
> The air grows proud for honor of that sound,

or Barnaby Barnes complimenting Parthenophe:

> Mistress, behold in this true-speaking glass
> Thy beauty's graces, of all women rarest,

or William Percy complaining of his Coelia:

> Judged by my goddess' doom to endless pain,
> Lo! here I ope my sorrow's passion,

or William Smith's shepherd addressing his Chloris:

> Whole Showers of tears to Chloris I will pour
> As true oblations of my sincere love,

or Alexander Craig sighing for Pandora:

> Go you, O winds that blow from north to south,
> Convey my secret sighs unto my sweet.
> Deliver them from mine unto her mouth,
> And make my commendations till we meet. . . .

And so it goes. Sometimes a new note is struck. Some of the poems
in Barnaby Barnes' *Divine Century of Spiritual Sonnets* are lively
and interesting, with a certain freshness of imagery.

Daniel's sonnets to Delia show a uniformly high level of smoothness and flexibility, and occasionally rise to something more, as in:

> When men shall find thy flower, thy glory, pass,
> And thou, with careful brow sitting alone,
> Receivéd hast this message from thy glass,
> That tells the truth and says that all is gone. . . .

—a variation on a theme of Ronsard's which Yeats was also to use.
and Drayton's *Idea* contains, among many splendid and brilliantly
phrased sonnets, one of the most memorable that the age produced:

> Since there's no help, come let us kiss and part—
> Nay, I have done: you get no more of me;
> And I am glad, yea, glad with all my heart,

That thus so cleanly I myself can free.
Shake hands for ever, cancel all our vows,
But when we meet at any time again,
Be it not seen in either of our brows
That we one jot of former love retain.
Now at the last gasp of love's latest breath,
When, his pulse failing, Passion speechless lies,
When Faith is kneeling by his bed of death,
And Innocence is closing up his eyes,—
   Now, if thou wouldst, when all have given him over,
   From death to life thou might'st him yet recover!

Of Shakespeare's sonnets, perhaps all that need be said is that they are not so obviously or immensely superior to other good Elizabethan sonnets as his plays are to those of his contemporaries and successors, but they *are* superior, and represent a most remarkable achievement; in the unfolding of a dramatic story, in the apt mingling of thought and passion, in the turning of the Petrarchan conceits ironically back on themselves to produce a whole new area of expression, in the bittersweet exploration by means of imagery of the mutations of passion, in the careful balancing of the sonnet on the concluding couplet, which often rings out like a sardonic epigram, and in the sheer mastery of phrase, these sonnets reveal a degree of poetic maturity and subtlety which none of his contemporary sonneteers possessed. At the same time, it should be noted that Shakespeare chose the simplest possible sonnet scheme (*abab, cdcd, efef, gg*) and did not, as both Sidney and Milton in their own ways did, enlarge the potentialities of the sonnet form.

Christopher Marlowe, who is of course better known for his plays and receives fuller discussion in the following chapter, deserves mention among the Elizabethan poets if only for his popular "Passionate Shepherd to His Love" (beginning "Come live with me and be my love"), which appeared in *England's Helicon* and his remarkable narrative poem, *Hero and Leander*. The richness and magnificent flow of this unfinished eight-hundred-word poem, the luxuriant facility with which the story unfolds, is typical of one aspect of Elizabethan poetry. It is too much, really; this easy (or easy-sounding) eloquence requires a more astringent touch to subtilize and mature it; but it is wonderful in its way, and a remarkable technical achievement. The unfinished poem was completed by George Chapman in his more sober and less sensual style, but with considerable power and subtlety. *Hero and Leander* appears to have set a fashion for love stories based on classical mythology. Lodge's *Glaucus and Scylla* (1592), Shakespeare's *Venus and Adonis* (1593), Drayton's *Endimion and Phoebe* (1594), and Marston's *Metamorphosis of Pygmalion's Image* (1598) are later examples of this form. Shakespeare's scintillating exercise in amorous narrative has all of Marlowe's sensuality but has, too, an intellectual quality in its images and "conceits" which provides a greater stiffening than Marlowe's verse possesses. It is a brilliant exercise; and the same can be said of Shakespeare's other narrative poem, *The Rape of Lucrece* (1594), in which he demonstrated that virtue assailed and overcome by lust is as amenable to such treatment as love triumphant.

The emulation of foreign models, which in some degree lay behind these English renderings of classical story (Marlowe's *Hero and Leander* professes to be a paraphrase of a poem by Musaeus), runs right through Elizabethan literature and is responsible for those numerous Tudor and Elizabethan translations, both in prose and in verse, in which the literary language was exercised. Sir Thomas North's translation of Plutarch's *Lives* (1579) made them available to Shakespeare; William Painter's *Palace of Pleasure* (1566, 1567), a rich and varied collection of stories from classical, Italian, and French sources, provided abundant material for the Elizabethan dramatists, and numerous other translations from Latin and from Italian put more and more of the wisdom of the classical world and of Renaissance Humanism within the reach of the literate but unlearned Englishman. Of verse translations, Arthur Golding's rendering in "fourteeners" of Ovid's *Metamorphoses* has at least the merit of fluency, and he brought Ovid's compendium of classical mythology to many who might not otherwise have had access to it. Shakespeare knew Golding's Ovid. Thomas Phaer's *Aeneid* (1583) was also in fourteeners, as was Chapman's *Iliad,* a vigorous and swinging version much more Elizabethan than Homeric in tone. These long lines soon become monotonous, however vigorously handled, and for his translation of the *Odyssey,* Chapman employed rhymed iambic pentameter couplets. Sir John Harington's translation of Ariosto's *Orlando Furioso* (1591), in an *ababab cc* stanza, has verve and flexibility and sometimes achieves an almost Byronic tone; Edward Fairfax's rendering of Tasso's *Gerusalemme Liberata* (*Godfrey of Bulloigne,* 1600), in the same stanza that Harington had used for Ariosto, is a conscientious but on the whole pedestrian performance, though praised by Dryden for the "harmony of its numbers." These are but samples; Elizabethan translations, though not always achieving high literary merit in their own right, both helped to exercise the language and to make available to Elizabethan drama and to Elizabethans in general the riches of classical history and story, of Italian epic, and continental Humanist thought. To read them helps us—no less than an appreciation of such things as the secular pageantry which in large measure replaced medieval church ritual in Elizabethan life—to understand more fully the range and the sources of the Elizabethan imagination.

CHAPTER EIGHT

Drama from the
Miracle Plays to Marlowe

THE MAIN GLORY of English literature in the late sixteenth and early seventeenth century was its poetic drama. English drama before the sixteenth century is of mainly academic and historical interest, though there are occasional plays which possess charm and liveliness. But the early history of English drama, however uninteresting to the literary critic, is of the first importance as illustrating how the instinct for dramatic representation finds its outlets; in addition, it tells us a great deal about the workings of the popular imagination, and it throws some light on the themes and conventions of later drama. The details of the story are not always clear—our picture of the development of medieval drama is dependent on records which are far from complete—but enough material survives to enable us to see the outlines as well as a few remarkable details.

The ultimate origins of all drama are the concern of the anthropologist rather than of the literary historian. Drama and religious ritual seem to have been bound up with each other in the earlier stages of all civilizations; folk celebrations, ritual miming of such elemental themes as death and resurrection, seasonal festivals with appropriate symbolic actions—these lie in the background (sometimes far in the background) of all drama, though a sophisticated literary tradition may go far to obliterate their traces. So far as we can write the history of English drama, it begins with the elaboration of the ecclesiastical liturgy in mutually answering dialogues. Of the other sources—pre-Christian seasonal festivals, St. George and Robin Hood plays, Maypole dances, and similiar folk activities—we can say little more than that they undoubtedly existed. Nor can we establish any continuity between the origins of European drama in the early Middle Ages and the drama of Greece and Rome, which had already run its course by the time the Christian era began and only influenced vernacular European drama after the Renaissance had directed new attention to the literature of the ancient world. The early Church fathers saw Roman acted drama in its last immoral and degenerate phase and understandably condemned it; and even this decadent theater disappeared, with so much else, under the impact of the barbarian invasions of the sixth century. Strolling minstrels and other varieties of itinerant entertainments perhaps preserved for a time some of the traditions of the last phase of the Roman theater, but they eventually became absorbed in the miscellaneous repertory of the profession long before it contributed anything to the vitality of the acting of miracle and morality plays.

The ritual of the Christian Church, with its two great festivals of Christmas and Easter and its celebration of the significant points in Christ's career from birth to resurrection, was itself inherently dramatic. Indeed, the Christian year commemorated more than the career of the founder of Christianity, looking before it to the Annunciation and beyond it to the Ascension. The ceremonies with which these events were commemorated lent themselves naturally to dramatization; from simple antiphonal chanting between priest and choir or two sections of the choir to more elaborate acting out of a scene between two characters or sets of characters was but a step. These "tropes," or dramatic elaborations of part of the liturgy, represent the beginnings of medieval drama. We have a record of an "Easter trope" dating from the early tenth century: this is a Latin dialogue between the three Marys and the Angel at the tomb of Christ, introduced before the introit of the Easter Mass. "Quem quaeritis in sepulchro, Christicolae?" ("Whom do you seek in the sepulcher, Christians?") the Angel asks, and the women reply that they seek the crucified Jesus. "Non est hic," replies the Angel; "surrexit sicut praedixerat; ite, nuntiate quia surrexit de sepulchro." ("He is not here; he has arisen as he said he would; go and announce that he has arisen from the sepulcher.") Bishop Etholwold of Winchester describes the *Quem quaeritis* trope in his *Regularis Concordia* (written about 970) as a dialogue between one sitting holding a palm branch by the sepulcher and three others who enter with censers in their hands, as if seeking something. Later, the trope received additions and elaborations, with more characters added. Other simple plays representing other phases of the life of Christ followed the same model. A play bringing the shepherd to the crib of the infant was introduced at Christmas. An Epiphany play introduced the three kings and a mechanical star. A Passion play developed but, surprisingly enough, not (as far as we know) until the thirteenth century. The liturgy, biblical story, and other varieties of Christian literature contribute to the development of other simple plays with characters from both the New Testament and the Old.

The trope thus grew into the liturgical drama, which was fully developed in the twelfth century. So far they were in Latin, as the liturgy was, but as they increased in popularity and indeed tended to overshadow the original devotional ritual of the feast-days, vernacular elements began to appear. At the same time the elaboration of the plays made it difficult to confine the performance to the choir where, like their liturgical sources, they had originally been spoken, and the performance therefore extended down the nave, using appropriate parts of the church building as rudimentary properties. Finally, it moved out of the church altogether, first into the churchyard and then into the marketplace or a convenient meadow. Once outside the church, the vernacular ousted Latin and the story element moved away from the liturgy to make free use of the whole range of sacred history from the Creation to the Last Judgment. Liturgical drama, acted within the church as embellishment of ecclesiastical ritual, thus gave way to plays in English, performed in the open and completely divorced from the liturgy though still religious in subject-matter. These are known as "miracle plays." It is at this stage that elements from minstrel performances and older folk festivals begin to come in and provide new vitality for a drama whose primary function is now quite simply entertainment.

It is impossible to document adequately the transition from liturgical drama to miracle play, but we have three fragmentary Anglo-Norman miracle plays dating from the twelfth century and we know that in 1244 Robert Grosseteste, Bishop of Lincoln, ordered his archdeacons to stamp out the performance of miracle plays by clerks and that some sixty years later William of Wadington, in his *Manuel des Pechiez*, distinguished between plays about Christ's burial and Resurrection acted modestly as part of the Church service, which he approved, and miracle plays, which he denounced as sinful folly. Miracle plays must have developed rapidly in the thirteenth century; there are records of cycles of miracle plays in many regions of England during the fourteenth and fifteenth centuries and well into the sixteenth.

These cycles of plays were developed by extending the themes of liturgical drama both backward and forward, to include the

Creation, the Fall, and early Old Testament story at one end and Doomsday at the other. Once out of doors, the presentation of plays could not be indifferent to the seasons; so that they were no longer acted at the different church festivals. The establishment of the feast of Corpus Christi (falling in May or June) in 1264, confirmed in 1311, provided a suitable day for the acting of miracle plays, though some cities preferred Whitsun. Corpus Christi Day was suitable not only because of the time of the year when it fell but also because, being a processional observance with the Host carried about and displayed at various stations, it proved naturally hospitable to dramatic performances, which were generally given on wagons (known as "pageants")—stages on wheels which went from one station to another. Each "pageant" presented a different scene of the cycle, and the wagons followed each other, repeating their scenes at successive stations. With the plays no longer associated with ecclesiastical ritual, their organizing and financing passed into lay hands. It was the trade guilds—important in so many ways in the social and economic life of the Middle Ages—that took over the sponsoring of the plays (which were probably written by some local cleric). Each guild would make itself responsible for a wagon with its scene, which involved considerable effort and expense. Though a wagon stage could not be more than primitive by modern standards, considerable ingenuity was shown in the arrangement of the superstructure and of the stage properties.

Almost complete cycles of miracle plays survive from Chester, York, and Wakefield; two plays from the Coventry cycle survive, in late and corrupt texts; and we have also a Noah play from Newcastle, a play on the creation of Eve and the expulsion from the Garden of Eden from Norwich, and an Abraham and Isaac play (dealing with the sacrifice of Isaac) which has been preserved at Brome Manor in Norfolk. There is also a cycle of forty-two plays generally known as *Ludus Coventriae*, though they have nothing to do with Coventry, which seems from its dialect to have come from a town in East Anglia. All this represents but a small fragment of the large number of cycles of miracle plays produced by the trade guilds of the different towns of England, but what remains is sufficient to give us some idea of what these plays were like.

The Chester cycle contains twenty-five plays, beginning with the Fall of Lucifer and ending with Doomsday: it includes plays dealing with the Creation, the Fall, Noah, Cain and Abel, Abraham and Isaac, Balaam and Balak (with Balaam's ass); a group on the life of Christ beginning with the Annunciation and ending with the Ascension, and including a Nativity, a shepherds' play (*Pastores*), a Slaughter of the Innocents, a Raising of Lazarus, a play dealing with a number of events from the entry into Jerusalem to the conspiracy of Judas, a Last Supper and Betrayal, a Passion play, a Harrowing of Hell, and a Resurrection play with the *Quem quaeritis*. The plays are written in an eight-line stanza with *rime couée*, derived from the Romances (the shorter fourth and eight lines rhyming with each other, and lines one to three and four to seven rhyming). The development of the dialogue and action is naïve enough, with the story presented in simple outline. There are a few realistic touches, but they are slight compared with what some later miracle plays do with such characters as Noah's wife, Balaam's ass, and the midwives at the Nativity. The York plays are probably later; forty-eight survive out of an original cycle of fifty-four. Four groups have been distinguished within the cycle. Eighteen plays seem to be earlier than the others; they are fairly crude and simply didactic in tone; twelve of them are written in a twelve-line stanza divided into an octave and a quatrain, and the other six in four or eight-line stanzas. These earlier and less interesting plays include an Adam and Eve, a Building of the Ark, an Abraham and Isaac, Exodus, Annunciation, *Pastores*, Three Kings, Christ disputing with the Doctors (*Doctores*), Lazarus, Last Supper, Passion, Pentecost, Assumption, and Last Judgment, though this last may belong to a later group. A second group, by an author distinguished by his metrical skill—the verse is clearly differentiated from that of the other plays in the York cycle and shows the influence of the alliterative revival—includes some revisions of plays in the earlier group as well as new plays. In this group belong the Fall of Lucifer, the Death of Christ, the Death of the Virgin, the Resurrection, and others. The revisions and new work of this metrically skilled author apparently date from the very early fifteenth century, and to the same period belongs the work of a third York author or authors, who introduced elements of realistic humor into the plays dealing with Noah and with the Shepherds. Finally, a little later than these, there is the work of an author who had a more powerful dramatic sense than any of the others: he apparently revised the Passion play, where his hand is clearly discernible in the heightened tension, and he handled also the Conspiracy of Judas, the Agony in the Garden, the Betrayal, and the Condemnation. This writer has a real feeling for character (he has a fine portrait of Pilate, for example), though his metrics are confused and he has a tendency to splutter.

The Wakefield cycle contains thirty-two plays (sometimes known as the Towneley Plays because the manuscript was once owned by the Towneley family). These deal with the usual themes, though there are some gaps. The literary merit of the Wakefield plays is higher than that of any of the other cycles which have survived. The stanzas are handled with some assurance, there is an occasional note of real poetry, and in five of the plays there is a lively ironic humor and realistic characterization that show a sense of comedy and of satire to a degree unparalleled in any other existing miracle plays. Among these plays are a Noah and two shepherd plays (the *Prima Pastorum* and the *Secunda Pastorum*). The story of Noah is treated as broad realistic comedy, with Noah's wife portrayed as a talkative shrew who refuses to enter the ark. In the shepherd plays there is much talk of the oppression of rustic laborers by rich landlords and sharp, realistic painting of the lives of the poor. The *Secunda Pastorum* includes a lively comic episode which is an irreverent anticipation of the actual Nativity: Mak steals a sheep and brings it home to his wife, who puts it in a cradle so that it will appear to be a new-born baby. When the shepherds come in, looking for the stolen sheep, they find nothing but two empty platters and a baby in its cradle. They leave, but one of them returns to give the baby a sixpence. He bends over the baby to kiss him and—"What the devil is this? He has a long snout." Mak's fraud is discovered, and the three shepherds toss him in a sheet, and then leave. Then they hear an angel singing of the divine birth, and they go to the stable to find the infant Jesus. The language throughout is full of verve, and the story is presented against a sharply etched background of fifteenth-century rural life. The "Wakefield Master," as the anonymous author of the five outstanding Wakefield plays has been called, is the first English writer of realistic comedy. His main inspiration was clearly the realistic *fabliau* and his own observation rather than the Bible or the liturgy.

Revisions and additions make the text of the *Ludus Coventriae* as we have it somewhat confusing; the literary interest of the plays is confined to some short passages of lyrical or dramatic vitality. More interesting is the Brome Manor Abraham and Isaac, which, in spite of its doggerel verse, has more than the simple pathos of some other versions of the story: the characters of father and son, with the former's anguish of mind and the latter's childish trustfulness, are presented with some force. The two surviving Coventry plays are fragments of a New Testament cycle; a series of revisions has left the text in a state of metrical chaos. The Newcastle Noah, dealing with the building of the ark, has its moments of liveliness,

though nothing as humorous as the Wakefield or even the York
Noahs. Other surviving miracle plays include one dealing with the
conversion of Saint Paul and one on Saint Mary Magdalen.

While the miracle plays were still in their heyday, another medieval dramatic form emerged, a form which has more direct links
with Elizabethan drama. This is the morality play, which differs
from the miracle play in that it does not deal with biblical or pseudo-
biblical story but with personified abstractions of virtues and vices,
who struggle for man's soul. The *psychomachia*, the battle for the
soul, was a common enough medieval theme and intimately bound
up with the whole development of medieval allegory. The allegorical habit of mind was so dominant in the Middle Ages that it is
hardly surprising to see it emerging in the drama. The morality play
handles the subjects that were most popular among medieval
preachers and draws considerably on contemporary homiletic technique. The theme of the seven deadly sins was a commonplace of
medieval art and literature as well as of the pulpit, and the notion
of Mercy and Peace pleading before God for man's soul against
Truth and Righteousness, which developed in the twelfth century,
also played its part. There are references to morality plays in the
fourteenth century (the earliest is to a "Pater Noster" play, which
was apparently a treatment of the conflict between the seven deadly
sins and the seven cardinal virtues), but the fifteenth century seems
to be the period of its full development. A theme almost as common as the struggle of virtues and vices over man's soul is the
"Dance of Death," also a common medieval motif, which treats
of Death, God's messenger, coming to summon all, high and low
alike: it is a dramatic rendering of the *ubi sunt* theme which figures
so largely in the literature of the Middle Ages. In the earliest extant
morality play, known as *The Pride of Life*, a king, *Rex vivus*, boasts
of his power and freedom of action, refuses advice to think of his
latter end, and disports himself with Mirth. A bishop reproves him,
but the king dismisses him with abuse and sends Mirth to proclaim
defiance of Death. This is as far as the existing fragmentary text
goes, but we know from the prologue that at the end Death claims
the king and his soul goes to the Devil, to be redeemed finally by
the prayers of Our Lady.

The earliest complete extant morality play is *The Castle of Perseverance*, written probably about 1425, a relatively elaborate affair
with thirty-four characters: the theme is the fight between Mankind's Good Angel and his supporters and his Bad Angel supported
by the Seven Deadly Sins, and the action takes Man (*Humanum
Genus*) from his birth to the Day of Judgment. *Mundus* (the world)

claims Man's first allegiance, with Folly and Lust acting as Man's servants. The struggle goes this way and that; and at the end of the first part the Good Angel, aided by Shrift and Penitence, rescues Man from the Vices and lodges him in the Castle of Perseverance, which is then besieged by the Vices. At first the Virtues are victorious, but Covetyse seduces man afterward, and finally Death comes for him, and he has to leave all his worldly goods behind. Mercy, Peace, Truth, and Righteousness, the Four Daughters of God, dispute over Man's salvation before God's throne, and the play ends with God's reminder that "king, kaiser, knight and champion, Pope, patriarch, priest and prelate" must all answer at the great Judgment. An extant diagram shows that the play was staged in a ring in the center of which was a "castle" and round it five "scaffolds" for *Deus*, *Caro* (the flesh), *Mundus*, Belial, and Covetyse.

The Castle of Perseverance is one of three plays found in the Macro MS; of the other two, dating from the mid-fifteenth century, one has no title in the text, but is generally known as *Wisdom*, and the other is *Mankind*. In the former, the five Wits (i.e., senses), together with Mind, Will, and Understanding, are attacked by Lucifer in the guise of a worldly gallant. Lucifer convinces Mind, Will, and Understanding of the advantages of the worldly life, and a great number of personified vices are introduced to show them in their evil conduct—Mind led into sins of violence and oppression, Understanding to dishonesty, and Will to sensuality, all of which are represented by dances, in which the appropriate vices take part. After further developments, Mind, Understanding, and Will, together with the five Wits and Anima (the soul), are brought to repentance by Wisdom: the regeneration of Anima concludes the play. *Mankind* shows the hero, Mankind, urged to good works by Mercy and tempted into vice by Mischief and a group of representatives of the worldly life. The latter characters engage in coarse language and horseplay, and the play as a whole is characterized by the mingling of coarse comic elements with the serious morality. In the end Mankind is saved by Merey, who speaks the epilogue. Both the plays are in stanzaic verse.

The best known and in many ways the most appealing of surviving fifteenth-century morality plays is *Everyman*. Here the action is developed with a simple dignity and the personified abstractions play their part with forceful dramatic logic. Everyman is summoned by Death to a long journey from which there is no return. Unprepared, and unable to gain a respite, he looks for friends to accompany him, but neither Fellowship nor Goods nor Kindred will go; Good Deeds is willing to act as guide and companion, but Everyman's sins have rendered her too weak to stand. She recommends him to her sister Knowledge, who leads Everyman to Confession, and after he has done penance Good Deeds grows strong enough to accompany him, together with Strength, Discretion, Five Wits, and Beauty. But as the time comes for Everyman to creep into his grave, all the companions except Good Deeds decline to go with him. Knowledge stands by to report the outcome while Everyman enters the grave with Good Deeds. An angel announces the entry of Everyman's soul "into the heavenly sphere," and a "Doctor" concludes by pointing the moral. The play appears to have some relation to the Dutch morality play, *Elckerlijk,* and may be a translation of it. The verse form is naïve rhymed couplets, often effective in their very naïveté.

Toward the end of the fifteenth century there developed a type of morality play which dealt in the same allegorical way with general moral problems, though with more pronounced realistic and comic elements. This kind of play is known as the Interlude, though that name is also given to some much earlier secular moralities, such as the fragmentary thirteenth-century *Interludium de Clerico et Puella,* which is based on the *fabliau* of Dame Siriz, and the equally fragmentary *Dux Moraud* which preserves the speeches of the title character in a strange story of incest, murder, and repentance. These earlier "interludes" are perhaps not to be regarded as morality plays at all, but as dramatized versions of *fabliaux.* But the later kind of interlude, the secular morality play, develops its comic and realistic side and by the sixteenth century comes to include scenes far removed from the theme and atmosphere of the medieval morality. It is perhaps simplest to use the term *interlude,* whatever its origins and varying earlier uses—the term perhaps originally denoted a playlet performed between the courses of a banquet—as it is now employed by literary historians to denote those plays which mark the transition from medieval religious drama to Tudor secular drama. It is difficult to document that transition adequately, because so many of the texts have not survived. But there does seem to have been a continuous dramatic tradition, with the simple native drama absorbing foreign influences to become more secular and more sophisticated. Particularly significant is the development of the character known as "the Vice" from that of a diabolic tempter to a purely comic figure.

In Henry Medwall's *Fulgens and Lucres,* at the very end of the fifteenth century, we have the earliest extant purely secular play in English. Medwall had already written a morality play, *Nature,* of a more sophisticated kind than earlier moralities, and the transition from that kind of play to one with a "romantic" love interest must have seemed less significant at the time than it appears to later historians. Medwall was one of a group of early Tudor playwrights associated with the household of Cardinal Morton and thus with Sir Thomas More, who was known for his interest in amateur dramatics when he was a page in Morton's household. Medwall was at one time the Cardinal's chaplain. John Rastell (ca. 1470–1536) who printed *Fulgens and Lucres* and wrote plays himself, married More's sister, while John Heywood (ca. 1497–ca. 1580), the most important dramatist of the group, married their daughter, More's niece. The More-Heywood group of Tudor dramatists thus spanned two generations; its work bridges medieval and Elizabethan drama.

Fulgens and Lucres derives from a Latin short story by the Italian humanist Bonaccorso, which tells how Lucretia, daughter of the Roman senator Fulgentius, is wooed by a rich and worldly aristocrat and by a poor but virtuous man. She refers them to her father, who puts the choice between the two suitors up to the Senate, before whom each of the suitors pleads his cause. The story had already been translated into English by John Tiptoft, Earl of Worcester, and in turning it into a play Medwall very properly takes the decision away from the Senate and gives it to the girl (whom he calls Lucres). She chooses the poor but virtuous suitor. There is thus a morality element in the story, though it is not stressed. Medwall made a more significant change than this: he added a comic subplot, in which the servants of the two suitors are rivals for the love of Lucres's maid. This subplot parallels the main story on a lower and comic level, and is thus an early example of a tradition of mingling serious with comic scenes in English drama that was to become characteristic of the Elizabethan play and reach its highest point of development in Shakespeare. In his epilogue Medwall explains that his purpose was both to edify and to amuse. The verse form of the play varies between rhyme royal and, in the comic scenes, a shorter-lined stanza.

John Rastell's interlude, *The Nature of the Four Elements*, published anonymously early in the sixteenth century, is what might be called a Humanist morality play: various allegorical characters instruct Humanity in the new science and geography, with interesting reference to recent geographical discoveries. There are the usual low-life scenes with the Vices. Another Humanist morality play is John Redford's *Wit and Science*, dating probably from the 1530's. Wit, a student, seeks to marry Science, daughter of Reason and Experience, and before doing so must conquer the giant Tediousness and make a pilgrimage to Mount Parnassus. His adventures with these and other allegorical characters, good and bad, illustrate the ideals and difficulties of education as conceived by Redford. This emphasis on education (as distinct from salvation) clearly distinguished the Humanist interlude from its medieval predecessor. We have reached the age of secular plays written by schoolmasters and other educated laymen for purposes of entertaining and instruction.

John Heywood's interludes were often written as part of an evening's entertainment at a nobleman's house, and the emphasis is more on amusement than instruction. *Witty and Witless* and *The Play of Love* are lively debates between types; *The Play of the Weather* is an amusing presentation of how Jupiter sends round Merry-Report to find out what weather people want, and each person asked, because of his different occupation and interests, wants a different kind of weather (e.g., the water miller wants plenty of rain and no wind, the wind miller wants wind and less rain, the hunting gentlemen wants it "dry and not misty, the wind calm and still," and the schoolboy wants snow to make snowballs). Jupiter's decision is to leave things as they are, and everyone will get his share of his favorite weather. The moral here is slight, but it is there, reminding us of the older morality out of which the brief and lively Tudor interlude grew. In *The Play Called the Four PP,* a palmer, a pardoner, apothecary (quack doctor), and a pedlar introduce themselves, quarrel, and eventually agree that three of them should hold a lying competition with the pedlar as judge. The apothecary tells a bawdy tale of a marvelous cure, and the pardoner then tells in vivid detail how he visited Hell to find a neighbor, one Margery Corson; Lucifer and his comrades are only too glad to get rid of the woman, who is an insufferable shrew, and asks the pardoner to see to it (as he can in the course of his profession) that no more women come to Hell. The palmer, calmly accepting the detailed account of the visit to Hell, merely remarks that he fails to understand the part about women being shrewish and difficult, for he has never seen or known "any one woman out of patience." This thundering lie at once wins the competition. *A Merry Play between Johan Johan the husband, Tyb his wife, and Sir Johan the Priest* is on the ancient theme of the meek husband, the shrewish and unfaithful wife, and the wife's lover, a priest. The whole play is pure farce, knock-about domestic comedy, with no pretence at edification. Heywood's art thus matures into something resembling the modern music-hall or vaudeville sketch; drawing on a great variety of sources, both native and foreign, for his plots, he produced amusing dramatic anecdotes. The plots are rudimentary; he showed no sign of being able to contrive a sustained piece of dramatic structure; even his best pieces must thus be called sketches rather than comedies.

The shift of interest from salvation to education, which has already been noted as marking a distinction between the medieval morality play and the Tudor interlude, was accompanied by a parallel shift from religion to politics. And when religion *is* treated, it is treated in the spirit of controversy produced by the Reformation and the great debate about the true form of Christianity which raged throughout the Tudor period and later. Such controversial or propagandist morality plays inevitably abandoned the large universal moral and religious themes of the older moralities and were liable to make the vices into representatives of a degenerate Catholicism. John Bale (1495–1563) wrote a number of Protestant propagandist plays, one of them, *King Johan,* being at the same time a history play (of sorts): its hero is King John, who is treated as a Christian hero who defied the Pope in the interests of an independent Bible-reading England. Abstractions and historical figures are curiously mingled in *King Johan.* The situation is confused by the fact that the play survives only in a much revised form, but the movement to and fro between an historical and allegorical treatment of the characters seems to be an integral part of the play's method. Thus Usurped Power, Sedition, Dissimulation, Commonalty, Nobility, Clergy, and Civil Order are characters, some of whom at times become historical figures (Usurped Power, for example, being the Pope and Dissimulation Archbishop Stephen Langton). This play can in a sense be called the first English history play, but it is history treated in a very special way, and *King Johan* is thus not to be taken as an early example of the Elizabethan chronicle history play, which will be considered later. Bale's other plays include three on biblical themes in the manner of the miracle plays and one using allegorical figures in the morality tradition: all are strongly Protestant in tone.

The ethico-political theme preceded Reformation controversy in English drama. Skelton's *Magnificence* (ca. 1515), aimed at Cardinal Wolsey, shows the rise, fall, and final repentance of a worldly prince who is seduced and in the end redeemed by allegorical figures representing different virtues and vices. Though it ends on a conventional religious note, its main lesson is not that of the medieval moralities but rather the Aristotelian virtue of measure, or moderation—a Humanist rather than a Christian virtue. The treatment of ethical and political themes is closely bound up with the Renaissance interest in education, particularly the education of princes, and in Skelton's *Magnificence* and Bale's *King Johan* we can see the tendency to present such subjects through the lives of individuals which is reflected in such a work as the *Mirror for Magistrates*. But once dramatic interest is focused on an individual, whether as an awful warning or as an example of the fall of princes, the possibilities of more exciting and more profound exploration of human fate are likely to suggest themselves, and in the end we arrive at new conceptions of both comedy and tragedy. The political, ethical, and religious moralities of the early Tudor period, insofar as they led on occasion from allegorical personification of virtues and vices to the presentation of the fate of a single historical character, do represent, however faintly, a movement toward greater dramatic maturity.

But the movement is not one of simple chronological development. Allegorical, biblical, and historical morality plays existed side by side in the middle of the sixteenth century. *Respublica*, perhaps by Nicholas Udall, was first performed in 1553; it mingles the older kind of religion with new political themes. A decade later, plays which handled biblical stories from a Protestant propagandist point of view (under the influence of Bale) seem to have been popular. At the same time classical influences were making themselves felt, providing new themes and a new sense of structure. Nicholas Udall, at one time headmaster of Eton and at the end of his life headmaster of Westminster, wrote *Ralph Roister Doister* about 1553, taking its theme from the *Miles Gloriosus* of the Roman playwright Plautus, thus bringing the braggart soldier for the first time into English drama. Roister Doister is the braggart who courts Dame Custance, a lady of some fortune already engaged to Gawin Goodluck. His servant Matthew Merrygreek is both the "parasite" of Latin comedy and the Vice of the morality plays. (The Vice in the moralities had long since developed into a clowning practical joker.) Roister Doister's fatuous courtship, continually prompted but never really helped by Merrygreek, ends with his defeat at the hands of Dame Custance and her lively maids. Everything ends happily, with reconciliation all round. The plot is simple enough, but it does include a complication and a resolution and thus shows a firmer grasp on structure than had yet been displayed in an English comedy. *Gammer Gurton's Needle* was written by "Mr. S.," probably William Stevenson of Christ's College, Cambridge, a few years later, and produced at the College. Here again Plautine themes and characters are domiciled in a comedy of English rural life. The plot is crude: it concerns Gammer Gurton's loss of her needle, out of which a variety of complications develop until the needle is accidentally discovered sticking in the seat of Hodge's breeches (Hodge is Gammer

Gurton's farm servant). But the construction, in five acts, is ingenious and effective and the low-life comedy genuinely amusing. Diccon the Bedlam, the central comic figure of the play, again combines medieval Vice and classical parasite, but he is a thoroughly English character for all that. The verse form is primitive—rhyming "fourteeners"—but the accent of conversation gets through with remarkable vitality. Verse was still the regular medium for English plays, often doggerel yet also often surprisingly lively. It was not until George Gascoigne produced his play *Supposes* at Gray's Inn in 1566 that prose made its appearance in English drama. Gascoigne's play is another comedy adapted from a foreign source, this time from the Italian, Ariosto's *Gli Suppositi*, though Ariosto himself was indebted to Plautus. The plot concerns a student and his faithful and ingenious servant managing by disguise and intrigue to outwit the older generation so that the student finally gets his girl; before the witty confusions produced by the behavior of the hero and his servant are finally cleared up, there is such a muddle of suppositions and countersuppositions on all sides that the play almost explodes in a riot of misunderstanding. This is a much more sophisticated piece of work than *Ralph Roister Doister* or *Gammer Gurton's Needle:* its Italianate subtleties and its extraordinary plays on words are far removed from the bluff humors of English rustic comedy or domestic farce. Gascoigne's play reminds us that the native popular tradition of English drama was now to be modified both by classical influences and by the tastes of more sophisticated audiences at the Inns of Court, the universities, the country houses of noble patrons, and the Court of Queen Elizabeth. *Supposes* is the first of a series of witty Italianate comedies in English which includes Shakespeare's *Taming of the Shrew* (which draws on Gascoigne for its subplot), *The Two Gentlemen of Verona,* and *Much Ado about Nothing,* in which the *genre* reaches its climax.

We have already noted how Humanist influence showed itself in the educational and ethical interests of the Tudor interludes, and we have noticed, too, the domesticating of themes from Plautus in English comedy. It was inevitable that Humanist interest in the Latin and Greek classics should also produce a new kind of English tragedy. There were no tragedies, of course, among either the miracle or the morality plays; indeed, there was nothing that could be called tragedy in English drama before the classical influence made itself felt. The favorite classical writer of tragedies among English Humanists was not Sophocles or Euripides but Seneca, the Stoic Roman, whose nine tragedies, never meant to be acted, adapted the old Greek myths to produce violent yet somber treatments of murder, cruelty, and lust. (They were translated into English by Jasper Heywood and others in the mid-sixteenth century.) Written in a polished yet monotonous verse, Seneca's tragedies combine powerful rhetoric, Stoic moralizing, and horror; the emotional crises are punctuated by epigrams; the characters are not subtly drawn but are carried along by the violence of their emotions: altogether they present a strange mixture of sophistication and crudeness (suggesting the rather exhibitionist work of a bright young man), and were certainly no happy model for a young drama moving at last toward some concept of tragedy.

But Senecan tragedy was, in its own way, ordered and concentrated. English attempts to handle classical themes in the native way can be seen in Richard Edwards' *Damon and Pythias* (played in 1564) which handles the famous story of friendship with an extraordinary combination of fooling and moralizing. John Pickering's *New Interlude of Vice Containing the History of Horestes* (printed in 1567), tells the story of Orestes' revenge on his mother and Aegisthus ("Egestus") with a remarkable mixture of military violence ("make your battle lively," says a direction to the players), allegorical action with the Vice acting as both clown and tempter, and realistic English characters. A similar combination is found in *Apius and Virginia* by "R.B." (printed in 1575 and described on the title page as "a new tragical comedy") and in Thomas Preston's *Cambises* (ca. 1570), which is described as "a lamentable tragedy, mixed full of pleasant mirth." These are typical of a group of plays produced in the 1560's and 1570's and still popular in Shakespeare's day. The lumbering "fourteeners," with their padding and repetitive rhetoric, were mocked by Shakespeare both in the play given by Bottom and his companions in *A Midsummer Night's Dream* and in Falstaff's "for I must speak in passion, and I will do it in King Cambyses' vein" in *Henry IV, Part I.*

Sir Philip Sidney, in his *Defence of Poesie*, objected strenuously to this sort of thing, and approved only the Senecan tragedy *Gorboduc*, by Thomas Sackville and Thomas Norton, produced both at Inner Temple and before the Queen at Whitehall in 1561-62. "Our tragedies and comedies (not without cause cried out against), observing rules neither of honest civility nor of skilful poetry, excepting *Gorboduc*, . . . which notwithstanding, as it is full of stately speeches and well sounding phrases, climbing to the height of Seneca his style and as full of notable morality which it doth most delightfully teach." And again, after complaining that the English plays move freely from place to place and jump long periods of time, he continues: "But besides these gross absurdities, how all their plays be neither right tragedies nor right comedies, mingling kings and clowns, not because the matter so carryeth it, but thrust in clowns by head and shoulders to play a part in majestical matters, with neither decency nor discretion. So as neither the admiration and commiseration, nor the right sportfulness, is by their mongrel tragi-comedy obtained." Sidney was not merely pedantically defending the "unities" of time and place and action on which the Renaissance Italian critics had so insisted (deriving the notion of unity of action from Aristotle's *Poetics* and expanding it to insist that plays should represent action as taking place in a single locality and during a single day); he was voicing a very natural exasperation with the complete lawlessness of native English drama. Shakespeare was to discipline this in his own way, and show the potentialities of the native tradition; but Sidney, writing in the early 1580's, could only hail the dreary Senecan *Gorboduc* as a herald of better things.

Gorboduc (also known as *Ferrex and Porrex*) is a tale of a divided kingdom, civil war, and the awful consequences of split authority in a state, which takes its plot from that mythical region of early English history which the Tudor chroniclers regarded as fact and which Spenser occasionally used in *The Faerie Queene* and Shakespeare drew on in *King Lear*. It is divided into five acts: it follows the classical manner in avoiding violence on the stage; and it is written in a wooden blank verse. It is sententious, rhetorical, and supremely dull. Though historically important as the first English play in blank verse and as an attempt at a purely "regular" form of tragedy which proved to have no real future in England, it is a play which nobody today would read for pleasure. There were imitations of *Gorboduc*, including *Jocasta*, by Gascoigne and Francis Kinwelmersh, presented at Gray's Inn in 1566, and *Gismond of Salern* (later revised as *Tancred and Gismund*), with a plot from the *Decameron*, which was first written in rhymed verse and then rewritten "according to the decorum of these days" in blank verse by Robert Wilmot. They too are "regular" and sententious and dull. The fashion remained popular for some time among certain "highbrow" groups, but no major dramatist ever wrote this kind of neoclassic play in Elizabethan England and, however the literary scene may have looked to Sidney in 1580, English drama was not to go that way.

From church to churchyard to "stations" in the town; from ecclesiastical auspices to those of town guilds; from amateur clerical authorship to professional authorship and professional acting—this was the progress of English drama from the early medieval period to Tudor times. At the same time the schools, the Inns of Court, the universities, houses of noblemen, and the Queen's Court provided opportunities for more sophisticated or more learned plays than were possible in the more public entertainments given by itinerant players in town innyards or on village greens. Nicholas Udall was a schoolmaster who wrote plays for his boys to act; and it was common enough in schools which had come under Humanist influence to have the boys act Plautus or Terence in Latin as part of their education. *Gorboduc, Jocasta,* and *Gismond of Salern* were first presented at Inns of Court. Latin comedies, derived largely from the Italian, were popular at Cambridge in the 1580's. It was at Cambridge, too, that *Gammer Gurton's Needle* was first acted, and that university also produced at the turn of the century a series of academic comedies about scholars, their way of life, and their prospects. Meanwhile, Oxford was producing Senecan tragedies in Latin.

As, with the progress of the sixteenth century, drama became more abundant and more various, professionalization developed both among authors and among actors. Some groups of actors were independent companies plying their trade where they could and doing so for their own profit. Others were servants of some wealthy nobleman and were under his protection. In 1583, Queen Elizabeth's Master of the Revels decided to form a company of players for the direct service of the Queen, and accordingly picked a number from among the companies attached to different noblemen—the Earls of Sussex, of Leicester, and of Oxford, among others—to form the Queen's men. This was perhaps a move on the part of the Court to defeat the claims of the Corporation of the City of London to control plays and players in the area under their jurisdiction. The Corporation shared some of the Puritan objections to the acted drama, and in addition, consisting as it did of employers of labor in the City, it objected to employees and apprentices being seduced by plays from their work. The opposition between the City and the stage had been developing steadily in the 1570's. In 1576, James Burbage, leader of the Earl of Leicester's men, had erected the first permanent theater (called simply the Theatre) on a field near Shoreditch, outside the City boundaries and so beyond the control of the Lord Mayor and Corporation. The Corporation kept restricting and even forbidding plays, but, with the Court on the players' side, they fought a losing battle. Other permanent theaters soon followed the Theatre—the Curtain, also in Shoreditch, in 1577, one at Newington Butts about 1580, the Rose, on the south bank of the Thames, about 1588, the Swan in Southwark about 1595, and the Globe in 1598. These theaters were built by companies of players who had begun as itinerant "vagabonds" but who were all now servants, theoretically at least, of noblemen, wearing their livery and free of the legal penalties of vagabondage. The structure of the theaters derived from the innyards which had served as their predecessors. They were round or octagonal, with the pit (or yard) open to the sky. Tiers of covered galleries ran round the yard, except for the section occupied by the stage, which was a large platform jutting well out into the yard and divided into an outer stage and an inner stage behind, which could be curtained off. Above the inner stage was the "upper stage," a gallery over which, supported by columns on the main stage, a thatched roof projected. Though costumes were often elaborate, properties were few and scenery in the modern sense nonexistent: the whole burden fell on speech and action. This platform stage of the Elizabethans must be clearly distinguished from the later picture-frame stage with its scenes "realistically" localized by means of a painted backcloth as well as from the more elaborate modern attempts to build up a complete illusion of physical realism on the stage. The Elizabethan stage was in essence a platform which could symbolically represent any place: it was up to the dramatist to create the proper illusion by his language. Often it was not necessary for the scene to be precisely localized at all. There were no actresses: boys took women's parts.

These were the public theaters; in addition there were "private" theaters, distinguished from the others by being roofed and by somewhat more complicated interior arrangements. They also charged rather more. The private theaters were originally used by child actors, drawn from the choirs of St. Paul's and the Chapel Royal. The first private theater was the Blackfriars, opened in 1576 for the children of the Chapel Royal, and we find it a few years later used by boy actors from other choirs as well (and in 1609–10 by Shakespeare's company). These boys, who were highly trained professionals, acted in more scholarly plays in the Humanist tradition with somewhat more elaborate staging than was employed in the public theaters. At times, they became serious rivals to the adult companies, as Shakespeare's reference in *Hamlet* to "an aery of children, little eyases, that cry out on the top of question, and are most tyrannically clapped for 't" makes clear.

There was thus the public theater, which produced popular plays appealing to all tastes; the private theater, where players, often boys, put on more sophisticated pieces for a more sophisticated audience; and the Court itself, as well as the halls of individual noblemen, where many kinds of entertainments, including plays, were produced to celebrate such occasions as visits by foreign notables, weddings, coronations, royal and other distinguished marriages, and visits by the Queen to different cities or country houses. The Court—which had had a permanent Master of the Revels since 1545—also put on entertainments at such festive seasons as Christmas, New Year, Twelfth Night, and Shrovetide, and could call on professional or semiprofessional companies attached to the royal household. The Master of the Children of the Chapel Royal had his carefully trained children available (Richard Edwards held this office, and his *Damon and Pithias* was played before the Queen by the Children of the Chapel), and the children of the choir school of St. Paul's (to be distinguished from the Grammar School also associated with the Cathedral) also performed at Court as well as joining the Children of the Chapel for public performances at the Blackfriars theater. As we have seen, the Queen's men were formed in 1583. These, and the companies in the service of noblemen, were available for Court and other private festivities and at the same time gave professional performances in the public theater.

The growing popularity and diversity of the drama, its secularization, and the growth of a class of writers and scholars who had no desire to be in holy orders (as the medieval scholar was bound to be) combined to produce a new literary phenomenon—the secular professional playwright. The group of writers known as the "University Wits," young men who had graduated at Oxford or Cambridge with no patrons to sponsor their literary activities and no desire to enter the Church, were the first to exploit this situation. They turned to playwriting to make a living, and in doing so they made Elizabethan popular drama more literary and in some respects more dramatic. Not all of them turned to the public theater: in writing plays for the Children of the Chapel to present at Court or at Blackfriars there was always the chance of attracting royal attention or achieving a noble patron. The University Wits thus had an important influence both on the public and the private theater; they wrote both roaring popular successes and sophisticated confections for connoisseurs. It could perhaps be claimed that they were the first to associate English drama permanently with *literature*. There is no necessary connection between plays and literature, and both in public and private entertainments the emphasis had often been as much on the action or the rant or (in Court performance) the splendor of the sheer *show* as on the dramatic effectiveness of the language itself. The University Wits, educated, ambitious, and opportunistic, often reckless bohemians in their personal lives but always professional men of letters, set the course for later Elizabethan and Jacobean drama and, in particular, paved the way for Shakespeare. The group consists of

John Lyly, Robert Greene, George Peele, Thomas Lodge, Thomas Kyd, Thomas Nashe, and Christopher Marlowe.

Lyly, who was born about 1554 and died in 1606, turned to drama after his success with *Euphues,* adapting his courtly artificial prose to the stage to produce a new kind of court comedy. It was for the Children of St. Paul's that most of his plays were written, to be performed at Court before the Queen. His intricately balanced and stylized prose is not the most suitable medium for dramatic dialogue, but it did at least impose some order on dramatic speech, even if his tendency to interrupt the action by cunningly wrought monologues is less agreeable to modern taste than it apparently was to that of those who saw the first Court performances; and in any case a move toward a polished prose, however overmannered, was an improvement over the doggerel "fourteeners" of his predecessors. The wit and grace of the prose of Shakespeare's "middle" comedies owe much to Lyly. For his plots, Lyly turned to Greek legend, but he did not simply dramatize well-known classical myths; he used characters and themes from mythology in a wholly original way. *A most excellent Comedy of Alexander, Campaspe, and Diogenes* (as the title page of the 1584 edition calls it) introduces characters from Greek history; its theme is the rivalry in love between Alexander the Great and the painter Apelles for the Theban captive Campaspe, and it is handled with a mixture of mythology and sentiment. Mythology is more pronounced in *Sapho and Phao, Endimion,* and *Midas,* which interweave more realistic subplots (in which Lyly shows that he could write a more vigorous, colloquial prose when he wanted to) with the main mythological theme, and in which also, perhaps, allegorical references to contemporary affairs are to be traced by the initiated. *Gallathea, Love's Metamorphosis,* and *The Woman in the Moon* are pastoral plays. The first is laid in Lincolnshire, the second in Arcadia, and the third in Utopia, but in fact the scene is the same in all three—a pastoral dreamland against which allegorical and mythological action concerning nymphs, swains, soldiers, monsters, goddesses, and a variety of human lovers and supernatural characters is played out. *The Woman in the Moon* is Lyly's only play in blank verse, and it is more satirical in tone than any of his others. *Mother Bombie* (if it is Lyly's) stands apart from his other plays: this is a comedy in the tradition of Plautus and Terence, where scapegrace young men and their ingenious servants outwit their more prudential elders in bringing their love affairs to a successful conclusion. The mythological and pastoral plays include some charming lyrics, which are not, however, certainly by Lyly, since they are first included in a posthumous edition of his "court comedies" in 1632. The phrase that comes to mind with reference to Lyly's plays is "faded charm." They are unequal; the subplots are not always effectively tied up with the main story; the euphuistic prose is often tedious; but there is a delicate imagination at work here, a sense of form, and a new conception of comedy, all of which held rich promise for later Elizabethan drama.

George Peele (ca. 1558–ca. 1596) began his career as a dramatist with a courtly mythological pastoral play in the same vein as many of Lyly's. This was *The Arraignment of Paris*, played by the Children of the Chapel before the Queen in the early 1580's. Peele takes the familiar story of the judgment of Paris, handling the love of Paris and Oenone and Paris's subsequent faithlessness with a smooth lyrical grace. The love of Colin for his hardhearted Thestylis provides a subplot, with rustic characters (whose names are derived from Spenser's *Shepherd's Calendar*) introduced to provide a more realistic level of action. Paris is summoned before the Council of the Gods, at the instance of Pallas and Juno, to be accused of partiality in his judgment. He defends himself in vigorous blank verse, and in the end Diana awards the disputed golden apple to

>   a gracious nymph
>   That honours Dian for her chastity,
>   And likes the labours well of Phoebe's groves;
>   The place Elizium hight, and of the place
>   Her name that governs there Eliza is.

And so the play is turned into a compliment to Queen Elizabeth. It is written in a variety of verse forms, including "fourteeners" and blank verse, and includes some fine singing lyrics, notably the duet sung by Paris and Oenone, "Fair and fair, and twice so fair," which is sadly echoed later in Oenone's lament for her desertion by Paris. Peele's *Old Wives' Tale* is a play of wicked enchantment and true love which begins as a story told by Madge, wife of Clunch the blacksmith, to three gay fellows who have lost their way in the wood and whom she is entertaining at her cottage; but soon after she begins to tell the story the characters appear to act it out, so that Madge's story becomes the play. The introductory scene is in vigorous colloquial prose; the main part of the play is partly in a more mannered prose and partly in blank verse. Though the whole has a quaint charm, the different elements of which it is composed are too loosely connected to produce a satisfactory drama. *The Battle of Alcazar* is a crude piece of bombast, and *Edward I* a loosely linked, episodic treatment of history. *The love of King David and Fair Bethsabe* dramatizes the biblical story of David's love for

Bathsheba and Absalom's rebellion in richly ornamented and slow moving blank verse. Peele was a poet of skill and charm, who experimented with drama in order to further his career. He had little theatrical sense or gift for dramatic structure, but he had facility and versatility and his flowing lyricism brought something new to Elizabethan drama.

Robert Greene (ca. 1558–92), a prolific and versatile bohemian, is better known for his graphic autobiographical prose than for his plays, but he, too, turned to the drama as a source of livelihood. Greene himself tells in *A Groatsworth of Wit* how he came to write for the stage. Once, sitting by a hedge lamenting his misfortunes and poor prospects, he was overheard by a player who told him he required the services of a scholar to write plays, "for which you will be well paid if you take the pains." To which proposal he agreed, thinking it best "in respect of his present necessity to try his wit." The result was a group of plays characterized by a craftsmanlike plotting, a skillful mixture of a realistic native background and an atmosphere of romance, and an ability to portray a heroine who is both charming as a personality, attractive as a woman, and convincing as a human being. *The Honorable History of Friar Bacon and Friar Bungay* deals with Bacon's proof of his magical powers (which he ultimately renounces) before King Henry III and the Emperor of Germany and combines with this not only some colloquial humor but also a love idyll between Margaret, the fair maid of Fressingfield, and Lacy, Earl of Lincoln. The two plots are neatly fitted together; the action moves between Margaret's Suffolk, Friar Bacon's cell in Oxford, and the Court, with a simple fluidity that the platform stage, with its lack of scenery, made possible; the dialogue, mostly in workmanlike blank verse but occasionally in lively prose, carries the story along vigorously, in spite of some moments of unnecessary classical ornamentation in the love speeches. *The Scottish History of James the Fourth* is not, as its title might suggest, a history play, but a serious comedy derived from a story by the Italian Giraldi Cinthio. The play opens with a rather unusual piece of machinery: it is presented before Oberon, King of Fairies, by Bohan, a Scot, to prove his cynical view that the world is no place for a wise man to live in. The main story concerns King James' love for Ida, daughter of the Countess of Arran, and the evil (including countenancing an attempt on the life of his queen) into which this leads him. But Ida's steadfast discouragement of her royal wooer and Queen Dorothea's constancy to her erring husband (she is driven from court disguised as a page and wounded by a hired assassin) bring the story to a happy ending at last.

Dorothea combines the patience of Griselda with something of the self-reliance as well as the constancy of Shakespeare's Viola and Imogen, and the play, though slow moving, has some charming and some tenderly pathetic moments. Greene's other plays are less interesting (though *George a Green, or The Pinner of Wakefield,* which may well be Greene's but cannot be certainly attributed to him, shows many of his best qualities), *Orlando Furioso* (based on Ariosto) and *Alphonsus, King of Arragon* showing the influence, not very happily, of Marlowe's *Tamburlaine.* Unlike Lyly but like Kyd and Marlowe, Greene wrote for the public stage and aimed at popular success rather than Court favor. Like Lyly, he taught Shakespeare something about comedy, his plays being the first English examples of the *genre* to which critics have given the name "romantic comedy" —a *genre* of which Shakespeare's *Twelfth Night* and *As You Like It* represent the highest development.

Thomas Lodge (ca. 1557–1625) is much less important as a contributor to the development of the drama. His most interesting work is his euphuistic prose romance, *Rosalynde,* the source of Shakespeare's *As You Like It.* He wrote a considerable amount of miscellaneous prose and some accomplished sonnets, and collaborated with Greene in *A Looking Glass for London and England,* a moral play about a vicious tyrant called to repentance. His one certainly known wholly original play is *The Wounds of Civil War,* "lively set forth in the true tragedy of Marius and Scilla." This treatment of the civil war between Marius and Sulla is interesting as an early dramatic handling of Roman history, but on the whole it is a confused performance, despite some Marlovian moments. Thomas Nashe (1567– 1601) had a hand in some plays by more than one author (collaboration being a not uncommon practice at this period), but the only complete extant play of his is *Summer's Last Will and Testament,* an allegorical play about the seasons which mixes satire with courtly compliment; it has incidental songs and some lively moments, in spite of a general weakness in both plot and character drawing. Nashe's most important work is his picaresque tale, *The Unfortunate Traveller,* which is discussed in Chapter 13.

If Greene founded what has been called "romantic comedy," Thomas Kyd (1558–94) was an even greater popular success as the founder of what might be called "romantic tragedy." Mingling the themes of love, conspiracy, murder, and revenge, Kyd found a way of adapting some of the main elements of Senecan tragedy to roaring melodrama. *The Spanish Tragedy,* probably first produced in the early 1580's, is the first, and in its own melodramatic way the most

powerful, of the series of revenge plays which so captured the Elizabethan and the Jacobean imagination. It opens with a prologue, in
which the ghost of Andrea, a Spanish nobleman slain in battle against
Portugal by the Portuguese Prince Balthazar, tells how Proserpine
in Hades has promised him revenge against his slayer, and Revenge,
a spirit who accompanies him, confirms that he will see vengeance
duly executed on Balthazar. But in fact, though revenge is a main
theme of the play, it is only incidentally Andrea's revenge, and the
prologue is somewhat misleading. As the plot unfolds, we find Bell-
imperia, daughter of the Duke of Castile and beloved of the dead
Andrea, being comforted by Horatio, son of Hieronimo, marshal of
Spain, and Andrea's faithful friend during his lifetime. But Lorenzo,
Bell-imperia's sister, and Balthazar, the Portuguese Prince now an
honorable prisoner in Spain, become suspicious of the growing affection between Horatio and Bell-imperia. Balthazar is himself in
love with Bell-imperia, and later it emerges that the new treaty of
friendship between Spain and Portugal calls for the marriage of the
two. Lorenzo, with the assistance of Balthazar, murders Horatio in
an arbor where he is making love to Bell-imperia. Hieronimo, driven
distracted by the death of his son, whom he discovers hanging dead
in the arbor after Bell-imperia's cries have summoned him from his
bed, plans his revenge with a mixture of madness and cunning (there
is a blending of real and feigned madness here which Shakespeare
was to use in *Hamlet*). He eventually achieves his revenge by arranging a play as part of the festivities celebrating the reconciliation
between Spain and Portugal: the play is a tragedy in which Hieronimo, acting the part of a Turkish pasha, slays Erastus, knight of
Rhodes (played by Lorenzo) to enable his friend the Turkish emperor (played by Balthazar) to possess Erastus' beautiful wife (played
by Bell-imperia). The wife then slays the emperor and stabs herself.
Hieronimo and Bell-imperia arrange that the killing shall be in
earnest, and thus Lorenzo and Balthazar are slain before the ad-
miring eyes of the King of Spain, the Duke of Castile, and the Vice-
roy of Portugal, who think it is all a show. Bell-imperia also really
slays herself, though Hieronimo had not intended that. Hieronimo
then gloats over his revenge, and when seized and told he will be
forced to tell the details of his crime, he bites off his tongue and
spits it on to the stage, to make sure that he will not talk. They then
say that he will be tortured until he writes the truth, but he defeats
them by calling for a knife on the pretense of mending his pen: with
it he stabs the Duke of Castile and then himself. Several minor

characters are also killed in the course of the play: the total list is happily recited by the ghost by way of epilogue:

> Ay, now my hopes have end in their effects,
> When blood and sorrow finish my desires:
> Horatio murdered in his father's bower;
> Vild Serberine by Pedringano slain;
> False Pedringano hang'd by quaint device;
> Fair Isabella by herself misdone;
> Prince Balthazar by Bell-imperia stabb'd;
> The Duke of Castile and his wicked son
> Both done to death by old Hieronimo;
> My Bell-imperia fall'n as Dido fell,
> And good Hieronimo slain by himself:
> Ay, these were spectacles to please my soul! . . .

But a summary of the plot gives little idea of the power of the play. Violence is everywhere, passion and intrigue work themselves out in every kind of horror and cruel cunning. The blank verse mingles exclamatory rhetoric with morbid sententiousness. After the witty love play in the dialogue between Bell-imperia and Horatio in the arbor—

> Bel.   If I be Venus, thou must needs be Mars;
>   And where Mars reigneth there must needs be wars.
> Hor.   Then thus begin our wars: put forth thy hand,
>   That it may combat with my ruder hand.
> Bel.   Set forth thy foot to try the push of mine.
> Hor.   But first my looks shall combat against thine.
> Bel.   Then guard thyself: I dart this kiss at thee. . . .—

we get the sudden intrusion of the murderers, the dispatching of Horatio, Bell-imperia's outcry, Lorenzo's callous, "Come, stop her mouth; away with her," and then the sudden entry of the aroused Hieronimo:

> What outcries pluck me from my naked bed,
> And chill my throbbing heart with trembling fear,
> Which never danger yet could daunt before?
> Who calls Hieronimo? Speak, here I am.
> I did not slumber; therefore 'twas no dream,
> And here within this garden did she cry,
> And in this garden must I rescue her.—
> But stay, what murd'rous spectacle is this?
> A man hang'd up and all the murderers gone!
> And in my bower, to lay the guilt on me!

This place was made for pleasure, not for death.
                                    He cuts him down.
Those garments that he wears I oft have seen—
Alas, it is Horatio, my sweet son!
O no, but he that whilom was my son!
O, was it thou that call'dst me from my bed?
O speak, if any spark of life remain:
I am thy father; who hath slain my son?
What savage monster, not of human kind,
Hath here been glutted with thy harmless blood,
And left thy bloody corpse dishonoured here,
For me, amidst these dark and deathful shades,
To drown thee with an ocean of my tears? . . .

In spite of the long rhetorical outbursts, the speed of the action
is tremendous, event following on event with the grimmest kind of
irony. The characterization in the play is crude to the point of non-
existence; the characters have passions and nothing else; but their
passions do carry them on, making them dissemble and hate and go
frantic as well as love and murder. *The Spanish Tragedy* was immensely "good theater"; it was one of the great successes of the Elizabethan public stage, and was continually being revived. Shakespeare
of course knew it as a popular theatrical piece, and took many devices from it. Indeed, it might almost be said that *The Spanish
Tragedy* is the great property-room of Elizabethan tragic devices: the revenge theme, the play within a play, the madness real
and feigned, the Machiavellian master of malicious plotting who
begins with Lorenzo and culminates in Iago. Time and time again
later Elizabethan plays use or refer to something in *The Spanish
Tragedy*. When, in *A Midsummer Night's Dream*, the bewitched
Titania awakes and hears Bottom singing, she exclaims:

> What angel wakes me from my flowery bed?

—which is surely a deliberate parody of Hieronimo's

> What outcries pluck me from my naked bed?

It is supposed that Kyd wrote a *Hamlet* (which has not survived),
on which Shakespeare based his *Hamlet;* but even without this pre-
sumed lost play of Kyd's we can see his kind of sensational melodrama lies behind the infinitely subtler and profounder Shakespearean tragedy. *The Spanish Tragedy* was sensational stuff all right,
Senecan though it was in some respects (though not in its having
violent physical action on the stage). But it was tragedy of a sort—

the first truly popular tragedy of the English stage, and one of the most influential.

Two other tragedies, both at one time or another wrongly ascribed to Shakespeare, date from this period. One is *Locrine,* a Senecan treatment of a story from legendary British history: it deals with Locrine, son of Brutus and King of Britain, his wife Gwendolen, and his paramour the fair Estrelda. As Spenser told the story, in Book II of *The Faerie Queene:*

> . . . He lov'd fair Lady Estrild, lewdly lov'd,
> Whose wanton pleasures him too much did please,
> That quite his heart from Gwendolen remov'd,
> From Gwendolen his wife, though always faithful prov'd.

Gwendolen seeks revenge in battle, and prevails. In the end, Estrelda and her daughter Sabrina are drowned in a river.

> Which of her name now *Severn* men do call:
> Such was the end, that to disloyal love did fall.

Spenser's brief telling of the story and Milton's introduction of Sabrina in *Comus* testify to the popularity of the theme. As handled by the anonymous author, the tragedy shows the Senecan style adapted for the public theater with less theatrical liveliness than Kyd succeeded in introducing into *The Spanish Tragedy* but with similar machinery. Much more interesting as a play than *Locrine* is another anonymous tragedy, *Arden of Feversham,* the first example of what has been called Elizabethan domestic tragedy. It deals with a real-life murder, which had occurred in 1551 and was recorded by Holinshed in his *Chronicles of England, Ireland and Scotland* (1578). Thomas Arden of Feversham, a prosperous gentleman, has a wife Alice who has become enamored of a low-born and ill-bred fellow named Mosbie. To enjoy Mosbie's sole love she plots, with him, to murder her husband. While her motive is infatuation, his is desire for wealth. The story is presented with remarkable psychological realism, concentrating on the changing passions and doubts and fears of the principal characters with an insight into character that *The Spanish Tragedy,* for all its theatrical brilliance, never displays (though the play has been attributed to Kyd and to Kyd and Marlowe jointly). The atmosphere of Elizabethan middle-class life is vividly presented: this is no story of Spanish noblemen or Italian intrigue, but a grimly convincing account of domestic crime. In spite of some crudities of sentiment and expression, *Arden of Feversham* is an impressive play which anticipates many later developments in Elizabethan and Jacobean tragedy.

English tragedy had not yet, however, found a blank verse eloquent and musical enough to add the effect of poetic conviction to that of rhetorical excitement. Nor had it yet turned to themes that came truly home to the Elizabethan imagination. In the hands of Christopher Marlowe (1564–93) it advanced spectacularly toward the achievement of these two goals. Marlowe, the most striking personality and the most impressive dramatist among the University Wits, stormed his way into popular favor with *Tamburlaine the Great*, a play in two parts probably first produced in the winter of 1587–88 when the author was still in his early twenties. This flamboyant story of the conquering Scythian shepherd, presented in a richly declamatory blank verse abounding in colorful images of power and violence, brought a new kind of life to the English theater. Marlowe's prologue indicates his own notion of what he was doing:

> From jigging veins of riming mother wits,
> And such conceits as clownage keeps in pay,
> We'll lead you to the stately tent of war,
> Where you shall hear the Scythian Tamburlaine
> Threat'ning the world with high astounding terms. . . .

The presentation of a man slaughtering his way to world mastery, convinced of his own invincibility and drunk with a sense of his own conquering mission, might soon have become tedious if Marlowe had not found a form of blank verse whose sounding lines echoed sonorously across the stage and kept the play continuously at an emotional fever pitch. This is a study of lust for power and military achievement gloried in almost esthetically for its own sake: it requires—and receives—"a great and thundring speech." All the excitement of new geographical discoveries, all the richly luxurious implications which oriental splendor has held for the occidental imagination ever since the temperate Greeks faced the extravagant Persians or the restrained self-indulgence of Horace repudiated the "Persicos apparatus," all the new glory of Elizabethan poetic utterance, the Renaissance feeling for *virtù*, the fascination with what man can achieve along a single line of endeavor if he sets his mind and heart to it with sufficient fervor and lyrical enthusiasm; the interest in pride, in lust for power, in man as master of his own destiny, challenging and vying with the gods—"How noble in reason! How infinite in faculties! In form and moving how express and admirable! In action how like an angel! In apprehension how like a god!"—and imagining that by an effort of the will he can control Fortune's wheel—all this is in *Tamburlaine,* a play which ignores moral considerations to exhibit the impressiveness of boundless ambition coupled with determination and self-confidence that similarly know no limits.

We find in *Tamburlaine,* even in the speech of the minor characters, that resounding use of exotic place names which Shakespeare
was to develop in *Antony and Cleopatra* and which Milton was to
turn to his own rather different purposes in *Paradise Lost.* The
characters conquered by Tamburlaine are themselves first built up
in magnificence so that Tamburlaine's achievement in overcoming
them and assuming their power and titles can be seen as greater
still. When Cosroe supplants his brother as King of Persia he is
hailed thus by his followers:

> We here do crown thee Monarch of the East,
> Emperour of Asia and of Persea,
> Great Lord of Medea and Armenia:
> Duke of Africa and Albania,
> Mesopotamia and of Parthia,
> East India and the late discovered Isles,
> Chief Lord of all the wide vast Euxine sea,
> And of the ever raging Caspian Lake:
> Long live Cosroe mighty Emperor.

Images of power and multitude combine in Bassoe's description of
the power of Bajazeth, Emperor of the Turks, another powerful
ruler to be subdued by Tamburlaine:

> My lord, the great Commander of the world,
> Besides fifteen contributory kings,
> Hath now in arms ten thousand Janisaries,
> Mounted on lusty Mauritanian steeds,
> Brought to the war by men of Tripoly.

Orcanes, "king of Natolia," planning an already doomed expedition
against Tamburlaine with the most powerful allies he can muster,
admits that

> Slavonians, Almains, Rutters, Muffes, and Danes
> Fear not Orcanes, but great Tamburlaine,
> Nor he but Fortune that hath made him great.
> We have revolted Grecians, Albanees,
> Cicilians, Jews, Arabians, Turks, and Moors,
> Illirians, Thracians, and Bythinians,
> Enough to swallow forceless Sigismond
> Yet scarce enough t' encounter Tamburlaine.
> He brings a world of people to the field,
> From Scythia to the Oriental Plage
> Of India, where raging Lantchidol
> Beats on the regions with his boisterous blows,
> That never sea-man yet discovered:

> All Asia is in arms with Tamburlaine,
> Even from the midst of fiery Cancer's Tropic,
> To Amazonia under Capricorn,
> And thence as far as Aechipellago;
> All Afric is in arms with Tamburlaine. . . .

This, of course, is overdoing it, and there is no doubt that the young Marlowe does work his tricks to excess; but they are tricks that Shakespeare was to learn from:

> He hath assembled
> Bocchus, the king of Lybia; Archelaus,
> Of Cappadocia; the Thracian king, Adallas;
> King Malchus of Arabia; King of Pont;
> Herod of Jewry; Mithradates, king
> Of Comagene; Polemon and Amyntas,
> The kings of Mede and Lycaonia, with a
> More larger list of sceptres.

So Shakespeare gives the Roman view of the enormity of Antony's defection in "giving his empire up to a whore" and making common cause with strange and sinister barbaric powers. Milton was to use such geographical imagery in his own fashion:

> A multitude, like which the populous North
> Pour'd never from her frozen loins, to pass
> Rhene or the Danaw, when her barbarous Sons
> Came like a Deluge on the South, and spread
> Beneath Gibraltar to the Lybian sands.

Or, with the overtones more purely literary:

> For never since created man,
> Met such imbodied force, as nam'd with these
> Could merit more than that small infantry
> Warr'd on by Cranes: though all the Giant brood
> Phlegra with th' Heroic Race were join'd
> That fought at Thebes and Ilium, on each side
> Mixt with auxiliar Gods; and what resounds
> In Fable or Romance of Uther's Son
> Begirt with British and Armoric Knights;
> And all who since, Baptiz'd or Infidel
> Jousted in Aspramont or Montalban,
> Damasco, or Marocco, or Trebisond,
> When Charlemain with all his Peerage fell
> By Fontarabbia.

Geography, history, and romance came together in the Elizabethan and seventeenth-century poetic mind, with powerful effect.

The intoxication with power is perhaps the main theme of *Tamburlaine,* and images of power abound in the play.

> Is it not brave to be a King, Techelles? . . .
> Is it not passing brave to be a King,
> And ride in triumph through Persepolis?

But "the thirst of reign and sweetness of a crown" do not represent a desire for any attainable object; nor does Tamburlaine show much interest in the fruits of power once he has attained it. His is the Faustian urge, the urge to reach beyond the limits of mortality, and though his ambition manifests itself in military conquest and often in outrageous cruelty and is not, like that of Dr. Faustus, intellectual in its primary impetus, there are moments when he sees its purely symbolic nature:

> Our souls, whose faculties can comprehend
> The wondrous architecture of the world,
> And measure every wand'ring planet's course,
> Still climbing after knowledge infinite,
> And always moving as the restless spheres,
> Will us to wear ourselves and never rest
> Until we reach the ripest fruit of all,
> That perfect bliss and sole felicity,
> The sweet fruition of an earthly crown.

Tamburlaine's conquests have no material objective in view: they are, one might almost say, metaphysical in inspiration. His love for Zenocrate does not project any serious dramatic conflict in the play —like that between love and honor which Dryden made out of *Antony and Cleopatra*—but is presented in order that the claims of beauty should be sounded in the same eloquent style that celebrates military power and conquest. But the scenes which must have struck the Elizabethan audience with most force are those where the imagery of power is projected in concrete situations: Bajazeth, the Emperor of the Turks, and his wife kept like beasts in a cage and taunted to desperation by Tamburlaine for the amusement of himself and Zenocrate; Tamburlaine using Bajazeth as his footstool as he climbs on to his chair; or, in the second part, Tamburlaine with his chariot drawn by conquered kings—"Tamburlaine drawn in his chariot by Trebizon and Soria with bittes in their mouthes, reines in his left hand, in his right hand a whip, with which he scourgeth them," as the picturesque stage direction of the early editions has it. Bajazeth finally dashes his brains out against the cage, and his wife, seeing what he has done, follows his example after a fine exhibition of Elizabethan frenzy. The early spelling gives its flavor more fully:

O Baiazet, O Turk, O Emperor, give him his liquor? Not I, bring milk and fire, and my blood I bring him againe, teare me in peeces, give me the words with a ball of wildefire upon it. Downe with him, downe with him. Goe to my child, away, away, away. Ah, save that Infant, save him, save him. I, even I speake to her, the Sun was downe. Streamers white, Red, Blacke, here, here, here. Fling the meat in his face. Tamburlaine, Tamburlaine, Let the souldiers be buried. Hell, death, Tamburlaine, Hell, make ready my Coch, my chaire, my jewels, I come, I come, I come.

She runs against the Cage and braines her selfe.

This is, indeed, crude sensationalism—though we recognize in it the pattern of many wild and whirling words to be spoken by later Elizabethan and Jacobean dramatic characters—but it is done with an immense gusto which is worlds apart from the stiffness of earlier academic plays. And again and again the language raises the physical violence into some symbolic quintessence of dominion, as when Tamburlaine addresses the conquered kings who draw his chariot:

> Holla, ye pampered jades of Asia:
> What, can ye draw but twenty miles a day,
> And have so proud a chariot at your heels
> And such a coachman as great Tamburlaine?

Tamburlaine is the perfect illustration of the view maintained by Hobbes in his *Leviathan:* "I put for a general inclination of all mankind, a perpetual and restless desire of power after power, that ceaseth only in death." In Tamburlaine's case this perpetual and restless desire for power after power does literally cease only in death: even "the death of his Lady and Love fair Zenocrate," which occurs in Part II, does not deflect him from his course, though it moves him to passionate speech. Part II has greater variety than Part I, for not only does it contain the death of Zenocrate, which effectively though temporarily interrupts the by this time somewhat monotonous run of Tamburlaine's victories, but it is in general rather more diversified than the earlier part, where the interest lies solely in Tamburlaine's triumphant career and the resounding verse in which he and others express themselves. The only moment in the first part when the hero is forced by events into some kind of in-

trospection comes when he realizes that his love for Zenocrate must
lead him to spare the life of her father, the Soldan of Egypt:

> There angels in their crystal armours fight
> A doubtful battle with my tempted thoughts
> For Egypt's freedom and the Soldan's life,
> His life that so consumes Zenocrate. . . .
> What is beauty saith my sufferings then?
> If all the pens that ever poets held
> Had fed the feeling of their masters' thoughts,
> And every sweetness that inspir'd their hearts,
> Their minds, and muses on admired themes:
> If all the heavenly quintessence they still
> From their immortal flowers of poesy,
> Wherein as in a mirror we perceive
> The highest reaches of a human wit—
> If these had made one poem's period
> And all combined in beauty's worthiness,
> Yet should there hover in their restless heads
> One thought, one grace, one wonder at the least,
> Which into words no virtue can digest.

In *Tamburlaine* "Marlowe's mighty line" first comes into Elizabethan drama: its successor, *The Tragical History of Doctor Faustus*
(probably completed in the winter of 1588–89) is not as consistently
declamatory in its verse, if only because its hero is less the confident
extrovert than a man who seeks a more purely intellectual empire.
The Faustus myth reaches more profoundly into tragic aspects of the
human situation than the more purely spectacular story of Tamburlaine. Doctor Faustus is a Tamburlaine on the intellectual level; his
ambition is for ultimate knowledge; and if knowledge for him
means power, the same can be said in some degree of the view implicit in the whole Baconian tradition, that the function of knowledge
is control rather than mere insight and the scientist works for "the
relief of man's estate." But Faustus is not merely a man who seeks
the practical fruits of knowledge: his inordinate thirst for ultimate
understanding has something splendidly disinterested about it, and
if he sells his soul to the Devil in exchange for forbidden knowledge
there is an element of the heroic in the transaction which would be
lacking if all he was seeking was the perfect washing machine. Tamburlaine operates outside the sphere of moral values, but Faustus
comes up against them in their most elemental state, symbolizing in
his own behavior the story of the Fall of Man through eating of the
tree of knowledge. If he had had a less aspiring mind he would have
been a better man: less imaginative, less interesting, and less dar-
ing, he would also have been more virtuous. Here we have the germ
of a truly tragic situation—*corruptio optimi pessima,* the corruption

of the best becomes the worst—and we can almost see a pointing forward toward the great tragic heroes of Shakespeare who are led to self-destruction by the implication of their own virtues.

Like *Tamburlaine, Doctor Faustus* is full of the spirit of Renaissance ambition and *virtù*, but there is also a specifically Christian background, and the pact with the Devil with its resultant damnation effectively sets against the Renaissance zeal for limitless understanding the popular Christian notion of a forbidden knowledge, all the dark ideas of witchcraft and black magic, which had haunted the mind of Europe for centuries. Faustus retains many elements of the old morality plays; he has a Good Angel to exhort him to repentance and amendment as well as an Evil Angel to urge him on to damnation; and he is not irrevocably damned until he has succumbed to the final temptation of despair and given up all hope of the possibility of his repentance.

Tamburlaine and Faustus—and this is true of nearly all of Marlowe's heroes—are lonely souls; they have no real confidants, and they play a lone hand. And just as Tamburlaine began life as a Scythian shepherd, so Faustus was born of "parents base of stock" and rises by his own endeavors and his own brilliance. We first see him when he has run through all available human knowledge but remains dissatisfied and eager for more:

> O, what a world of profit and delight
> Is promised to the studious artisan!
> All things that move between the quiet poles
> Shall be at my command: emperors and kings
> Are but obeyed in their several provinces,
> Nor can they raise the wind or rend the clouds.
> But his dominion that exceeds in this
> Stretcheth as far as does the mind of man.

And so he turns to magic and forbidden knowledge.

There is rich dramatic irony when Faustus, having conjured up Mephistopheles, finds him "pliant" and "full of obedience and humility," and even more so when Mephistopheles has the truth about his real condition forced out of him and Faustus laughs at him for being superstitious and lacking "manly fortitude." Self-confidence has made him fatuous, and he signs his compact with Mephistopheles —gaining twenty-four years of knowledge and power and a life of "full voluptuousness"—with a braggart light-heartedness:

> Had I as many souls as there be stars,
> I'd give them all for Mephistophilis.

But the actual signing of the compact is delayed, while the suspense is maintained by keeping alive the possibility of Faustus' repentance.

And even when Faustus has signed the deed in his own blood, all is not yet irrevocably lost; it is only before the final climax, when he gives up hope, exclaiming, "But Faustus' offence can ne'er be pardoned: the serpent that tempted Eve may be saved, but not Faustus," that the end becomes inevitable.

Marlowe's real difficulty comes when he has to illustrate the kind of knowledge Faustus has obtained by his compact with Mephistopheles and to present the kind of life he is now able to lead. True, there are textual confusions which make it doubtful that we have the play exactly as Marlowe wrote it, but even so it is clear that Marlowe was at a loss to illustrate superhuman knowledge and power in concrete dramatic situations. Milton, faced with the problem of putting divine wisdom into the mouth of God Almighty, solves it with simple confidence by making God say what Milton had already been maintaining for some time; Bernard Shaw, presenting in *Back to Methusaleh* his Ancients who have achieved a wisdom beyond anything yet available to man, puts into their mouths the views that Shaw had long been arguing; but Milton and Shaw stand alone in English literature in their confidence that their own ideas represented ultimate understanding. Marlowe has to fall back on petty conjuring tricks only rarely punctuated with splendid poetic passages in which he suggests the atmosphere of Faustus' present way of life. Of these the most celebrated and the most successful is his speech to Helen of Troy, when she (or her appearance) has been conjured forth:

> Was this the face that launched a thousand ships
> And burned the topless towers of Ilium?
> Sweet Helen, make me immortal with a kiss:
> Her lips suck forth my soul, see where it flies.
> Come, Helen, come, give me my soul again.
> Here will I dwell, for heaven be in these lips,
> And all is dross that is not Helena. . . .
> O thou art fairer than the evening air
> Clad in the beauty of a thousand stars;
> Brighter art thou than flaming Jupiter
> When he appeared to hapless Semele,
> More lovely than the monarch of the sky
> In wanton Arethusa's azured arms,
> And none but thou shalt be my paramour.

But time is always moving on, and we are never allowed to forget that Faustus has only twenty-four years before the Devil comes to claim his own. The periodic urges to repentance by symbolic figures become more desperate, and after he has sunk into the final sin of despair, the terrible end blazes forth in a magnificent poetic passage which properly places more emphasis on Faustus' state of mind than on the details of what is to become of him when he is damned:

> Ah, Faustus
> Now hast thou but one bare hour to live,
> And then thou must be damned perpetually.
> Stand still you ever moving spheres of heaven
> That time may cease, and midnight never come;
> Fair Nature's eye, rise, rise again, and make
> Perpetual day, or let this hour be but
> A year, a month, a week, a natural day.
> That Faustus may repent and save his soul.
> *O lente, lente currite noctis equi:*
> The stars move still, time runs, the clock will strike,
> The devil will come, and Faustus must be damned.
> O I'll leap up to God: who pulls me down?
> See see where Christ's blood streams in the firmament.
> One drop would save my soul, half a drop, ah my Christ!
> Ah rend not my heart for naming of my Christ,
> Yet will I call on him: O spare me Lucifer!
> Where is it now? 'tis gone. And see where God
> Stretcheth out his arm, and bends his ireful brows.
> Mountains and hill, come, come, and fall on me,
> And hide me from the heavy wrath of God.
> No, no.
> Then will I headlong run into the earth:
> Earth gapes. O no, it will not harbour me.
> You stars that reigned at my nativity,
> Whose influence hath allotted death and hell,
> Now draw up Faustus like a foggy mist,
> Into the entrails of yon lab'ring cloud,
> That when you vomit forth into the air
> My limbs may issue from your smoky mouths,
> So that my soul may but ascend to heaven.
> Ah, half the hour is past: *The watch strikes.*
> 'Twill all be past anon.
> O God,
> If thou wilt not have mercy on my soul,
> Yet for Christ's sake, whose blood hath ransomed me,
> Impose some end to my incessant pain.
> Let Faustus live in hell a thousand years,
> A hundred thousand, and at last be saved.
> O no end is limited to damned souls,
> Why wert not thou a creature wanting soul? . . .

Curst be the parents that engendered me:
No Faustus, curse thyself, curse Lucifer,
That hath deprived thee of the joys of heaven.
                            The clock striketh twelve.
O it strikes, it strikes: now body turn to air,
Or Lucifer will bear thee quick to hell.
                            Thunder and lightning.
O soul, be changed into little water drops,
And fall into the Ocean, ne'er be found.
My God, my God, looke not so fierce on me.
                            Enter divels.
Adders and Serpents, let me breath a while:
Ugly hell gape not, come not, Lucifer,
I'll burn my books,—ah, Mephistophilis!

This passionate, highly charged blank verse, rich in a compelling imagery that searches the emotional condition of the speaker at each moment, is as far as dramatic verse was to go before Shakespeare. It is still end-stopped, with the pauses falling regularly at the end of each line, but there is more flexibility than in the declamatory speeches of Tamburlaine, and the shifts in tempo correspond to the rise and fall in the emotion far more effectively than in any of the *Tamburlaine* passages, where the emotion ran more evenly and the speeches were far more set recitations. Nevertheless, even in *Doctor Faustus* Marlowe can achieve effective dramatic verse only in great moments of crisis. He is the dramatist of the passionate moment, and has not yet mastered the subtler art of expressing poetically, dramatically, and continuously the general run of the play's action. The art of using dramatic verse with fine poetic effectiveness in moments of low emotional tension in a play was not to be adequately developed in English before Shakespeare, and not even by him until the middle of his career.

Of Marlowe's other plays, *The Jew of Malta* (ca. 1590?) is a dramatic presentation of a "Machiavellian" man, full of greed and cunning, who will stop at nothing to attain his ends. But the ambition of Barrabas, the Jew of Malta, lacks the central drive of either Tamburlaine or Faustus, and the play, though it has some effective moments of grim irony lacking in any of Marlowe's other works, falls apart into a series of uneven episodes. *Edward the Second* (1591?), though the main interest still concentrates on a central character—this time a study of weakness rather than of strength: Edward II is the sentimental weakling betrayed and done to death by the forces of ambition and cruelty—spreads the emphasis over a number of personalities and moves less in purple passages than the other plays. Marlowe is gaining a greater control over his dramatic material, and is moving toward a new subtlety in character portrayal; he is interested both in Edward's weakness and in "the proud corrupters of the light-brained king." As a work of sustained dramatic invention this is the best of Marlowe's plays. The scene in which Edward is murdered shows Marlowe dealing for the first time in the pathetic: the play as a whole moves between violence and pathos. For further advance in this direction we have to wait until Shakespeare's *Richard II*.

Marlowe has yet other plays, but nothing he produced in the later part of his brief life—nothing, indeed, after *Tamburlaine* and *Doctor Faustus*—had the impact on the contemporary dramatic world of his first two. It is these two plays that reveal Marlowe's characteristic splendor, and if his early death by violence in 1593 cut short a career which might, if spared to develop, have rivaled Shakespeare's, it can still be said that his dramatic debut was one of the most remarkable in English literary history, and one which has left a lasting impression. He remains a living and not an academic figure, even to the most casual student of Elizabethan literature.